Leading Learning

The notion that school transformation is dependent on exceptional leaders is increasingly seen as unrealistic and unsustainable. Instead, the idea of distributed leadership, which promotes the view that all stakeholders have complementary leadership roles to play in enhancing student learning, is now being promoted as a more useful framework for understanding schools and how they might be changed.

Subscribing to the notion of distributed leadership, O'Donoghue and Clarke identify two key groups: the 'leaders *of* learning' and the 'leaders *for* learning'. The leaders *of* learning – the focus of this book – are those working at school level to improve the quality of learning in the classroom such as teachers, principals, students and involved members of the local school community. The leaders *for* learning are the policy-makers and administrators whose support is crucial. The authors argue that in order to be effective leaders, both groups require an understanding of:

- broad trends in contemporary leadership theory
- recent views on learning theory
- the importance of teachers continually engaging in learning about their practice
- the significance of creating and sustaining schools as learning organisations
- forging links between leadership and learning.

The book's examination of the shifting approaches to leading learning in contemporary schools is enriched by innovative examples drawn from a range of international contexts.

Leading Learning will appeal to students involved in Masters and Doctoral courses relevant to the field and those undertaking programmes of school leadership preparation and development. It will also be of interest to academics working in the field of educational leadership and management.

Tom O'Donoghue is Professor of Education at the Graduate School of Education, The University of Western Australia.

Simon Clarke is Deputy Dean of the Faculty of Education, The University of Western Australia.

Leadership for learning series
Series edited by: Clive Dimmock, Mark Brundrett
and Les Bell

Also available:
Education Policy
Les Bell and Howard Stevenson

Forthcoming:
Human Resource Management in Education
Bernard Barker, Justine Mercer and Richard Bird

Leadership in Education
Clive Dimmock

School Leadership for Quality and Accountability
Mark Brundrett and Christopher Rhodes

Leading Learning
Process, themes and issues in international contexts
Tom O'Donoghue and Simon Clarke

Leading Learning

Process, themes and issues in international contexts

Tom O'Donoghue and
Simon Clarke

Routledge
Taylor & Francis Group

LONDON AND NEW YORK

First published 2010
by Routledge
2 Park Square, Milton Park, Abingdon, Oxon OX14 4RN

Simultaneously published in the USA and Canada
by Routledge
270 Madison Avenue, New York, NY 10016

Routledge is an imprint of the Taylor & Francis Group, *an informa business*

© 2010 Tom O'Donoghue and Simon Clarke

Typeset in Sabon by Swales & Willis Ltd, Exeter, Devon
Printed and bound in Great Britain by
TJ International Ltd, Padstow, Cornwall

British Library Cataloguing in Publication Data
A catalogue record for this book is available
from the British Library

Library of Congress Cataloging in Publication Data
O'Donoghue, T. A. (Tom A.), 1953-
    Leading learning : process, themes and issues in international contexts /
    Tom O'Donoghue and Simon Clarke.
    p. cm.
    1. School management and organization—Cross-cultural studies.
    2. Educational leadership—Cross-cultural studies.
    3. School improvement programs—Cross-cultural studies.
    I. Clarke, Simon. II. Title.
    LB2805.O335 2009
    371.2—dc22
    2008051482

ISBN10: 0–415–33612–0 (hbk)
ISBN10: 0–415–33613–9 (pbk)
ISBN10: 0–203–87696–2 (ebk)

ISBN13: 978–0–415–33612–3 (hbk)
ISBN13: 978–0–415–33613–0 (pbk)
ISBN13: 978–0–203–87696–1 (ebk)

Contents

Acknowledgements

We wish to acknowledge the support of the members of the Graduate School of Education, The University of Western Australia, in helping us see the book to fruition. We are also pleased to record our thanks to the staff at the library at The University of Western Australia for their patience and hard work in helping us locate vital source material. Finally, we wish to thank Mrs Zan Blair, Dr Ian Melville and Ms Michelle Striepe for all of the assistance they gave us.

Tom O'Donoghue and Simon Clarke
Graduate School of Education
The University of Western Australia

1 Introduction

In a world characterised by enormous change there is a perceived need for educational institutions to move from their traditional bureaucratic structures where the emphasis with regard to the educative process has tended to be placed on the management of teaching, to ones which are more flexible and responsive, and where the stress is on the promotion of learning. Concurrently, it is increasingly being argued that a form of distributed leadership is integral to achieving this outcome. One consequence of the persuasiveness of the argument is that programmes for professional learning in various parts of the world are beginning to highlight the importance of the leadership capabilities of all stakeholders within various educational institutions in order to enhance student learning. This book on leading learning was stimulated by such developments, particularly as they relate to students, teachers and the school as an organisation. A general overview of the broad directions taken in the book is now outlined in this chapter.

The underlying argument

The focus of this book is on schools, the most common of the educational institutions. The concern is primarily with the key personnel who interact daily within the schools' sector, namely, students, teachers and school leadership teams. These personnel, of course, do not go about their activities independent of other major stakeholders, particularly parents, local communities, system administrators and senior policymakers. However, while the influence of such additional personnel is recognised throughout, it is not foregrounded. Various types of analyses, including those of a critical theory nature, of current educational policies and practices, are also not foregrounded.

One might well ponder the outcomes of the analyses of significant critical theorists and argue that they should be heeded by politicians and bureaucrats. Recently, for example, Smyth (2006, p. 279) made the provocative suggestion that as conditions conducive to learning in schools deteriorate through emphases on "accountability, standards, measurement, and high stakes testing", an increasing number of students are making active choices that school is not for them. As Smyth sees it, there is evidence indicating that "muscular policies of testing, scripted and prescribed teaching, an ethos of competition, along with dehumanised and irrelevant curricula" are not working for the majority of students. Contentions like this are certainly very thought provoking. Our position, however, is that even if critiques of such a nature are warranted (and there are good reasons for arguing that, at the very least, they constitute an over-generalisation), it does not follow that school-level leaders cannot work within existing parameters in order to set about trying to improve the quality of students' experiences.

MacBeath (2006) presents a different challenge. In harmony with much of what we say throughout this book, he argues for a new vision of educational leadership that is more focused on fostering learning in schools than has historically been the case. We are not necessarily committed, however, to his notion that leadership, given contemporary educational structures, particularly within government education systems is, or needs to be, a 'subversive activity'. Rather, we take the stance that leaders of learning can work within many current system-level parameters, requirements and expectations, and at the same time operate 'openly' in a manner aimed at improving the quality of learning in the school with the best interests of students in mind.

The most serious challenge of all is presented by Dimmock. In his work, *Designing the learning-centred school* (Dimmock, 2000), he tackles a demanding task, namely, that of producing a generic model for the development of a learning-centred school which is also appropriate for different learning contexts. What is required, he argues, "is a cross-cultural framework for seeking to understand the degree to which theories, research funding policies and practices can be successfully adopted in culturally diverse settings" (2000, p. 43). As Soliman (2003) has summarised, Dimmock goes on to explain the need for school design in terms of demands for accountability for student learning outcomes in school systems and system-wide monitoring of students, changes in expectations of schools to educate students for an information-based technological and competitive global economy, increases in social problems, concerns for the number of students leaving school before graduating, the resistance in schools towards changing teaching and learning practices, and the need for schools to be inclusive in the pursuit of addressing disadvantage and social justice.

For Dimmock (2000, p. 9) 'design' consists of "forethought, planned, intended, deliberate and comprehensive change creating desired organisational patterns". He argues that a new and different configuration is now needed in school design to meet the changing expectations and requirements of schools in future societies. To this end, he advocates a collaborative institution-wide approach based on informed practice and a coherent mix of vision, intuition and research-driven knowledge. The core elements of his model include a curriculum based on student learning outcomes, learning processes and experiences, teaching approaches and strategies, and computer technology. He is also at pains not to neglect such elements as organisational structures, human and financial resources, leadership and organisational culture, performance appraisal, and community-school relations.

We are very much in sympathy with Dimmock's position. Also, we welcome his argument that at the point of implementation of his ideas, particularly in relation to teaching, learning and communication, it is up to each society to "work out its own adaptation and cultural interpretation of the school design precepts" (Dimmock, 2000, p. 287). The issue, however, is that in order to be implemented with fidelity senior policymakers need either to embrace his position in totality and ordain total system-level change, or else ensure their systems are devolved to such an extent that individual schools are free to redesign their approaches. While those with the power and influence should be encouraged to act along these lines, such proposals are not necessarily attractive to many who are set in their ways, nor to those like administrators in large government education systems who fear disruption. Such individuals could, however, be encouraged to promote change by focusing on leadership aimed primarily at trying to improve the quality of learning in the classroom.

Our argument is that there is much space within many contemporary education systems for adopting such a 'bottom up' and incremental approach to promoting initiatives aimed at improving student learning. This is to commit to the position of Smith and Lovat (2003, p. 209) that it is essential to "plan to achieve little change rather than to try to make large changes that do not eventuate". Their view is that a change plan that can be divided into sequential parts or phases, each of which is achievable in a moderately short-term, is likely to be more successful than a large plan which requires a long time to realise. This is a principle that needs to be heeded when planning to promote any change in relation to each of the levels of learning in the school. In other words, planning to promote change aimed at improving the quality of students', teacher and organisational learning – the three levels of learning – needs to result in a number of small-scale and achievable projects to be implemented rather than one grand scheme.

It is conceded that there does not seem to be any empirical evidence to justify the case for focusing on these three levels of learning in the school as opposed to any other area when taking the first step in promoting change aimed at developing the learning-centred school. Such a focus is, however, justified on other grounds. For one thing, it involves addressing the core activities of teachers, those that mostly occupy their time and are of most concern to them on a day-to-day level. Given the importance of commitment in any change process, it is reasonable to argue that should positive results manifest themselves in this domain, and should the key stakeholders feel successful in their efforts, then a very solid foundation will be laid for maximising the possibility of gaining success in other domains.

The outcome of adopting the position being advocated here could, to put it another way, result in a new set of practices with regard to leadership and learning becoming embedded in schools. This is a notion of 'embedding' as a set of approaches that become central to the configuration and culture of the organisation. As Fullan (1992), Hargreaves and Fink (2005) and Schein (2004) have conceptualised it, the associated processes involve a certain amount of dislodgement and reconceptualisation. Out of this, it is hoped, can emerge consensus. This, in turn, should provide the basis for change in other areas.

From considerations so far, it should be clear that we are very much in favour of current thinking on the need for schools to move their emphases from the management of teaching to leadership for learning. We see this as being essential in its own right, while also recognising that it can be viewed as the first step in major incremental change aimed at promoting whole-school reculturing and restructuring within a learning-centred agenda. Our main concern in this book is with providing an exposition on what this can mean in relation to student learning, teacher learning and organisational learning. Integral to this exposition is that learning at each level can be enhanced through distributed leadership.

The current emphasis on distributed leadership throughout much of the literature has been stimulated by disillusionment with the notion that the transformation of schools lies with exceptional leaders. As the latter notion proved to be unrealistic and unsustainable (Timperley, 2005, p. 395) the idea of leadership as distributed across multiple people and situations began to be promoted as a more useful framework for understanding schools and how they might be changed (Copland, 2003). The challenge in this alternative approach involves thinking of leadership, as Heller and Firestone (1995) and Smylie and Hart (1990) put it, as involving role complementarities and network patterns of control.

Central to the argument in favour of distributed leadership is that leadership resides in the potential available to be released within an organisation. It is the intellectual and social capital, sometimes dormant, or unexpressed, residing within its members. The role of the leader is to harness, focus, liberate, empower and align that leadership towards a common purpose and, by so doing, build and release capacity. As Harris and Lambert (2003) see it, however, the current leadership model for school systems is not marked by learning innovation, enquiry and knowledge creation. Rather, the focus is on structures, job descriptions, targets and performance management. For them also, the solution is to have the organisation of the school redesigned and activated through distributed leadership. They foresee that a profound mindshift is necessary for believing that everyone can contribute to leadership. Yet they insist that this belief can transform schools.

We take a much more modest position in this book. To argue that learning at the level of the student, the teacher and the organisation can be enhanced through distributed leadership is most definitely not to commit to such an approach to leadership for all of the activities of the school. In this regard, the fact that leadership is currently equated with status, authority and position cannot be overlooked. Also, this situation is unlikely to change in the foreseeable future with governments intensifying their leadership accountability measures. Thus, one can hardly expect those at the front line in the account-ability stakes to relinquish wholeheartedly much of their authority to others. Again, however, the one area in which a major step could be taken without providing a major threat to established modes of operating is in the area of teacher, student and organisational learning.

It is also important to highlight that throughout the book the emphasis on distributed leadership for learning at the three levels within the school changes slightly in various chapters depending on the particular level being addressed. Where student learning is the main focus three propositions in relation to leadership of learning in the school are stressed. They are as follows: leadership for developing flexible learners should promote student self-regulated learning; leadership for developing flexible learners should promote learning in community; and leadership for developing flexible learn-ers should promote learning which is problem-based. These embody ideas which we consider to be particularly helpful to educational leaders in shaping their thinking on the nature of student learning. Also, where teacher learning is the main focus, the position taken is that it is closely intertwined with stu-dents' learning. Particular emphasis is placed on the importance of teachers working collaboratively, being reflective practitioners and adopting a research stance to the classroom. This is in harmony with the observation of Hargreaves (1997, p. 99) that teachers' learning should be as constructivist as the learning of their students is meant to be. In a similar vein, where organisa-tional learning is the main focus, what is stressed is that while student learn-ing is dependent on teacher learning, and teachers' learning is enhanced by its receptiveness to students' learning needs, organisational learning is depend-ent on, and feeds back into, teacher learning (MacBeath, 2006). The follow-ing section elaborates on each of these three levels of learning.

The three levels of learning in the school

A useful way of conceptualising learning agendas that occur throughout the school is according to three levels (Knapp *et al.*, 2003). We have already described these as 'student learning', 'teacher learning' and 'organisational learning'. While they can constitute distinct foci, it is important to emphasise that they are also interdependent in a complex variety of ways; an interde-pendence that will vary with context, but one that always requires great sen-sitivity and attention on the part of school leaders. The nature of each learning agenda will now be elucidated as a precursor to the more detailed exposition presented in subsequent chapters where the implications of these specific learning agendas for a school's policy and practice are discussed.

Student learning

Put simply, the agenda for student learning is primarily concerned with build-ing the academic and social capacity of all students in the school. For this

purpose, priority of the school must be to provide the conditions and opportunities that serve to promote students' capacity in ways that will equip them
for survival, success and happiness in a rapidly changing society (Bowring-
Carr and West-Burnham, 1997). In this connection, it is especially important
for schools to support students as flexible learners. According to Cibulka *et
al.* (2003), there are three significant ways in which schools are better placed
to nurture students as flexible learners than might have been the case in the
past, namely, an enhanced understanding of individual students' innate
learning capacity, a clearer concept of learning transfer, and a more developed notion of levels of learner aptitude.

Enhanced understanding of individual students' innate learning capacity
highlights the importance of teachers being aware of their students' different
learning styles. Research has indicated that a number of learning styles exist
– such as learning by doing, or watching, or thinking – which are likely to
change over time and according to context. These styles might also be associated with specific kinds of behaviour that could account for students' degree
of engagement in classroom activities. Clearly, the acknowledgement that
individual students have a propensity for particular styles of learning has vital
implications for strategies adopted towards teachers' learning and organisational learning.

Encouraging students as flexible learners also entails a clearer concept of
learning transfer. This represents a shift from a traditional understanding of
learning as a demonstrated acquisition of facts to one that places more focus
on applying acquired knowledge and skills to different situations. In other
words, there seems to be an increasing acceptance by educators that learning
is a more complex process than the memorisation of an externally imposed
and restricted body of knowledge. Rather, learning and understanding need
to be deepened through the development of cognitive skills to enable the processing of knowledge and its practical application. This deepening of learning
and its capacity to be transferred is further enabled by recognising students'
prior knowledge. From this perspective, students are not blank slates on
which teachers' words are inscribed. On the contrary, students bring to the
classroom their own realities which create certain legitimate understandings.
What they learn, therefore, is conditioned by what they already know. Thus,
it becomes imperative to establish how new information can be aligned with
the student's existing reality.

The processing of knowledge and its practical application can also be promoted through the fostering of social skills. Vygotsky (1978), for example,
argued persuasively that an individual's understanding of the world is
extended by interacting and working with others, and he reinforced the
notion that learning is fundamentally a social activity. Clearer understandings of what is involved in enabling knowledge transfer also have profound
implications for teachers' and organisational learning.

We have argued here that the agenda of students' learning is influenced
heavily by the need to encourage students to be flexible learners. Such

learners are more likely to develop the knowledge, skills and dispositions required to learn in order to deal with the circumstances of rapid change that seem to characterise our times. As a corollary to the emergence of more sophisticated understandings of how students learn, there is now greater attention paid by schools to teachers' learning. In other words, there is recognition that the effectiveness of students' learning that occurs in the 'classroom' is inextricably linked to the effectiveness of teachers' learning that occurs outside the classroom. In a similar vein, Shulman (1997, p. 504) has commented that any effort at school reform must ask itself the following: "As I design this grand plan for improving the quality of learning in students, have I designed with equal care and concern a plan for teacher learning in this setting?"

Teacher learning

Put simply, the agenda for teacher learning is primarily concerned with building the intellectual and professional capacity of teachers in the school. The efficacy of this process will depend in the first instance on teachers, as well as principals, recognising that they are learners themselves. It seems axiomatic that the advancement in knowledge about students' learning necessitates an acceptance that teaching is a complex rather than a technical activity. Hence, it could be argued that continuous professional learning for teachers has become a *sine qua non* if they are to remain adept in the classroom. Indeed, ten years ago Hargreaves (1997) recognised the increasing complexity of teaching which he regarded as the crucible for teachers' learning, especially by means of collaboration. Factors such as an expanded knowledge base of teaching, increasingly diverse students in classrooms, and the broadening ambit of teachers' responsibilities serve to buttress the importance of teachers' continuous learning.

In order to enable teachers' learning as effectively as possible it is useful to refer to the principles of adult learning (andragogy), although we recognise that these principles are not significantly different from those deemed desirable for guiding the learning experiences of children (pedagogy). Szabo and Lambert have enumerated the principles of adult learning as follows:

- Learning is an active rather than a passive process;
- Learning is by nature social and is more likely to occur when learners share ideas, enquire and problem solve together;
- Learners need opportunities to make sense of new knowledge and create meanings for themselves based on individual and shared experiences;
- Reflection and meta-cognition contribute to the construction of knowledge and sense-making;
- New learning is mediated by prior experience, values and beliefs.

(2002, p. 204)

In the context of professional learning in schools these principles could well engender a fundamental shift in thinking about how teachers should do their work. In particular, the principles seem to highlight the need for teachers to engage in a number of activities to create opportunities for the kind of powerful learning that has the potential to improve teaching capability and performance. For example, there is a need for collaborative ways of working which promote teachers' learning by enhancing their sense of self-efficacy in being able to make a difference with their students (Hargreaves, 1997). As opposed to traditional arrangements whereby teachers have worked within a culture of individualism, opportunities for professional learning are more likely to occur when they engage in high level collaborative activities such as peer interaction, support and feedback (Harris and Muijs, 2002). When conducted on a regular basis, these interactions can create teacher communities within a school, as well as beyond, that have the potential to enable a deepening of knowledge and expertise as information and insights are shared, common issues are debated, innovative ideas are tested, and tacit understandings are developed. Collaboration can also represent a "marriage of insufficiencies" (Shulman, 1997, p. 515) insomuch as professional challenges increasingly becoming impossible for teachers to deal with individually, but are easily met in the company of others.

In these ways, teaching can become a highly reflective process, which constitutes another activity embedded in the principles of adult learning. The process of reflection is difficult to conceptualise, but engenders more than just 'thinking about' something uncritically (West-Burham and O'Sullivan, 1998). Instead, there needs to be a depth of deliberation involved that enables a new stage to be reached in one's thinking about practice. It is in this sense that Agyris and Schon (1978) argued that practitioners should be urged to reflect critically on their taken-for-granted assumptions as part of a process of learning and improvement in their practice. This exercise in critical reflection can lead to a reframing of theories-in-action through deliberation and heightened metacognitive awareness. Hence, the fundamental role of critical reflection (individually and collectively) in teachers' learning and development has become well-acknowledged (Day, 1999).

Closely connected with the exhortation for teachers to become 'reflective practitioners' is the notion of teachers acting as researchers in their own classrooms (Stenhouse, 1975) in order to assist them in deepening their understandings and enhancing their practice. Although the idea of teachers adopting a research stance to the classroom is hardly new, it does seem to have undergone resurgence over recent years. In accordance with the emergence of site-based decision making in many educational jurisdictions, teachers, local schools, and school districts have become more accountable to all stakeholders for the policies, programmes and practices they implement. Practitioner research represents a potent means of identifying the needs of the classroom, assessing resulting development processes and evaluating the outcomes of the changes that have been defined, designed and implemented.

One way in which teachers can engage in research that enables them to use data collected in classrooms to critique practice, which also contributes to their professional learning, is through action research. The process of action research involves thinking systematically about what happens in the class-room (or in the wider school environment), implementing action where improvements are thought possible, and monitoring and evaluating the effects of the action with a view to continuing the improvement. In crude terms, the process is based on a learning cycle comprising initial reflection, planning, acting, observing and reflecting. The literature on action research (Herr and Anderson, 2005; Johnson, 2008; McNiff *et al.*, 1996) indicates that there is a number of benefits to be derived from teachers participating in such projects associated with empowerment and willingness to change, the processes of which seem to be squarely aligned with the key principles of adult learning enumerated earlier.

Organisational learning

The efficacy of teachers' learning along the lines we have discussed will be dependent to a large extent on the general culture and values of the school. This observation has important implications for organisational learning. The concept of organisational learning, however, is a slippery one and "takes several forms, operates at several levels and follows several stages" (Morrison, 2002, p. 91). It is also an elusive concept because it is not organisations of themselves that learn. Rather, it is the inclination and capacity of individuals and groups within the organisation that create the potential for it to adapt to a changing environment (West-Burham and O' Sullivan, 1998).

Senge (1990) presents useful constructs for visualising organisational learning in schools through the concepts and application of the 'learning organisation'. He has defined a learning organisation as one:

> Where people continually expand their capacity to create the results they truly desire, where new and expansive patterns of thinking are nurtured, where collective aspiration is set free and where people are continually learning how to learn together.
>
> (Senge, 1990, p. 3)

According to Senge the learning organisation is made up of five disciplines:

*   *Systems thinking* focuses on wholes rather than parts, goes beyond events to their underlying structure and leads to experiencing the inter-connectedness and inter-relationship of things (Silins *et al.*, 2002);
*   *Personal mastery* relates to Senge's contention (1990) that organisations learn only insofar as individuals and groups learn. It is axiomatic, there-fore, that conditions and opportunities should be available for individuals and teams throughout the organisation to learn continuously and improve;

- *Mental models* refer to making explicit deep-seated frrameworks by which sense is made of the world and exposing the associated deeply ingrained beliefs, values, mind-sets and assumptions that determine the way people think and act. Being conscious of mental models and making them open to discussion enables them to be re-examined in the light of espoused beliefs and thus contributes to facilitating change;
- *Team learning* is created when teams share their experience, insights, knowledge and skills with each other about how to improve practice. In doing so, teams develop their skills in reflection, inquiry and dialogue to form the basis for a shared vision of change and common commitments to action. In the original Greek sense of the word, *dia-logus* engenders a free flowing of meaning through the group that allows it to discover insights not attainable individually (Voogt *et al.*, 1998);
- *Shared vision* is manifested in common understandings and genuine commitment which unleashes people's aspirations and hopes so that they identify with the vision not out of compliance, but because they are motivated to do so.

Senge (1990) argues that learning organisations are characterised by valuing and developing these five disciplines, which can collectively empower the organisation to be innovative. This is an important requirement as schools take on the changing, uncertain and ambiguous conditions that characterise the current educational environment.

To conclude this section, we have suggested that learning in schools may be conceptualised according to three different levels or agendas, namely, students' learning, teachers' learning and organisational learning. Our explanation of these three learning agendas illustrates the complexity of their interdependence, the identification of which presents a considerable challenge to educational leaders. As Knapp *et al.* (2003, p. 17) have pointed out, the nature of students' learning informs teachers' learning, which then influences classroom improvement. In addition, students' and teachers' learning contribute to organisational learning and *vice versa*. Knapp *et al.* (2003) also make the important observation that the efficacy of the three learning agendas will be determined by the environment in which they are pursued.

The international dimension

The word 'international' features in the sub-title of this book. This is because an international dimension is brought to bear at various points, but particularly at the beginning and towards the end of the work. In the very broadest sense, such a perspective is important because, as one renowned American educationalist has contended, it can deepen one's understanding of one's own society and education system (Noah, 1986). It is a perspective which is also adopted for three specific purposes. First, it is deemed important to contextualise what is advocated against a background where broad trends both historically and internationally in developments aimed at promoting the development of student learning are sketched out. Second, portraying a variety of developments internationally in line with some of the ideas presented has the potential to enthuse leaders of learning at the school level. Third, the portrayal of significant international experiences can also serve to impress on leaders of learning, and particularly those in more senior positions, the importance of listening to the voices of those at the level of the school if they wish to maximise the possibility that policies aimed at enhancing student learning will be successful.

For many years comparative educationalists have been stressing how in various instances apparently well thought-out ideas on curriculum change and initiatives aimed at improving student learning have floundered because they have involved inappropriate transnational educational knowledge transfer. This refers to a process which involves the exchange of theories, models and methods for academic or practical purposes among countries. It took off in earnest in the education domain during the nineteenth century with educators travelling to other nations to see what they could learn to improve the system at home (Fraser and Brickman, 1968). The Americans visited Europe in search of ways of improving American education. The British were also active in taking a close look at their neighbours' schools, while the French studied the Prussian educational system. Furthermore, the European and American models of education were exported to colonial dependencies (Crossley, 1984). At the other side of the world the Japanese launched "the greatest of all hunting expeditions in this period" (Thut and Adams, 1964, p. 3), reconstructing their educational system along Western lines.

The process of transnational knowledge transfer continued into the twentieth century. By the 1950s and 1960s the predominant model being adopted for such transfer between industrialised nations and developing nations was one of imitation and intervention; of attempting to solve problems in non-Western countries by utilising Western knowledge (Kumar, 1979; Useem and Useem, 1980). However, during the 1970s, with the emergence of dependency theory, the rise of Third World consciousness and the increasing cultural awareness of some Western social scientists (Lee *et al.*, 1988), this approach came in for major criticism. The failure of many ambitious educational innovations made donors, lenders, recipients and borrowers considerably more aware of the complexity and context-dependence of educational change.

Entering the last decade of the twentieth century, the literature on educational change, especially that which was written from the donors' and planners' perspective, began to speak of flexible, iterative and incremental strategies; of the importance of paying attention to culture, behaviours and values, and of the appropriate role of participatory, bottom-up processes and qualitative data in educational planning and evaluation (Rondinelli *et al.*, 1990). Little summarised the position as follows:

Only when prepared to spend the time doing our homework to learn and understand more about the situation on which advice is sought, and only when prepared to share responsibility when things go badly wrong, should we erect our 'for sale' signs. International consultancy work is difficult, and time and energy consuming, if it is done well.

(1988, p. 19)

At the same time, however, the message was not being heeded totally in all parts of the world. Teachers and lecturers continued to be sent overseas by state and voluntary development agencies without being properly trained for the reality of the education situation on the ground (O'Donoghue, 1991, p. 28). As a consequence, they often rushed headlong into adopting curriculum and pedagogical proposals eminently suited for their country of origin in a society where they were totally inappropriate.

Lately there has been a renewed curiosity about the folly of such practices. The research of Watkins (2000) has been particularly enlightening. He has pointed out that many of the findings presented in psychology textbooks around the world are based on research with American psychology undergraduates. He also points out that most of the major theories which are described are based on the values of Western culture and on an individualistic, independent conception of the person. This, he concludes, does not mean we should assume that such literature is inappropriate for other cultures, but rather that we should find out through research how to demonstrate its appropriateness.

Watkins goes on to provide some useful examples to illustrate his point. Regarding memorising, he states that without understanding it can lead at best to very limited outcomes. However, for Chinese learners the repetition involved is important in deepening understanding by discovering new meaning, unlike the Western students he studied who tended to use repetition to check that they had really remembered something. He also highlights the misperception of Western observers regarding how Chinese teachers use group work. The usual Western approach, he states,

> is to split the class up into pairs or small groups, say of four to five, and then have members of each group discuss an issue or work on a problem together at the same time as other groups. . . . many Western teachers try to involve students in the class through *simultaneous* pupil talk. Large class sizes are seen as a constraint on this teaching method. By way of contrast, Chinese teachers often use *sequential* talk for the purpose of involvement. . . . two pupils may come to the front of the class to perform a dialogue which has been prepared in advance to the teacher and the rest of the class . . . What makes this approach work in the context of the Chinese classroom is that the rest of the class consider they learn through listening to the teacher or their peers.

(2000, p. 169)

Watkins also points to the role of questions in the classroom. Whereas Western teachers expect questions to be asked by students during the process of learning "to fill in gaps in their knowledge, or to aid understanding of the reasoning involved", Chinese students ask questions after they have learnt independently of the teacher. The reason, for this, he states, is that Chinese students consider that questions should be based on knowledge. Finally, he points out that while there is a belief amongst many teachers from a Western tradition that children learn through being creative, Chinese teachers see creativity as a slow process that depends on solid basic knowledge (2000, p. 171).

The area of leadership has also benefited from the new-found interest in stressing the vital importance of not trying to impose uncritically Western models of thought and action without considering the cultural context. Dimmock and Walker (1997) have been particularly influential in placing this matter squarely on the research agenda, especially by way of highlighting the fact that different cultures have different approaches to leadership and that these have strong cultural foundations. More recently, Fitzgerald (2003a, 2003b, 2004) has made an equally significant contribution aimed at drawing attention to the importance of considering how educational leadership may be practised differently by females, by indigenous leaders and by female indigenous leaders.

We are convinced of the vital importance of being mindful of these perspectives. At the same time, we do not see a clash between them and the approaches to leading and learning which we are promoting. The key issue is the importance of taking cognisance of such positions when trying to bring about change. Hargreaves (1993, p. 149) put this most eloquently when he spoke of the importance of listening to, and taking account of, the voices of those expected to implement educational reforms. He contended that many social policies fail and nowhere is this more evident than in education, where, he held, innovations frequently fail quite disastrously. The one common reason for this, he argued, is as follows:

> . . . in grafting new ideas onto schools, we do it with so little knowledge about the nature of the everyday world of teachers, pupils and schools that our attempted grafts (and various forms of major and minor surgery) merely arouse the 'anti-bodies' of the host which undermine our attempts to play doctor to an educational patient.
>
> (1993, p. 150)

Hargreaves went on to argue that "only when we understand the precise nature of the host body can we design our innovatory grafts with any confidence that they will prove to be acceptable" (1993, p. 150). This was an echoing of Fullan's (1982) argument in his contention that to effect improvement, that is to introduce change that promises more success and less failure, the world of the people most closely involved in implementation must be understood.

Carron and Chau (1996, p. 268) also drew attention to the latter matter specifically in relation to teachers, arguing that they have their own ways of doing things and that "it is a mistake to think they are not without wills of their own, that they are easily manipulable". They went on to state that one of the foremost reasons for sub-optimal implementation is that planners do not consult with those who have to implement their plans. True consultation, they concluded, is intensive, laborious and time-consuming, but the consequences of neglecting it are almost inevitably far-reaching and severe. For us, this means that while we hold that our position has the potential to 'travel' across cultures as well as within them, we also recognise that they have no hope of succeeding unless they are implemented in a culturally sensitive manner.

The structure of the book

The focus of this book, as is clear from the exposition so far, is mainly on 'leaders of learning'. This group consists of those working at the school level to improve the quality of learning in the classroom. It is comprised primarily of teachers and school principals, but also includes students and involved members of the local school community. A major premise is that these personnel can be effective leaders of pedagogical change in many countries without there being a need for significant change in educational structures being initiated at the system's level concurrently. At the same time, however, it would be folly to think that the influence of middle and senior level policymakers and administrators can be overlooked. Indeed, the support of personnel in this group, those who can be termed 'leaders for learning', is crucial to the operations of leaders of learning.

Subscribing to this position, we hold that, in order to be effective, both leaders of learning and leaders for learning require an understanding of:

- General developments in the international context internationally so that they can locate their work within the contexts of time and space;
- Broad trends in leadership theory, including contemporary ideas on 'distributed leadership';
- Recent views on learning theory and on approaches to enhancing student learning;
- The importance of teachers engaging continually in learning about their practice;
- The significance of creating and sustainning schools as learning organisations;
- The value of engaging in deliberation on inspirational developments in student and teacher learning which have taken place in different parts of the world;
- The wisdom of giving voice to key stakeholders at the school's level regarding how they make sense of their educational world.

Each of the next nine chapters elaborates on these areas.

The chapters of the book can also be seen as being clustered in three sections, each corresponding to the general structure used in all of the books in the series to which this book belongs, namely, 'Leadership for Learning', edited by Professor Clive Dimmock and Professor Mark Brundrett. The first section deals with 'process' and consists of this chapter along with Chapters 2, 3 and 4. Chapters 2 and 3 focus on central concepts and broad trends internationally in developments in the learning and assessment contexts respectively. Together, they constitute a scaffolding which serves to contextualise the considerations in the remainder of the book. Chapter 4 goes on to detail a number of background considerations on leadership in education. A brief overview of one of a range of typologies that indicate some of the various positions on leadership which have impacted on education, including student, teacher and organisational learning, over the last 20 years, is then presented. The chapter concludes with a delineation of the basic ideas within the concept of 'distributed leadership', particularly as they apply to teachers and how they can improve the quality of learning in the classroom.

The second section of the book deals with 'themes' and is concerned solely with the three levels of learning in the school. Chapter 5 focuses on student learning. Specific attention is paid to both the constructivist perspective on learning and to the concepts of 'surface and deep learning'. Also, one way of making sense of the great array of theoretical ideas, constructs and practical theories which serve to inform thinking on the promotion of flexible student learning is detailed. In Chapter 6 the focus shifts to teacher learning. Here the exposition is centred on three main themes, namely, 'reflective practice, 'collaboration' and 'teacher leadership'. In Chapter 7, on organisational learning, the main concern is with expanding on those learning processes in schools that bring to fruition the hidden capital of their staff and students, thus creating and sustaining the kind of organisations that learn. The implications that organisational learning has for leadership are also examined.

The final section of the book considers 'issues' and also consists of three chapters. Chapter 8 takes up a point already made earlier in this chapter that we consider our position on each of the three levels of learning to be a pragmatic one for the current educational climate. We also hold that one way of enthusing leaders to espouse the position is to expose them to inspirational developments which have taken place in different parts of the world. To this end six such developments are outlined. This issue of being pragmatic is pursued further in Chapter 9, albeit in a very different sense. Here it is argued that while it is very valuable to deliberate on exciting curriculum innovations and on the implementation of innovative pedagogical practices in order to promote inspiration amongst leaders of learning, the facilitation of such deliberation needs to be accompanied by the promotion of the argument that it is vital to give voice to the key stakeholders involved in the educational enterprise, especially those at the school's level. Six cases are offered which illustrate how failure to take account of this position has resulted time and again in the failure of theoretically sound projects with great potential to enhance student learning. Finally, Chapter 10 concentrates on illustrating ways in which leadership and learning are indispensable to each other and considers implications for practice, with particular reference to the three levels of learning within the school.

2 International developments in the learning context

Introduction

This chapter is the first of the two which provide a scaffolding serving to contextualise the considerations in the remainder of the book. It does so by outlining general developments in the learning context internationally. Broad trends in the parameters within which the 'whole' curriculum is located, particularly across the Organisation for Economic Cooperation and Development (OECD) member countries, are first of all sketched out. Attention is then given to a range of influential policy positions united by the argument that it is not just the promotion of learning, but specifically the promotion of lifelong learning, which should constitute the overarching aim of those working within such parameters. Finally, the move towards emphasising that the educational enterprise should have learner-centred education at its core is considered. This sets the scene for locating the main exposition on leadership for learning in later chapters.

Broad trends internationally in the parameters of the 'whole' curriculum

The word 'curriculum' can be a broad or a narrow term depending upon the context in which it is used. A helpful approach, however, is to consider it according to four domains: the formal learning and teaching in classrooms; those activities which occur outside the classroom, such as sporting competitions, music and drama productions, outdoor education and public speaking; where the school intervenes and brings an ameliorating influence such as the implementation of policies on bullying, drug education and health issues; and the unplanned learning (the 'hidden curriculum') which occurs in many different forms. Curriculum, therefore, can be viewed as being fluid in the areas for which the school and the wider community takes responsibility. The rest of this section of the chapter is concerned primarily with international trends in the first domain, namely, the formal learning and teaching in classrooms. Also, the concern is with the 'whole' curriculum, rather than the curriculum for any particular subject, or teaching area. Thus, the focus is on the patterns that can be identified according to such fundamental areas as the values and beliefs that underlie schooling, the range of educational outcomes desired, the pattern of components into which the curriculum is divided, and the approaches that are used to evaluate the work of schools.

At this point it is important to emphasise that no curriculum is politically neutral. Rather, it has to be viewed as the product of a number of social, economic and political forces (Giroux, 1994). The 1970s was a period when this perspective was taken very seriously in the academic literature, influenced especially by work such as that of Bowles and Gintis (1976) which argued that schools prepare students to enter the current economic system via a correspondence between school structure and the structure of production, and Willis's (1977) introduction of the concept of resistance in demonstrating how the working class boys he studied in an English secondary school resisted both the official and hidden curriculum. During the next decade the work of Goodson became influential. Goodson (1987) argued that the 'formal' or 'prescribed' curriculum (his particular focus) is a site of contestation, where different interest groups struggle for influence and power. In a similar vein, he rejected the view of the written curriculum as a "neutral given", proposing instead that it is "a social artefact, conceived of and made for deliberate human purposes" (1987, p. 260). Thus, curricula have to be seen as continually changing bodies of knowledge, skills and beliefs reflecting diverse interests of sub groups and alliances which shift frequently over time.

To highlight this position is not to overlook Bartlett and Burton's (2007, p. 74) point that "teachers interpret the curriculum within the context of their own situation". In certain countries, however, they are having to conform to external constraints and behave in ways that are not always in accordance with their individual judgements. Commenting specifically on the United States, McKernan (2008, p. 5) argues that there has been a decided movement away from the strong concern since the 1950s for equality of educational opportunity. Instead, the neoconservatives have sold policymakers the notion that what is to count as 'official curriculum' is "a political strategy exercised to aid such causes as market ideology, personal choice of schooling, standards for literacy, school crime and violence" (McKernan, 2008, p. 5). This has resulted in a 'back to basics' emphasis, accompanied by a removal of power from teachers and professionals and giving it to special interest groups and government.

A similar movement has taken place in the United Kingdom. Here, as Vlaeminke (1998) has identified in a survey of the history of the primary school curriculum over 200 years, developments until the 1980s can be considered to have been evolutionary and piecemeal, as opposed to confronting such big issues as "what education is for and how much national effort should be invested in it" (1998, p. 13). Rather, the outcome of dealing with the "competing claims of nationalism, regionalism, social class and religious denominationalism have never been fully resolved", as well as responding to economic influences, resulted in "a long history of compromise, evasion and partial solutions" (Vlaeminke, 1998, p. 14).

By the mid-1950s the level of teacher autonomy in England was high, while there was also a view that government interference should be kept to a minimum. On this, Broadfoot (1996, p. 206) points out that additional freedom was given to schools with the introduction of the O and A level examinations in 1951 (a development which will be considered in the next chapter), the establishment of the Schools Council in 1964, and the emphasis within *The Plowden Report* of 1967 on the need for teachers to exercise their professional judgement in relation to the needs and interests of the child. By the mid-1970s, however, partly in response to the economic situation created by the 'first oil crisis', central government became more and more concerned about what it saw as a need to take much greater control of curriculum and assessment strategies. This was indicated nationally in the famous 1976 Ruskin College speech of Prime Minister, James Callaghan, where he called for a 'core' national curriculum to address what were perceived to be falling academic standards in schools.

Over the next 12 years the momentum for change developed to such an extent that in 1988 the National Curriculum was introduced. This curriculum, with its key stages, its 'core' and 'foundation' subjects in the first two key stages, its inclusion of a modern foreign language in key stage 3, its 'entitlement' subjects in key stage 4, and its numeracy and literacy strategies for the primary curriculum, was the principal indicator of a radical change in the British educational landscape. The institution of the Office for Standards in Education (Ofsted) in 1993, with the remit to inspect every school at least once every four years, reinforced this change. Bartlett and Burton have summarised the scenario as follows:

> [There was] great pressure on teachers to ensure that they covered all aspects of the curriculum and left them little time to deviate from it. Effectively, they had to 'teach to the test' in order to ensure the highest possible scores in the assessment. Clearly this led to a narrowing of the range of pedagogic methods teachers could employ and to some extent stifled the creativity of both teachers and schools.
>
> (2007, p. 74)

In other words, while decisions regarding how to teach the curriculum were officially to be made by teachers, the requirement that all pupils be assessed and the results made public, greatly shaped what actually went on in classrooms.

It would be remiss, however, to view the move to a national curriculum in the United Kingdom as part of a new international movement. On the contrary, the notion of a broadly-based, general, non-specialised curriculum embracing the vernacular language and literature, mathematics, a second language and science, had for quite some time been the common pattern in a range of European countries, promoted largely on the grounds of its necessity in order to ensure equality of opportunity in education. For example, uniform curriculum prescription had been official state policy in the USSR since 1918, while throughout much of Europe in the post-Second World War years, there emerged various new institutions in which common provision of basic subject matter was the determining principle of curriculum planning and design. Amongst these were the colleges d'enseignement secondaires in France and the unit schools in Scandinavia. Also, in the Federal German Republic, despite the strong regionalisation which existed there in the political and administrative spheres, inter-Lander arrangements over the years ensured high uniformity in curriculum policies.

This latter observation indicates the importance of considering developments in the curriculum field in a broader international context. In this regard, a valuable benchmark historically depicting the broad pattern in relation to the 'whole' curriculum areas across many countries in the developed world was identified by the OECD in 1989 (Skilbeck, 1989) in a report entitled *Schools and Quality: An International Report*. It also indicated the extent of the desire of governments to utilise state-provided education, often in the name of quality control. This, as Skilbeck (1992) saw it, was an intensification of a trend that can be traced back to the inception of most systems of public education. Thus, while academics in the United States, England, Australia and New Zealand are wont to point to what they often term the unprecedented desire of central governments to direct the school curriculum, and to speak of this as an alarming situation, such direction has long been the norm elsewhere.

The trend identified in 1989 and the associated 'whole' curriculum patterns have been maintained up to the present. In certain countries this applies even in relation to private schools, since they are often not free of governmental influence even though they enjoy greater independence than state schools. At the same time, of course, 'government' does not always mean 'national government', since in certain jurisdictions it is the region or province which has responsibility for public education. Professional bodies and teachers' unions are also often involved in the decision-making process by government under a social partnership model of consultation.

The general trend has not just been one of seeking control over the curriculum, but also of attempting to channel it and associated approaches to learning in specific directions. The strategies adopted for doing so have varied from country to country, primarily because of different national cultural traditions. The motivation in most cases, however, has been largely the same, namely, to promote economic and social change. Regarding the former, the main concern has been with trying to maintain economic growth, while in the case of the latter it has been an attempt to achieve high employment and maintain social stability. The capacity of education to play a major part in this enterprise is not only assumed, it is often held up as being the 'magic potion'. This, of course, is not surprising given the extent to which we now live in a knowledge-based economy.

Three of the common themes of national level reform identified by the OECD (1989) nearly 20 years ago have persisted (Kamens *et al.*, 1996) and are still strongly evident (Hoffman *et al.*, 2008). These are increased involvement of community interests in the processes of curriculum making, validation and appraisal; the emphasis on standards, levels of attainment, procedures of assessment and the articulation of qualifications; and the maintenance of the notion of a 'broad general education' intersecting with competencies and skills for the adult world. Each of these themes merits brief consideration.

Regarding the increased involvement of community interests in the processes of curriculum making, validation or appraisal, it is noteworthy that traditionally the curriculum in most countries has been mandated by central government, whether at national or regional level. This has also tended to be done without much consultation with various other educational groups, except perhaps, in certain political jurisdictions, with teachers' unions. Over the last 20 years, however, this has changed. Increasingly community interest groups have been brought into the processes of curriculum design and development. These include business and industry interests. Along with making recommendations on the direction that the curriculum should take, including suggesting the content which should be taught and the teaching and learning approaches which should be utilised, they are also involved in validating and appraising various proposals. A significant spin-off has been the development of business-industry school partnerships in various countries.

Increasingly, also there has been a trend to consult with parents and parent bodies, while in some countries particular attention has been paid to conferring with ethnic groups. Equally, teachers and teacher educators have not been excluded from the consultation process. In addition, they have been charged with more responsibility than previously in overseeing curriculum improvement, a move which, at least within the policy rhetoric, has led to an improvement in the portrayal of their professional role. This is particularly the case in those societies where teachers are expected to operate within general curriculum frameworks and assume more responsibility for the selection of content and pedagogical strategies, as opposed to the more traditional practice whereby they have had to operate by responding to highly specific central prescriptions.

At the same time, there has been much more of a tendency internationally for central government to become involved in monitoring and evaluation. This is aimed primarily at trying to ensure that the educational goals which are set are being pursued and, hopefully, achieved. Accordingly, the role that central inspectorates played in previous eras has been largely restored. School inspectors are once again charged with seeing that schools and teachers are complying with the outcomes and standards which are set, especially in relation to the performance of students (Australia and much of the USA are notable exceptions in not having such personnel).

The second overall trend in international developments in the learning context, as noted already, is the increased emphasis being placed on standards, levels of attainment, procedures of assessment and the articulation of qualifications (Goldstein, 2004). A consequence of associated developments is that the mode of school assessment has become a major force orientating students' approaches to learning and teachers' approaches to teaching. Much of this is driven by the stress which governments now place on consulting international league tables which compare the results of assessment of national standards of educational attainment, and particularly what are termed "output standards related to student achievement" (Gipps, 1998). Such attention is often justified on the grounds that it helps to ensure that the curriculum has quality and relevance through benchmarking against international standards and criteria.

The trend has also allowed governments to claim that they are responding to calls for greater accountability in the spending of public money on education. In particular, a variety of approaches are taken to communicate to 'the general public' what it is schools should be trying to achieve. The approaches adopted also provide for greater visibility and there is more transparency than ever before about what is going on. This is especially so in the case of those educational systems which have produced nationally defined and assessable levels of student achievement (Holger, 1997; Hubert and Phillips, 2006).

The third common theme of national level reform relates to the maintenance of the notion of a 'broad general education' intersecting with competencies and skills for the adult world. While some might hold that there has been a shift in policy across many countries towards a narrow utilitarian approach to the curriculum, it is arguable that the pattern is rather more complex. Certainly, there is greater emphasis now on the knowledge and skills that are considered relevant for adult life, including the world of work (Bagnall, 2000). Nevertheless, such knowledge and skills are embedded in curriculum frameworks which draw upon a wide range of knowledge forms and academic disciplines (Paris and Kimball, 2000). Also, while they have a large skills component, the tendency is to prescribe the teaching of generic skills rather than highly specific ones (Wirth, 1994). Thus, the tendency, as Skilbeck first identified it in 1992, is "more akin to a contemporary form of work-related general education than to the older idea of preparation for a precisely defined occupation" (1992, p. 13). Schools have also been re-equipped to deal with this trend and, in general, have responded positively.

So far, considerations have centred on the broad trends in relation to the 'whole' curriculum, particularly across OECD member countries. A related development, however, is also evident, namely, the great emphasis which has been placed on the notion of education for lifelong learning. Many countries have seized upon this notion as an overall guiding aim to give coherence to the wide range of activities taking place within their educational systems. We now turn our attention to what is meant by lifelong learning.

An emphasis on lifelong learning

In a growing number of countries the concept of nurturing students who have attained the skills, knowledge, values and understanding to become lifelong learners is promoted as the major purpose of the educational endeavour. Indeed, such a concept of lifelong learning is becoming a focal point around which many of the developments outlined in the previous section are given clearer focus. Also, it is promoted to address the needs of the twenty-first century in a manner which suggests it only came into prominence in what has been variously termed the 'information age' (Blackmore, 1999), or the 'learning age' (Blunkett, 1998; Longworth, 1999). Those who advocate the need for all citizens to become lifelong learners argue that in just about all aspects of our lives the pace of change and innovation continues to escalate at a rapid rate. No longer, it is stated, can we simply rely on our traditional ways of doing things and on proven strategies to address evolving issues and trends.

Contemporary factors such as the advent of the global economy, the rapid advancements in technology which have facilitated greater access to information and communication, the world's burgeoning population and changes in demographics, and the evolution of new types of employment which require a varied range of skills and competencies are all exerting enormous influence on economic and social development. Lifestyles for many are also being influenced by comparatively high levels of unemployment, frequent job changes which require retraining and flexibility, the need for multi-skilled employees, and an emerging desire for greater personal fulfillment. As a result, governments in a range of countries have been developing policies and implementing strategies to bring lifelong learning precepts into action, corporations and small businesses have acknowledged that the habit of continuous learning in the workplace is important, and cities and regions have started to orient their information, environmental, educational and civic policies to develop the human potential of all their inhabitants.

Yet the concept of lifelong learning is not a new one. Even though we are in the midst of an era of rapid advancement, the call to create lifelong learners in order to keep pace with the changing world has been regularly made throughout history. As Longworth (1999, p. 3) tells us, the notion has been around for many thousands of years, having been embraced by Plato, Kuan Tzu, Comenius, Seneca, and many others. Over the past decade, however, there has been a renewed focus to ensure that lifelong learning opportunities are provided for all. At the same time, the literature reveals that there is some disagreement as well as confusion about what the term means.

Back in the 1960s the term 'lifelong learning' was synonymous with other terms which became popular at that time, such as 'adult education', or 'careers education'. It was in the middle of that decade that the UNESCO International Committee for the Advancement of Adult Education considered a paper on *Education Permafaente* (Jessup, 1969). As a result of the arguments put forward, the Committee recommended endorsing the principle of 'lifelong education', which it defined as "the animating principle of the whole process of education, regarded as continuing throughout an individual's life from . . . earliest childhood to the end of his [*sic*] days, and therefore calling for integrated organisation" (Jessup, 1969, p. vii).

Soon the concept of 'lifelong education' began to attract the attention of international policymakers and practitioners (Goad, 1984). As a result, the UNESCO Institute for Education (UIE) commissioned a series of studies on the implications for curriculum development (Dave, 1973; Hameyer, 1979), learning strategies (Hawes, 1975) and teacher education (Dove, 1982; Lynch, 1977). These were grounded in the following list of characteristics which were documented (Dave, 1975, p. 8) as constituting the most recognisable features of lifelong education:

- *Totality:* A comprehensive view of activities and experiences that contribute to education throughout a lifetime;
- *Integration:* Understood from the viewpoint of curriculum integration, the integration of teacher training and community life;
- *Flexibility:* Variety or diversity of educational content, modes of learning and time of learning;
- *Democratisation:* Free access to educational opportunities for all members of the community;
- *Opportunity or Motivation:* Necessary societal and personal conditions for the development of lifelong education;
- *Educability:* Learning to learn;
- *Operational Modality:* Recognition that education can be carried out through formal, non-formal and informal channels;
- *Quality of life and learning:* The recognition that the central societal function of education is that of developing human potential to the full.

These characteristics have a correspondence with many of the more contemporary definitions of lifelong learning. Yet, as Chapman and Aspin (1997) have argued, the term 'lifelong education' as it was used by writers like Gelpi (1984), lacked clarity, with the use of the word 'education' indicating something akin to a formal process undertaken at the conclusion of compulsory schooling. Thus, 'lifelong education' was used largely to refer to provision, whereas contemporary notions of 'lifelong learning' focus more on the needs and ongoing development of the individual.

Longworth (1999, p. 14) clarified the latter point by noting that "learning is as different from education as following instructions is from thinking, as having information is from knowing, as reading words is from communicating ideas". He defined the specifics of lifelong learning as:

- *'Lifelong'* – from cradle to grave, from 0–90, from birth to earth, from maternity to eternity, from hatch to dispatch;
- *'Learning'* – it focuses on giving learners the tools by which they can learn according to their own learning styles and needs;

- *'For all'* – it excludes no one and pro-actively creates the conditions in which learning develops creativity, confidence and enjoyment at each stage of life.

A definition with similar focus was provided by the European Lifelong Learning Initiative (ELLI) in a report for the 'First Global Conference on Lifelong Learning' conducted in Rome in 1994. Here lifelong learning was stated to be:

> a continually supportive process which stimulates and empowers individuals to acquire all the knowledge, values, skills and understanding they will require throughout their lifetimes and to apply them with confidence, creativity and enjoyment in all roles, circumstances, and environments.
> (European Lifelong Learning Initiative, 1994, p. 5)

The contention was that provision for the whole being includes the continued refinement of social skills, emotional and physical well-being, enhanced self-esteem, positive values and attitudes, and other essential life-skills.

The expression of such views in the 1990s was reflective of a renewed interest in, and further development of, the concept of lifelong learning by a range of organisations. In 1990, a UNESCO 'World Conference on Education for All' held in Jomtien, Thailand identified the necessity to promote the concept. The gathering also precipitated further work and major international lifelong learning conferences throughout the ensuing decade. For example, the Education Ministers from the OECD countries conducted a significant meeting in 1996 under the theme of 'Making Lifelong Learning a Reality For All' (OECD, 1996). At this meeting, ministers were encouraged to develop policies in their own countries that would coordinate all government departments in order to foster the development of 'learning societies' based on the philosophy of lifelong learning.

The new level of significance and commitment directed towards the establishment of a lifelong approach to learning for all was clearly indicated by the European Parliament and the Council of the European Union when the year 1996 was designated as the 'European Year of Lifelong Learning'. This designation was based on the need to provide a more educated and skilled workforce in order to enhance national economic growth, international competitiveness and a greater capacity for individuals to improve their employability. The European Ministers were very concerned about the potential for large numbers of unemployed to create levels of social unrest through societal acceptance of xenophobic behaviour, violence, and the entrenched use of drugs and alcohol. Responding to this situation, the European Parliament described the purpose of lifelong learning as follows:

> To develop each person's personality, to teach values of private, social and public life as solidarity, tolerance and understanding of cultural

diversity, to promote the ability of various cultural groups to communicate and to promote the involvement of all the citizens of Europe in democratic decision making.

(1995, p. 2)

Lifelong learning, then, according to the European Parliament, is much more
than just a national strategy to achieve economic goals. Rather, it is also the
path to greater fulfillment, contribution and satisfaction for the individual, as
well as being the path to social cohesion and the development of a more tol-
erant and accepting society.

Lifelong learning can be viewed, therefore, as having a broad platform with
a variety of underlying assumptions. Instead of learning being considered to
be an instrument utilised to produce an extrinsic goal, lifelong learning and
education itself may also be seen as being something which brings its own set
of intrinsic rewards. That is, education can provide individuals with
expanded horizons which will continue to develop and grow throughout life
as skills and competencies are continually refined and as required learning is
absorbed. Developing an individual's ability and motivation to continue to
learn throughout life can, it is held, lead to greater fulfillment, satisfaction,
enhanced employment opportunities, greater remuneration and a range
of additional benefits which improve the quality of life. In this regard,
Blackmore (1999) explained that lifelong learning is fundamental as individuals move in and out of work, training, community, home and leisure
activities. The theory is that learning becomes a lifestyle through the interaction of the individual with learning communities, learning cities and a learning society. In this view, education and training are organised along seamless
pathways on which individuals progress according to interest, need and
aptitude.

It would be remiss to overlook the concerns raised by certain commentators about the proclaimed vision of lifelong learning (Dehmell, 2006; Hake,
1999; Livingstone, 1999; Schuetz and Casey 2006; Walters, 1999). These,
however, have been tiny voices in comparison to the continuing loud
proclamation of the stated economic and personal benefits of lifelong
learning opportunities for all. Societal advantages to be realised have also
been articulated. It has been strongly argued that members of a better
educated and more highly skilled workforce would have a major interest in
contributing towards the good governance of the world in which they live.
This could translate into an increased commitment and participation by
more enlightened citizens in democratic processes which ensure that values
such as tolerance, freedom, security, openness and honesty are strongly
enshrined. These central, or core elements have been termed the 'triadic
nature of lifelong learning' (Chapman and Aspin, 1997). Specifically, the
elements emphasise the importance of lifelong learning for economic
progress and development, for democratic understanding and activity and
for personal development and fulfillment. Also, it is held that there is a

complex interplay between them. Clearly, none of these aims can stand alone as all three elements are interdependent. For example, a competent lifelong learner who has developed an expanding array of flexible skills and competencies will have the potential to attain a high level of personal satisfaction in all aspects of his or her life which could be in part derived from a contribution to a democratic society. In turn, economic development and global competitiveness will be very much enhanced for countries with such citizens (Chapman, 1995, p. 61).

There has also been no shortage of prescriptive blueprints being put forward indicating how the notion that learning is a continuous process can be put into practice to ensure ongoing success. In particular, it is becoming commonplace for principles along the following lines to appear in curriculum documents produced to guide primary and secondary school education in a range of educational systems:

- Students learn when they are challenged and motivated;
- Learning occurs when students are able to build on existing knowledge, skills and values;
- Learning involves making connections between different areas of knowledge and experience;
- Students learn best when they can see a purpose for what they are doing;
- Learning involves both action and reflection;
- Individuals differ in their styles and rates of learning;
- Learning involves interaction with others;
- Students need a supportive learning environment.

(Curriculum Council of Western Australia, 1998, p. 37)

Schools also began to report how they put such ideas into practice, often guided by related developments in theories seen to have relevance to the production and enhancement of student learning. To take just one of a multitude of examples, Greany (2000) reported on Camborne School's History Department in the United Kingdom after using Gardner's (1991) theory of multiple intelligences to help students develop their learning preferences.

The literature is replete with many such examples of interesting projects. The problem is that they constitute a set of disparate and often only vaguely connected innovations from which it is difficult to extrapolate any model of how to proceed in a holistic manner. UNESCO, however, came up with a solution when, in 1996, it advocated the notion of four supporting pillars of lifelong learning for all in *Learning The Treasure Within* (UNESCO, 1996). These pillars were stated to be 'learning to know', 'learning to do', 'learning to be' and 'learning to live together', and collectively they were defined as the symbols for the interpretation of the purposes of education. A brief overview of what is fundamental to each pillar is now provided.

Learning to know

The first of UNESCO's lifelong learning pillars is termed 'learning to know'. This 'pillar' is underpinned by the view that pleasure can be derived from understanding, knowledge and discovery. Such intellectual pursuit, so it is argued, encourages the development of intellectual curiosity and sharp critical faculties, and enables people to make their own independent judgements about the world around them (UNESCO, 1996). Equally, the broader our knowledge, the better we can understand the major aspects of our environment. Senge (2000) argues that schools need to ensure that students learn how to learn, are encouraged to understand their own learning and are given time to achieve intended learning outcomes. He further stresses the need for processes to be designed to facilitate success and development towards independent learning and autonomous responsibility. This has echoes of Postman's (1992) earlier argument that the most important contribution schools can make to the education of our youth is to give them a sense of coherence in their studies and a sense of purpose and connectedness in what they learn.

It can be argued further that the notion of 'learning how to learn' is built upon students having developed a range of core concepts to utilise as 'tools' for thinking. On this, Ausubel (1968) contended over 40 years ago that the most important single factor influencing learning is what the learner already knows. Taking up this point in more recent times, Treagust *et al.* (1996) hold that the key to learning is to determine what the student knows about a concept and then to build learning experiences from the student's view. To put it another way, teachers need to connect the students' core concepts with what they want them to learn. This, as NeSmith (2001) points out, means starting with the students' experiences and demonstrating how new concepts can be assimilated into them.

Learning to do

UNESCO's second pillar of lifelong learning, 'learning to do', was a response to the question of how the education process can be adapted so that it can equip people to do the types of work needed in the future. Such an education, so the argument goes, involves more than just training people to perform very specific occupational tasks. Rather, it also requires a level of personal competence that involves well-developed interpersonal skills which facilitate the intensive application of information, knowledge and creativity (UNESCO, 1996).

This pillar is described by Boston (1999) as being a basis for lifelong learning. He is of the view that "success in a good general and vocational education is the best foundation for subsequent learning, together with the integration of knowledge with know-how and skill through key competencies" (Boston, 1999, p. 3). Also, as he sees it, the core element of this lifelong learning 'pillar' is to provide relevant learning experiences that will enable young adults to obtain places in the workforce at an early age.

A trend in many Western countries especially in relation to this 'pillar' has been to emphasise the importance of the learning of generic skills, a development already noted in the first part of this chapter. The sorts of associated 'key competencies' promoted as essential for all young people to learn in preparation for the world of work are usually identified in the areas of language and communication, mathematics, scientific and technological understanding, cultural understanding, problem solving, and personal and interpersonal characteristics. A particularly enduring set of such competencies developed in Australia consisted of the following: collecting, analysing and organising information; communicating ideas and information; planning and organising activities; working with others and in teams; using mathematical ideas and techniques; solving problems; and using technology (Mayer, 1993). Here it was argued that these generic competencies should also form the basis for more specialised skills determined by the vocational pathway one eventually chooses.

At the same time, various scholars were drawing attention to the likelihood that such developments would be unlikely to win student commitment without also paying attention to their experiences of the world. Thus, there was renewed interest in the importance of motivation in promoting student learning, with Young (2000) emphasising how crucial it is to a person's wish, ability, or need to become engaged and to continue with learning. This led to a reawakening of a recognition of the importance of engaging a student's interest and responding to its many different dimensions. The argument is that teachers must make contact with students' lives, ensure they feel that the content of the classroom experience is something of value and significance to them, and make clear that the school personnel value their experience (Nuthall and Alton-Lee, 1994, p. 8).

Learning to be

The third of the UNESCO pillars of lifelong learning relates to the development of independent, critical ways of thinking and making judgements so that individuals can make-up their minds on the best courses of action to take in different circumstances of their lives. On this, it is argued that more than ever before the essential task of education is to make sure that all people enjoy freedom of thought, judgement, feeling and imagination to develop their talents and to keep control over as much of their lives as they can. Thus, students should be provided with opportunities for aesthetic, artistic, scientific, cultural and social discovery and experimentation in order to develop their own sense of independence and personal development.

A related argument is that it is imperative that schools now look to providing students with the skills that enable them 'to learn how to learn' in order to continue to meet life's challenges, many of which cannot yet be anticipated or predicted. This point was clearly articulated not only by UNESCO, but also by the Nordic Council of Ministers. For example, in *The golden riches in the grass* the latter stated:

> Nobody knows tomorrow's curriculum and the range of subjects to be included in it. Nobody knows the specific technical skills that will be required. Thus it is today a question – more so than at any other stage of history – of learning to learn; at school, in everyday life and at community level.
>
> (Nordic Council of Ministers, 1995, p. 12)

The notion is that education is not simply about preparing people to take their place in the knowledge-age economy of the twenty-first century, but is also about enlarging their minds, stimulating their imagination, arousing their curiosity, and assisting them to learn how to think.

At the beginning of the new millennium Ryan (2000) proclaimed that the need to develop higher order thinking skills among all students has never been greater. Such skills he identified as being "reasoning, argument, problem-solving, collaboration and so on" (Ryan, 2000, p. 1). The need to promote metacognition was also highlighted, with NeSmith (2001) arguing that teaching students to analyse their intellectual strengths and weaknesses, and how to accommodate them, is to provide them with a powerful learning tool.

Learning how to live together

The fourth of the UNESCO pillars of lifelong learning is 'learning how to live together'. This relates to the view that students need to be taught tolerance, non-violence and the value of human diversity (UNESCO, 1996). The argument follows that by teaching from early childhood the need to accept and understand other people and communities, such empathy can have a positive effect on a person's social behaviour and allow groups of people to strive for common goals. UNESCO also took the initiative in promoting in-depth discussion on the implications of such a perspective by devoting three issues of its scholarly journal, *Prospects* (one in 1998, one in 2001, and one in 2002), to a series of papers on how the associated ideas might translate themselves into solid curriculum and pedagogical practices. School subjects identified as having the potential to provide such an orientation include human geography, foreign languages, history, religion and literature. Citizenship, civic education, values and morals are other elements that are incorporated under the edifice of this lifelong learning pillar, as are many forms of sport. The view is that working towards common goals in partnerships enables the acceptance of differences and promotes the value of teamwork.

From considerations so far it is clear that lifelong learning, while something of a contested concept, has provided the basis for developing an influential blueprint to guide educational developments throughout much of the world. It was seized upon by policymakers in a variety of countries because of its attractiveness as an overall aim to give coherence to the wide range of activities taking place within their educational systems. Its particular attraction is that it can be seen as both a process and a product of the educational enterprise. This, however, is not the only sense in which 'learning as process' has come centre stage in educational debates internationally. What is being referred to here is the concurrent emphasis which has been placed on viewing student learning as being at the absolute core of educational considerations. The catalyst for this development broadly has been cognisance that as society moves from the industrial age to the information age it requires education to change from a 'factory system of delivery' to a 'knowledge system'. The argument is that there has been a shift in worldview from a clockwork, mechanistic concept of the universe to that of a living organic system. Thus, new learning structures are needed to reflect the changes that are occurring in both our institutions and ourselves so that they can accommodate the move from reductionist, linear thinking about schools and learning, and the ways in which we interact with one another. This third development in the learning context internationally is now considered briefly.

Learning-centred education

Cotgrove (1997) describes industrial age schools as concentrating masses of children into heavily routinised, regulated and controlled classes, where they were taught by teachers held in high regard by a largely uneducated society. They were the product of a masculine society which valued dominance and exploitation, and where institutions were hierarchical, homogenous and conformist. What is needed for today, however, so the argument goes, are schools that are more flexible and modular in their functions so that they reflect the societal attitudes of stewardship and conservation where sustainability and quality of life are important, and where institutions are more heterogeneous.

Beare (1997) was at the forefront in criticising the current system for perpetuating industrial concepts such as 'egg-crate' classrooms, set class groups based on age-grade structures, division of the school day into standardised slabs of time devoted to particular subjects, the linear curriculum which sequences knowledge, the parcelling of knowledge into predetermined subjects and the division of staff by subject specialisation, the limitation of learning to a place called 'school', the division between school and home, and the isolation of the school from other aspects of the community. Spady (2001, p. 55) also weighed into the fray, stating that the "mechanical, standardised, command and control, industrial age model of instruction is profoundly flawed because it is contrary to human potential [and] human learning". He concluded that education operates on an agrarian and industrial age delivery system that is counter to ensuring learning.

Adopting a similar position, Hancock (1997) outlined six requirements of an information age school: interactivity; library-media specialists; continuous evaluation; the presence and easy accessibility of information technologies, the teacher's role being that of coach and guide; and the encouragement of a high level of self-initiated learning. These, and a host of other recommendations relating to the need to place student learning at the very core of the educational enterprise could be elaborated on in a major tome. However, it is sufficient within the present context to outline the main thrust of the associated movement. This can be achieved by briefly considering three major associated developments, namely, the shift towards an outcomes-based approach to learning, the stress which is placed on taking cognisance of learning conditions and learning styles, and the promotion of concepts of the learning organisation and the learning-centred environment.

An outcomes-based approach to learning

Over the last 10 to 15 years there has been a major increase in the stress placed internationally on the promotion of an outcomes-based approach to learning. The focus in this approach is on success, but the means by which this success should be pursued is not made clear. It is an approach which is underpinned by three premises: all students can learn and succeed, but they learn in different ways and at different rates; if students experience success they are more likely to be motivated to seek further success; schools can control the conditions for success by establishing a context which facilitates learning. The thrust of recommendations based on these premises has resulted in a shift in many countries from a teacher-input model to one in which the curriculum emphasis is on what students are expected to learn and achieve. The claim is that through adopting such a model, students will be empowered in their learning and concentrate on success.

An outcomes-focused system, then, is one that is based on a clearly developed set of student-learning outcomes around which the school is organised and where the conditions and opportunities that enable all students to achieve these outcomes are established. The outcomes are performances that embody and reflect learner competence. If practised as recommended, it is held, outcomes-based learning provides schools and teachers with a great deal more freedom to create a curriculum and learning environment suited to the needs of the learner than has traditionally been the case. It provides a curriculum framework that defines the skills and understandings to be developed and the performance criteria for judging achievement. At the same time, it does not define the learning experiences and opportunities to be provided. This is the domain of the teacher (Darling-Hammond, 1997).

A stress on taking cognisance of learning conditions and learning styles

Dimmock (2000) impresses that the physical learning environment needs to be conducive to student learning. This includes such factors as adequate fresh air, bright and cheerful presentation of classrooms, display of student work, ambient temperature, exclusion of distractions such as external noise, and adequate space for arranging furniture. Control of these factors can lead to the production of a safe and comfortable learning environment that can stimulate learning. Ornstein (1995) has also emphasised the importance of heeding a number of conditions when attempting to provide an appropriate psychological environment to foster student learning. In particular, he has stressed the importance of trying to ensure that the student has a positive self-concept, is motivated to learn, is goal-focused, recognises the connection between prior knowledge and new information, is in a state of 'developmental readiness' for learning the matter in hand, is given opportunities for appropriate practice or rehearsal, is provided with opportunities for transfer of learning, receives appropriate reinforcement, and receives positive feedback and encouragement.

The importance of heeding students' learning styles has also received much emphasis. What is often highlighted is the notion that learners operate from one of four main learning styles: active, reflective, pragmatic and theoretical. A great deal of research aimed at identifying such styles has been conducted over the last 30 years. As early as 1975, for example, Dunn and Dunn (1975) identified 4 stimuli and 18 elements of learning styles. Later, McCarthy (1990) developed and applied the 4MAT system to identify learning styles and Mamchur (1996) developed an instrument for assessing student learning styles based on the Myers-Briggs Type Indicator. The large corpus of such work which developed came to be emphasised strongly by those advocating learning-centred education.

The emphasis by those who foreground the importance of taking into account students' learning styles is on a view that such a position can enable a teacher to organise learning experiences in response to students' needs. While the traditional classroom environment, it is argued, suits the analytic learner, it often cannot provide a stimulating environment for other types of learners, and this can lead to frustration. The implication for teachers is that they need to be able to identify the learning styles of their students and to provide experiences to accommodate all kinds of learning styles. They also need to expose students to all learning styles and to encourage them to operate on more than one style, as well as to advise that they work with people who operate using a learning style other than their own.

The promotion of the concepts of the learning community and the learning organisation

Alongside the advocacy of the notion of a more integrated and multi-dimensional approach to learning has been the promotion of the concept of a 'learning community'. McGilp (2000, p. 15) expressed the view that the creation of learning communities is based upon "a declaration of a vision of . . . learning which necessitates upholding values of open-mindedness and integrity in relationships and creating a passion for and love of learning". The argument is that education is not confined within the walls of traditional institutions. Rather, opportunities for learning need to be provided at all hours of the day in formal and informal situations, and in a variety of traditional and non-traditional settings.

The latter position is very much in line with the recommendation of the European Round Table of Industrialists' (1997) report that to ensure learning is relevant, schools will need to expand their boundaries and become an integral part of a community that provides collaborative learning opportunities for the benefit of everyone. It stated that "the learner will be at the core of the learning process and this will require close co-operation of all the links of the Education Chain as well as the intensive interaction between the formal education system and the outside world" (European Round Table of Industrialists, 1997, p. 3). The outcome of this process, it was argued, will be the 'learning community'. Put simply, the learning community is a composition of all the places where learning takes place and would include traditional sites of education in addition to places such as work-sites, the home, various clubs, community centres, cultural centres such as museums and art galleries, churches and local libraries and telecentres.

Even more prominently promoted has been the notion of the 'learning organisation'. This was defined by Garvin (1993, np) as "an organisation skilled at creating, acquiring and transferring knowledge, and modifying its behaviour to reflect new knowledge and insights". In a similar vein, Senge, in his book *The Fifth Discipline* defined it as "an organisation that is continually expanding its capacity to create its future" (1995, p. 14). Overall, the concept generated the notion that learning is also an integral part of work and is a foundation of a successful organisation's culture and philosophy.

Conclusion

A number of broad developments in the learning context internationally have been outlined in this chapter. These have included an outline of general trends in the 'whole' curriculum, the emphasis on lifelong learning as an overarching aim of education for those working within such parameters, and the encouragement of a view that the educational enterprise should have learner-centred education at its core. They have been put forward so that the various components of the position articulated in later chapters may be located contextually. Before moving on to consider these components, however, it is necessary to outline the extent to which any associated proposals and practices also need to be evaluated in light of current developments internationally in the assessment of student learning. This is the concern of the next chapter.

3 International developments in the assessment of student learning

Introduction

Broad trends in the learning context internationally, as demonstrated in the previous chapter, are influencing much that is going on in schools. These trends are complemented, and to various degrees influenced, by developments pertaining to assessment practices. This chapter, the second aimed at contextualising the considerations in the remainder of the book, provides a broad overview of these developments. A brief account of the historical background is outlined first. Some of the main concepts related to assessment are then clarified. This is followed by an overview of the main argument advocating a practice which balances 'assessment of learning' with 'assessment for learning'. The chapter concludes by considering how current approaches in various educational systems can act to constrain the realisation of such a balance. Two phenomena in particular are considered in order to illustrate this issue, namely, the growth in international assessments in students' performance and the role of school inspectors. Attention is also given to the fact that the extent to which 'assessment for learning' is constrained by 'assessment of learning' can vary significantly from country to country.

Historical background

Throughout much of the twentieth century the discourses on assessment, especially in countries whose educational systems were based on the British tradition, were centred largely on two phenomena, namely, the school report and the written examination. In many instances, the school report consisted of a set of marks achieved in in-house examinations on the various subjects studied in school, accompanied by a few comments on behaviour and the often used phrase 'could do better' (Bryce, 2003, p. 710). In Britain itself, at least up until the advent of comprehensive schools, examinations also loomed large even at primary school level. These did very little to help in the emotional development of the child. A recent summary of autobiographical writings attests to this, highlighting in particular the extent to which the 11-plus examination brought great anxiety to generations of children and their parents (Crook, 2007, pp. 156–57).

In many other countries, by contrast, assessment remained low key in primary schools. The situation in secondary schools, however, was quite different, with examinations providing the major focus to much of what went on. As is still the situation today, the important secondary school examinations were often externally set by examination boards. Working within such a context, teachers and students joined together to work against "the unknown, external examiner, second-guessing what could come up this year, and so forth" (Bryce, 2003, p. 709). Much time was spent preparing for the examinations, including undertaking trial-runs or 'prelims', engaging in a lot of cramming, and trying to deal with a great deal of nervousness.

These practices, which were an integral part of the institutionalised curriculum, have roots which go back a long way. For example, Pinar *et al.* (1995) recall the evidence indicating that rigorous forms of assessing educational performance were developed in China by the Sui emperors during the period 589–613 AD. In attempting to establish control over "an entrenched aristocratic system" they sought a way to "allow those with natural ability to enjoy equal opportunity with the aristocracy" (Pinar *et al.*, 1995, p. 796). The solution they arrived at was to test candidates for official government positions according to their knowledge of Confucian tradition and they were successful because of the prestige of this heritage in the society.

Pinar *et al.* (1995, p. 787) point out that in the nineteenth century Prussia became the first European nation to rely on written assessments for the selection of public officials. Historians also suggest that the British East India Company held the Chinese examination system in such high regard that it decided to introduce a similar system for the selection of its own personnel. Not all examinations in the past, however, were of the written variety; there is also a tradition of oral examinations. In some societies these were prized over written examinations, in others they had no place, while in most some form of them existed alongside the written ones. The origin of the tradition is that of the classical Greek and Judeo-Hebraic notion that knowledge is "developed through disciplined conversation and argumentation" (Pinar *et al.*, 1995, p. 797). Spreading throughout the Mediterranean region, this rhetorical tradition has left its mark in a number of Continental European countries to the present, where most final examinations include an oral component. It also manifests itself in England and the USA where the interview is a mandatory part of the admission process to undergraduate degrees at the prestigious universities.

Other traditions also developed with the growth of external examinations, including that traced by Madaus and Keelaghan (1992) to what they claim was the first recorded instance of evaluation which occurred in Europe. This took place in one of the German states in 1444 in a contract between town officials and the town schoolmaster, which stipulated that the teacher's salary would vary according to the achievement of pupils in the school, as measured by an oral examination. Thus was formalised, they argue, the idea that learning is labour to be rewarded financially (Madaus and Keelaghan, 1992). The idea won popularity amongst politicians and educational policymakers, particularly over the last 200 years, as did the associated notion that the reward for what is achieved should be based on some kind of assessment. Thus, payment-by-results was very popular in the nineteenth century in Ireland, Britain, Australia and Jamaica. Also, as Pinar *et al.* (1995, p. 787) point out, variations of the idea include "the performance-contracting movement of the 1960s, present day efforts to link merit pay to the test scores of students and proposals to remunerate those students who score well on tests".

Cummings (1990), on reviewing the broad pattern of developments historically, concluded that many present examination procedures and patterns can be traced to nineteenth-century developments. The remainder of this section of the chapter consists of an overview of the work of Broadfoot (1996, pp. 168–216) which illustrates this conclusion in the case of England. Such an examination serves to contextualise further the trends in assessment outlined later in the chapter.

Broadfoot points out that soon after the beginning of the nineteenth century there was a great desire to maintain law and order in the new industrial cities and also to prepare workers for the industrial capitalist economy. Schooling was seen to be one important solution. Assessment in various forms also developed over time as part of the response. For example, the first of Her Majesty's Inspectors (HMIs) was appointed in 1840 to oversee the maintenance of standards in elementary schools. The introduction of examinations of various kinds, including for the Home and Indian Civil Service, followed later in the century.

Examinations became ever more important with the establishment in 1917 of the Secondary School Examination Council. While this was a central council to control school examinations, the main power was wielded by the universities through their school examination boards. Success in these examinations now became the main route to economic and social advancement, leading, especially for the aspiring middle classes, to a free-place scholarship to a grammar school. Once enrolled, further avenues were opened up through success in the Lower and High School certificate examinations. These, as Broadfoot (1996, p. 175) has put it, "placed a premium on the reproduction of knowledge, passivity of mind and a competitive or even mercenary spirit". This, of course, was no accident; the type of individual produced was precisely what was required to ensure a compliant workforce. On the other hand, those human abilities which were neglected, such as the capacity to make independent judgements and engage in creative thinking and criticism, had to be suppressed lest their promotion led to the emergence of a class interested in the overthrow of existing power structures in the interest of creating a more just and equitable society.

The year 1944 was most significant in the history of English education as it witnessed the introduction and provision of 'secondary education for all'. Public examination now became more important than ever, as increasing numbers aspired to obtain a place in the more prestigious grammar schools as opposed to the alternative secondary modern schools. The 11-plus examination, which included tests of English and Mathematics, as well as of intelligence, was the central mechanism in the sorting process. The 'back-wash' effect of developments on the primary school curriculum was that "'streaming' in the primary school was common from the age of seven onwards, to give 'bright' children the maximum chance of developing their abilities and passing the 11-plus – and thus gain entry to grammar school" (Broadfoot, 1996, p. 180). This remained very much the pattern until the widespread introduction of the non-selective comprehensive secondary schools during the 1960s and 1970s.

New examinations were also introduced at the secondary school level, most notably, the General Certificate of Education, Ordinary and Advanced levels, in 1951. This was followed in 1965 by the Certificate of Secondary Education (CSE) which was designed "to provide the goal of a pass in at least one subject for about 60 per cent of the year group, the top grade of the CSE being equivalent to an O level pass" (Broadfoot, 1996, p. 185). Over the following two decades there was a desire to provide relevant information for employers and to have an assessment system which would be within the grasp of most pupils. Four significant policy developments have been identified in this regard: "the pursuit of a common system of examining at 16-plus; the rise of teacher assessment; a series of attempts at broadening and vocationalising post-16 qualifications; and, perhaps, most of all, the 'profiles' movement" (Broadfoot, 1996, p. 186). By the mid-1970s, however, as has already been noted in Chapter 1, a view was also being circulated by politicians of the 'Right' that standards were falling and a major contribution to recitifying the situation should involve the introduction of a national curriculum which would be under the control of central government rather than being left to the professional judgement of teachers, with 'product-based accountability' being enhanced through national assessment. The market model of education which eventuated under successive Conservative governments and continued under 'New Labour' has dominated developments to the present although, as is pointed out in a later section of this chapter, it is now coming under severe criticism, with a major charge being that teachers are required to spend so much time assessing their pupils there is not enough time left for teaching.

Clarifying the concepts related to asssessment

Historically, as assessment became more formalised and technical it developed around it a particular set of concepts which are now used internationally. These were originally articulated by senior policymakers, those responsible for designing tests and examinations, and academics specialising in the field. Over time, however, they proliferated to become part of the general parlance of school principals, administrators and teachers, even if they still have not entered the discourse of 'the general population'. As Fraser (1989) noted in the latter half of the 1980s, some of the key concepts in question date from the late 1960s. The origins of the associated terminology is a fascinating area of exploration in itself, as are the various interpretations of, and contestations around, much that is expounded. Here, however, it is sufficient to provide an overview of the basic concepts so that they can be used to inform not only considerations in the remainder of this chapter, but also those throughout the book as a whole.

One of the most basic distinctions made is between information gathering, assessment and evaluation. The first of these, information gathering, relates to such matters as what students think, what they feel, and what they are able to do. This encompasses many activities, including making observations about performance, administering tests, and requiring students to express their ideas in writing. In general, it involves measurement, which is defined by Smith and Lovat (2003, p. 171) as being "concerned with making comparisons against some established scale", often using a numerical score.

The second major process is that of student assessment. This involves interpreting measurement information. Traditionally, this has meant giving a mark or grade to a student's performance, although it can also involve the assignment of qualitative comments about the work. The outcome of assessment allows one to compare a student with himself or herself at some previous period in time, and with other students at the present time and previously, as well as against some notion of the ideal performance in what is assessed. The purpose which usually lies behind making comparisons of these types is to inform decision-making in relation to the performance of students and teachers.

Traditionally, two major approaches to assessment have prevailed. These are norm-referenced assessment and criterion-referenced assessment. In norm-referenced assessment the performance of one student is compared with another, using the same measuring 'tools' and taking steps to try to ensure that the contexts within which the data are collected are as similar as possible. The most usual forms which such assessments take are external examinations and standardised tests. In relation to the former, the same questions are asked of the particular cohort of students on the same day and at the same time within similar physical environments, and the responses are then assessed by a group of examiners who have been prepared to mark according to a standard approach. The other form, standardised tests, are "measuring devices that have been normed on one population and then used to measure the performance of those in another population" (Smith and Lovat, 2003, p. 176).

Internationally, most external systemic examinations tend to be norm-referenced, whereas criterion referencing is most used for within-school testing and charting individual student progress. In criterion-referenced assessment, comparison is made against a standard set of criteria. These criteria, as Smith and Lovat (2003, p. 183) point out, may relate to the content of the material measured, the process of arriving at the result, or both. Also, their specification is a subjective matter, although in many cases they are arrived at through the agreement of experts in the field. The advantage of involving teachers in the process is that it can force them to think seriously and reflect on their teaching so that they can make very clear to students the grounds on which their work is being assessed. Also, while it is not a common occurrence, there is much to recommend involving students in a criterion-referenced assessment system, including being participants with their teachers both in negotiating the criteria and the assessment process (Smith and Lovat, 2003, p. 205).

Marsh (2008, p. 261) argues that currently throughout much of the world assessment can take many forms and has "a much wider scope than traditional forms of objective tests and essay tests". This is because assessment is now undertaken for a variety of reasons, including diagnosis of learning and monitoring progress, grading students, motivating them, predicting future outcomes, diagnosing teaching and, particularly at upper secondary school level, predicting students' eligibility for selection in future courses. He also emphasises the close links between reasons for assessment and their intended audiences. These intended audiences, to quote him directly, include:

1   Learners – these should be the main audience, but typically they are not given a high priority. They are rarely involved in planning the assessment activities;
2   Teachers – teachers need feedback about the effectiveness of their teaching. Student assessment data are being used increasingly as a data source for appraising teachers;
3   Parents – parents want regular feedback. Media efforts to publicise school results and 'league tables' of schools has led to increased clamouring for assessment information;
4   Tertiary institutions – universities and technical and further education colleges require specific assessment information from applicants intending to enrol;
5   Employers – employers are demanding more specific information, especially in terms of literacy and numeracy and key competencies.

(2008, p. 263)

Here it is also opportune to note that in some countries, including England, assessment for one purpose has, because of misunderstanding and misuse, evolved into another purpose. On this, Rochex (2004, p. 165) uses the market economic model to point out that what has happened in certain education systems is an "evolution from an evaluation of 'products' (students' knowledge and ability linked, to a certain extent, to the curriculum studied or the competencies judged necessary for a 'successful' life)" to an "evaluation of the 'producers' (the different school systems and the different schools, teachers and practices" (2006, p. 165). Thus, the aggregation of assessment results for individual students to give whole-school results are used to rank schools, which are then published in national and regional newspapers. This is justified on the grounds that it gives information to parents so that they can make informed choices when deciding on the school to which they should send their children.

Such an approach is often embraced wholeheartedly by governments, particularly those of the neo-liberal ilk. The problem, however, is that the published results make no reference to the extent to which they may be owing to the different social contexts in which teachers work and in which schools are located. West and Pennel have commented on this as follows:

> The focus on results of tests and examinations and pupils' education progress . . . does appear to have resulted in a focus on internal school processes as the key means of improving learning and knowledge, rather than, for example, addressing structural issues to do with pupil mix or structural inequalities within society.
>
> (2005, p. 195)

This development means that governments can shift the blame for poor performance from their own unwillingness or inability to address disadvantage to the performance of the teachers in the schools.

The third and final major concept to be discussed in this section is that of evaluation. It involves bringing together much of the information gathered and much of the assessment undertaken in order to arrive at an overall composite judgement. This, in turn, may lead to a decision. One of the most popular and useful distinctions which has developed around the concept is between 'formative evaluation' and 'summative evaluation'. Formative evaluation involves the making of judgements on the basis of the results of assessment undertaken as students engage in learning activities. A major function of engaging in such evaluation can be to assist the teacher "to discover what the students know about a topic already, whether students have understood the task set and whether instructions are clear and sufficient" (Smith and Lovat, 2003, p. 170). Thus, it can play a diagnostic role. Also, the outcomes can be provided to students as a motivational device. Equally, they can assist students and their parents in monitoring their progress. Summative evaluation, on the other hand, takes place at the end of a unit, programme, or course. The purpose is to try to determine if, in fact, students engaged in the intended activities and if the intended outcomes were realised. It is often concerned also with investigating possible reasons for the processes which actually took place and for the outcomes realised.

Popham (1995, p. 14) clarifies another distinction between formative and summative evaluation when he states that while the audience for the former consists of the designers and developers of a programme, the audiences for the latter are the "the consumers. . . . or those charged with the consumers' well-being". He goes on:

> The summative evaluator would, for instance, gather evidence in order to help a school faculty decide which of three commercially distributed

mathematics textbooks to adopt. There is no question about improving the math book. They come from a publisher, well bound in hard covers. They are to be bought and used as is. The summative evaluator's job is to help the teachers decide which of the completed books will do the best job.

(1995, p. 14)

He concludes by stating that the formative evaluators should do everything in their power to help a programme work better. In contrast, summative evaluators should "behave in a nonpartisan fashion", avoiding the tendency to be co-opted by those who have devised the programme (Popham, 1995, p. 14).

The case for 'assessment for learning'

For a variety of reasons indicated in the historical exposition at the beginning of this chapter, the attention of teachers, students and parents for many years was firmly on summative evaluation, especially the crucial examinations which were the gateway to middle-class occupations, university entrance, and the professions. In recent decades, however, formative assessment has been receiving much more attention than in the past, particularly through the popularisation amongst the academic community of the notion of 'assessment for learning'. This can be attributed partly to the influence of the research evidence by Black and William (1998) that formative assessment, when suitably employed, is a potent means to improve student learning. The central aspects of this conclusion have been summarised by Stiggins as follows:

. . . achievement gains are maximised in contexts where educators increase the accuracy of classroom assessments, provide students with frequent informative feedback (versus judgemental feedback), and involve students deeply in the classroom assessment, record keeping, and communication processes.

(2002, p. 8)

More recently, the same point has been made by Broadfoot and Black (2004) when summarising the evidence on studies demonstrating improvements in student achievement.

While 'assessment for learning' is a very attractive notion, it has generated certain differences of view in terms of what is involved. Earl (2005a), for example, has stressed that 'assessment for learning' involves two processes: providing information to teachers to help them modify their teaching and learning activities, and developing and supporting students' metacognition. This is a view, as she puts it, of "students as active, engaged and critical assessors" who "make sense of information, relate it to prior knowledge and use it for new learning" (2005a, p. 10). Perrenoud (1998), on the other hand, while recognising the existence of both processes, makes clear that the teacher modifying teaching and learning activities should not be confused with arguing for a need to concentrate on the regulation of the on-going activities of students. To engage in the latter, he holds, would be to do students a disservice by denying them "the right to hesitate, make mistakes, reflect, enter into dialogue, and thus learn" (1998, p. 88). The main concern, he argues, should be with the regulation of learning processes. On this, he states:

> It no longer suffices to talk, to explain, or to show; one needs to take into account the representations acquired and the cognitive functioning of the subject. One needs to accompany him or her in a 'metacognitive' journey, in the form of a dialogue which, being anchored in the activity, separates itself to concentrate knowledge and the learning process.
>
> (1998, p. 89)

The sorts of practices identified by James *et al.* (2007, p. 6) as being likely to assist in this process include clarifying goals and criteria, reflecting on learning, and promoting peer- and self-assessment. It may also be argued that these sorts of practices contribute to supporting students as flexible learners, a theme that will be considered in greater detail in Chapter 5.

In the USA, Stiggins (2002) has been a key player in emphasising the importance of engaging in 'assessment for learning'. As he sees it, it is not the same as formative assessment because, while it involves teachers testing more frequently and providing students with evidence so that instruction approaches can be revised, it must also involve students (2002, p. 5). Successful practitioners of this approach, he holds, when they assess for learning, use the classroom assessment process and the continuous flow of information about student achievement that it provides in order to advance, not merely check on, student learning. They do this, he points out, by:

- Understanding and articulating in advance of teaching the achievement targets that their students are to hit;
- Informing their students about those learning goals, in terms that students understand, from the very beginning of the teaching and learning process;
- Becoming assessment literate and thus able to transform their expectations into assessment exercises and scoring procedures that accurately reflect student achievement;
- Using classroom assessments to build students' confidence in themselves as learners and help them take responsibility for their own learning, so as to lay a foundation for lifelong learning;
- Translating classroom assessment results into frequent descriptive feedback (versus judgemental feedback) for students, providing them with specific insights as to how to improve;
- Continuously adjusting instruction based on the results of classroom assessments;

- Engaging students in regular self-assessment, with standards held constant so that students can watch themselves grow over time and thus feel in charge of their own success; and
- Actively involving students in communication with their teacher and their families about their achievement status and improvement.

(2002, p. 5)

The outcome of such an approach, he argues, is that students keep learning and remain confident that they can continue to learn at productive levels, rather than giving up in frustration, or hopelessness.

Stiggins is not so naive as to assume that such practices can be brought about simply by bringing them to the attention of teachers. Also, he does not argue that in the promotion of 'assessment for learning' we should neglect 'assessment of learning'. Rather, in referring specifically to the situation in the USA, he states that what is needed is the following:

- Match every dollar invested in instruments and procedures intended for 'assessment of learning' at national, state and local levels with another dollar devoted to the development of 'assessment for learning';
- Launch a comprehensive, long-term professional development program at the national, state and local levels to foster literacy in classroom assessment for teachers, allocating sufficient resources to provide them with the opportunity to learn and grow professionally;
- Launch a similar professional development program in effective large-scale and classroom assessment for state, district and building administrators, teaching them how to provide leadership in this area of professional practice;
- Change teacher and administrator licensing standards in every state and in all national certification contexts to reflect an expectation of competence in assessment both of and for learning; and
- Require all teacher and administrator preparation programs to ensure that graduates are assessment literate – in terms of promoting and of documenting student learning.

(Stiggins, 2002, p. 9)

He concludes by arguing that Federal education officials, state policymakers, and local school leaders need to allocate resources in equal proportions to ensure that teachers engage in 'assessment for learning' along with 'assessment of learning'.

Constraints on 'assessment for learning'

The emphasis placed by Stiggins and others on the importance of trying to achieve a balance in schools between 'assessment of learning' and 'assessment for learning' cannot be overemphasised. At the same time, it is important for leaders of learning to recognise that various forces operate to constrain this happening. For example, it has been recognised for decades that external examinations can restrict the curriculum, with objectives and material often being excluded from or neglected in the classroom. More recently, Broadfoot and Black (2004) and Harlen (2005), have concluded that the main obstacle to more widespread use of 'assessment for learning' is the current high stakes 'assessment of learning', such as the growth of large-scale international assessment studies. This section draws attention to the development of these tests and the importance they have attained. It also seeks, however, by drawing attention to the continuing existence of school inspectors in certain contexts, to illustrate that other obstacles can equally exist. Furthermore, it highlights that there is no discernible pattern in how both areas are dealt with across nations and hence no clear blueprint for practice in all cultural contexts.

International tests as constrainers of 'assessment for learning'

There is no homogeneity across nations in terms of the methods they use to measure and assess student achievement. Rather, significant variation exists on such matters as the nature of the tests utilised and the age-levels of those tested. Consequently, it has been difficult for many years to draw meaningful comparisons of the levels of achievement of students across nations. Ornstein and Levine (1989) drew attention to this over 20 years ago when they reviewed the results of a project on student testing practices in 17 industrialised countries. The conclusion was that because there was so much variation there was hardly any scope for making comparisons.

Very little has changed on this matter since then, with the only common denominator still being that curriculum policy and practice in many countries continues to be driven, as it has been for a long time, by examination results. On the other hand, there has been an enormous growth in the last 10 years in international assessments of students' performance. The foundations for this movement were laid down over 50 years ago with the establishment of The International Association for the Evaluation of Educational Achievement (IEA) in 1961. Since then the Association has been involved in conducting a great number of assessments of the effectiveness of different educational systems, along with identifying factors related to student achievement (Owen *et al.*, 2004, p. 4). The approach taken in reporting results was, from an early stage, to rank countries using national average scores on assessments in a host of different subject areas. This was driven by certain technical requirements of in-depth analyses. Unwittingly, however, it acted to spur competition between countries, thus initiating a movement which seems to accelerate with each passing year.

The international assessment movement itself has also accelerated greatly. During the 1980s individual studies were conducted on mathematics, science, written composition and classroom environment. Amongst the countries in which they had a major impact was the USA. The results from the mathematics assessment in particular were given extensive coverage and led to a cry for a return to basics and the rigorous implementation of traditional teaching methods. There was no let-up during the 1990s, which witnessed the following major developments identified by Owen *et al.* (2004, p. 7):

- Two administrations of the IEA's Trends in International Mathematics and Science Study (TIMS), which by 1995 was the largest study of student achievement undertaken to date;
- The IEA Reading Literacy Study (RLS), conducted in 1990–91 in 32 countries;
- Three waves of data collection for the International Adult Literacy Survey (IALS) in a total of 20 countries between 1994 and 1998;
- The IEA Civic Education Study (CivEd), expanding upon previous studies of civic education with the integration of both qualitative and quantitative methodologies.

In addition, the OECD began planning during this decade for engagement in similar projects. Network A of the OECD's 'Indicators of Education Systems' (INES) project became particularly active, with a group of countries cooperating to collate and publish cross-national comparative data. This led to the Programme for International Student Assessment (PISA) (Owen *et al.*, 2004, pp. 3–23).

By the early 2000s a number of claims were being made with regard to positive developments in the international assessment arena (Owen *et al.*, 2004, pp. 7–9). Amongst these were the harnessing of great advances in statistical methodology to enhance the validity of the comparability of assessments. New more reader-friendly forms of reporting were developed in order to bring the results to a wider audience. Furthermore, the development of an international system for education indicators supported the development of national indicator systems and the growth in national assessment. In some countries where there is no national assessment, such as the Czech Republic and Switzerland, international assessments provide the only available macro-level data on student outcomes. Furthermore, as Owen *et al.* (2004, pp. 10–11) pointed out, in countries like Spain where there is no clear definition of educational objectives or established curriculum at the national level, it is even more necessary to "have as a point of reference data from other countries that may have similar contexts". In similar vein, they state:

> Assessment results have also triggered changes in curriculum. In Finland, policy makers reported that international assessments have considerable influence on curriculum development and in the Netherlands results have spawned the establishment of study centres dedicated to particular curricular areas.

Such developments would seem to suggest that international assessments will receive widespread support for some time to come as individual governments continue to embrace the notion that having information comparing students in their country with those in others is necessary in order to produce educational policies aimed at ensuring economic competitiveness in a global environment.

On the other hand, certain associated developments have not been in harmony with the wishes of researchers involved in the early IEA projects. In particular, they had hoped that what some have now come to term the 'horse race amongst nations' would be prevented by somehow insulating the results from extensive media coverage aimed at generating the notion of successes and failures. It appears also as if they never expected the results to be used by those with a political agenda to legitimate practices that governments already wish to implement on ideological grounds. Furthermore, there is a small but vocal set of critics who continue to highlight technical matters aimed at questioning whether the tests measure what they claim to measure, the extent to which cultural differences may bias results, and the extent to which performance on tests can be generalised beyond the items on the test. Specifically in relation to developing countries, Rochex (2004, p. 164) has recently drawn attention to the fact that many African countries, keen to assess their school systems' outcomes, have taken part in PISA tests, but because of their own dire economic situation at home, their representatives have no influence to modify for their respective contexts the Western countries' tools which are used in the tests. There is also very little evidence from the many countries involved in such tests, both developed and developing, that the results are put to productive use as 'assessment for learning'. If anything, in fact, they appear to act to constrain the process by promoting a 'teaching to the test' approach, in the belief that this will help maximise the nation's results and increase its prestige in the international academic league tables.

Inspectors as constrainers of 'assessment for learning'

So far, this chapter, where it has been concerned with developments in Britain, has focused on England and Wales. Now, however, the attention moves north of the border. The concern is with exemplifying, through considering the situation in Scotland, how school inspectors can also have expectations which often add to the demands of teachers and generate anxieties. These can sometimes be so great as to require significant leadership within schools in order to try to maintain motivation and commitment to the profession.

While being part of the United Kingdom, Scotland's educational system is separate from England. Indeed, education has long been seen as a key element of Scottish identity. Amongst the features identified as part of this element are a concern for egalitarianism and for education as a public good rather than a private advantage (Munn, 2008, p. 62). It has also been claimed that because members of the educational policy community in Scotland may have broader social origins than their English equivalents (McCrone, 2003, p. 244) and because they themselves have been beneficiaries of the nation's largely government school system, any attack on the system is perceived as an attack on Scottish culture and identity itself. On this, Munn (2008, p. 62) recalls that in the 1980s, a number of attempts were made by the then British Conservative government, which was unpopular in Scotland, to introduce such market reforms to education as parental choice of school and the publication of attainment results school-by-school. However, these attempts were opposed by teachers and parents in combination, on the grounds of the 'Englishing' of the Scottish education system.

Scotland continued along its own path in education after the creation of a Scottish parliament in 1990, even though the British state retains control of economic, foreign and defence policy. A notable feature of recent policy is that divergence from England has continued. For example, there is no great desire for the establishment of different kinds of schools in order to create a quasi-market. The commitment to comprehensive public education is as strong as ever, with the aspiration being that every school should be seen as excellent. Also, Scotland, unlike England, did not go through a period where the work of HMIs was complemented (some might even argue undermined) by the work of the Ofsted until both sectors were eventually brought together. Instead, HMIs continued in Scotland to be the sole 'inspectors' of the educational work of schools. This, however, is not to argue that the work of inspectors has been less controversial than that which has been undertaken in England.

In a very comprehensive overview of their work, Weir (2003, p. 152) has noted that while historically state rhetoric has consistently portrayed HMIs in Scotland as independent, they have generally been seen by teachers as agents of state domination who arrived at a school to measure, judge and control them. Little seems to have changed in this regard. What has changed, however, is the criterion for appointment as an inspector. For many years the crucial criterion was scholarship. Gradually that was replaced, so that today the main criterion is that one has had significant and successful practice as a teacher. This drift away from scholarship has, Weir (2003, p 153) argues, "reduced the ability of HMIs to influence policy and practice through intellectual argument". Instead, he concludes, they have come mainly to be concerned with finding solutions based on technicist, or managerialist approaches.

HMIs in Scotland are now known as members of Her Majesty's Inspectorate of Education (HMIE) in Scotland. While they do not seem to be quite as adversarial as their counterparts who inspect in England (Barker, 2009, p. 58), they are equally as rigorous. Most of the work is of the 'whole school evaluation' type, where everything is inspected from school ethos, staffing, accommodation, curriculum, learning and teaching, and support for learning, to care and welfare, and leadership. The process normally takes place over a one-week period in the case of primary schools, while in second-ary schools it is usually two periods of four days' inspection, with a short break in between. Within 16 weeks a report is issued to the school inspected and four weeks later it is widely published. Also, the HMIE revisits the school after two years to see what has been the response to his or her recommenda-tions. The nature and level of the school's progress, if any, is then reported to parents.

The audit unit of HMIE also operates to involve schools in critically exam-ining themselves in relation to national priorities and targets, those of the local authority in which they are located, and individual school development plans, with the intention that they will build their own internal quality assur-ance frameworks. Such activity, however, along with the whole-school inspections, does not appear to act as 'assessment for learning', or to empower teachers. On the contrary, according to Bennett (2001), it is part of a broader agenda operating over the last 15 years aimed at deprofessionalis-ing teachers and increasing control over schools. She concedes that inspection does go some way towards delivering public accountability, providing an external perspective and forcing schools to pay more attention to their ongo-ing development. On the other hand, she considers the shift in the approach of inspectors from being that of 'allies' to being 'judges', to be a regrettable development.

At a more specific level, Bennett found that teachers are unhappy with inspection because they consider inspection time to be too short, they do not have enough contact with the HMIEs, and the inspectors themselves do not have sufficient knowledge of the contexts of specific schools. Regarding the activity of the audit unit, she states that the whole concept of self-evaluation "is still too controlled and too inflexible to encourage teachers to innovate and follow their own convictions" (Bennett, 2001, p. 463). Rather than being given the freedom to negotiate local standards with their local communities, teachers are told what standards they should reach. Her overall judgement is that the Scottish system of inspection is weak in not engaging teachers with each other and with external advice in pursuit of a school's own development priorities and evaluation strategies. Reflecting on this, Weir (2003, p. 158) concludes that the matter of how to reconcile the political need for schools to be accountable with the professional need for collegial support remains unresolved.

Country-specific constrainers of assessment practices

While the emphasis so far has been on the importance of balancing 'assess-ment of learning' with 'assessment for learning', and with recognising that this can be constrained in a number of ways, it is also important to highlight that there is no discernible pattern in how both areas are dealt with across nations. Hence, there are no clear patterns as to what 'would work' in any one country committed to ensuring such a balance. Black and Wiliam (2005) came to this view after conducting an investigation of a number of countries, including France, Germany, the USA and England. Regarding France, they highlighted that it has a national curriculum for all levels of compulsory education. The majority of students take the *brevet des colleges* examination at 15 years of age. Those who proceed to the *lycee* and wish to enter higher education are then examined in the *baccalaureat* after another three years of study.

Notwithstanding the importance of such examinations in students' lives, focusing on the results is not considered appropriate for monitoring standards of achievement in schools. Rather, the Ministry of Education's Office for Assessment and Forecasting uses surveys to monitor facilities, resources, classroom practices, students' achievements and school effectiveness, as well as students' attitudes and values. Also, at ages 8, 11 and 16, students are tested in their school subjects at the beginning of the school year to provide information to teachers to aid them in their teaching. On the other hand, the results on these and other summative tests are not, as Bonnet (1997, p. 303) has put it, to evaluate teachers and thus "antagonise the teaching profession".

The overall conclusion which Black and Wiliam arrive at in relation to France is that because teachers have no role in assessing students summatively, they are "free to concentrate on learning, and it is therefore probably not a coincidence that the role of assessment in the support of learning has been such a strong aspect of French teaching for many years" (Black and Wiliam, 2005, p. 254). The situation in Germany, however, is quite different. While education policy rests with each of the 16 *Lander* there is a great deal of similarity and cooperation in relation to curriculum and assessment. In grades 1 and 2, students are given report cards which document their work habits, special skills and areas for improvement. In the higher grades, results on formal tests and examinations are reported to parents and students scoring very low grades may be required to repeat the year. Also, it is the teacher who recommends the appropriate form of lower secondary school for those students in the final year of elementary school on the basis of their performance in a series of officially prescribed tests and examinations administered throughout the year. Thus, Black and Wiliam (2005, p. 249) conclude, in Germany there is "faith in the ability of tests to measure learning accurately and to allocate students to different educational pathways".

A different scenario yet again prevails in the USA. Here there is not one system, but 51 separate ones. They are all characterised by the existence of multiple demands for accountability at different levels, which "have resulted in multiple assessment systems", but these tend to be "focused on measuring the amount of learning that has taken place, providing little insight into how it might be improved" (Black and Wiliam, 2005, p. 249). Also, while great emphasis is placed on grades, and almost all students are assessed on the same literal grade scale, the grade "is usually not a pure measure of attainment, but will include how much effort the student put into the assignment, attendance, and sometimes even behaviour in class" (Black and Wiliam, 2005, p. 249). A particularly strong force militating against the use of effective formative assessment is the increase in pressure to test for accountability purposes from the state and federal sources which supplement the funding provided by tax-payers in local school districts. On this, Black and Wiliam (2005, p. 258) conclude that because most districts have developed 'curriculum, pacing guides' that detail which pages of the set texts are to be covered each week, "there are few opportunities for teachers to use information on student performance to address learning needs".

England is the final country examined by Black and Wiliam. Within the broad parameters of the national curriculum introduced in 1988, the assessment situation by 2005 was that all prescribed subjects were being assessed by teacher judgements at ages 7, 11 and 14, with externally set tests for the same age groups in English and mathematics, and for science at 11 and 14. When the national curriculum was introduced it appeared as if the requirement that teachers be involved in the assessment process as part of their normal teaching could serve both formative and summative functions. However, by insisting that teacher assessments "should be judged according to the definitions of reliability that had been developed for traditional tests, combined with a profound lack of trust of teachers" (Black and Wiliam, 2005, p. 252), the potential for teacher assessments to support learning was greatly eroded. Also, the lack of central guidance about what would constitute adequate records of student achievement resulted in the development of record-keeping systems geared more to providing comprehensive evidence of students' achievements than to supporting student learning.

Within a few years of its introduction it was being reported that the national curriculum was proving to be a traumatic event in the professional lives of many teachers. By early 2009, the emphasis in criticisms had shifted to the disservice being done to pupils. The most authoritative voice on this to date is the Cambridge Primary Review, which conducted a wide-ranging and independent enquiry into the condition and future of primary education in England. The evidence base of the Review (Cambridge Primary Review, 2009) is extensive: 820 written submissions, many from national organisations; reports on 87 regional and 9 national sounding sessions, and over 140 meetings; and 28 surveys of published research commissioned from leading academics and drawing on nearly 3000 published sources. On 20 February, 2009, *The Guardian* newspaper summarised the main findings of the Review as follows:

- Children are losing out on a broad, balanced and rich curriculum with art, music, drama, history and geography being the biggest casualties;
- The curriculum, and crucially English and maths, have been "politicised";
- The focus on literacy and numeracy in the run-up to national tests has "squeezed out" other areas of learning;
- The Department for Children, Schools and Families and the

Qualifications and Curriculum Authority, which sets the curriculum, have been excessively prescriptive, "micro-managing" schools.

It also highlighted the accusation in the Review that the government has been attempting to control what happens in every classroom in England and that this has led to an excessive focus on literacy and numeracy in an "overt politicisation" of children's lives. Thus, it is recognised that the problem of the curriculum is inseparable from the problem of assessment and testing. Among the major recommendations are that schools should be freed from having to focus on standard attainment targets and league tables to allow them to make more decisions about what they should teach and how they should teach it. Should the government take heed and give much more autonomy and flexibility to teachers, then one major area in which there is likely to be increased emphasis is on 'assessment for learning'. Indeed, there remains a paradox in many countries. On the one hand, governments are enthusiastically advocating educational leadership because of its crucial importance for learning. On the other hand, there is simultaneously a reluctance to change the policies which tend to promulgate a restricted notion of learning and necessitate that school leaders are preoccupied with managerial responsibilities. In the end, it might well be the case that policy reform is the key to making the connection between school leadership and learning in a more authentic manner.

To bring a close to this sub-section of the chapter which has provided a synopsis of the comparative study of France, Germany, the USA and England by Black and Wiliam (2005), it is important to highlight their conclusion that a 'royal road' cannot be identified which would indicate an assessment system that would effectively serve both 'assessment of learning' and 'assessment for learning'. This, they hold, is because in individual countries the overall impact of particular assessment practices and initiatives "is determined at least as much by culture and politics as it is by educational evidence and values" (Black and Wiliam, 2005, p. 260). Thus, they state, it might be folly to try to develop detailed plans for an ideal assessment policy for a country, even if the 'expert' community could agree on the principles and evidence to support them. Rather, the approach might "lie in those arguments and initiatives that are least offensive to existing assumptions and beliefs" in the hope that they might "serve to catalyse a shift in them while at the same time improving some aspects of present practice" (Black and Wiliam, 2005, p. 260).

Conclusion

A number of broad developments internationally in relation to assessment of student learning have been outlined in this chapter. These, along with the developments outlined in the previous chapter on broad developments in the learning context internationally, have been presented so that the various components of the position articulated in later chapters may be located contextually. One of the key components of that position is that leadership needs to be provided to promote a consideration and a realignment of conventional school-based learning. Accordingly, the next chapter will now consider the concept of leadership, with particular attention being given to the notion of distributed leadership aimed at improving student learning in the classroom.

4 Leadership

Introduction

The model of school leadership for many years was focused on authority, power, structures, job descriptions, targets and performance management. While this model has not been abandoned for various reasons, it is no longer the sole one advocated by enlightened policymakers. They recognise that in a complex and multi-layered world, the conventional idea of great leadership being the result of the effort of a single individual is no longer sufficient. Rather, attention is given to the plethora of research over the last decade in particular, which has led to a growing recognition that deep and sustained school improvement depends upon the leadership of the many rather than the few (Harris, 2003a). Concurrently, innovation, teacher capacity building, student-centred learning, enquiry and knowledge creation are promoted.

It is also being recognised that when it comes to improving the quality of student learning, teachers from every level should be involved, thus creating a highly enduring web of influence that binds the school together and makes it special. Teacher collaboration, it is held, develops capacity for fresh perspectives on existing knowledge and experience and generates learning among teachers and students leading to sustainable development. Also, the work envisages that there is no simple solution to school improvement. As schools are facing increased pressure to raise standards and to improve performance there is an impending need to share responsibility, build positive relationships and foster sustained improvement and positive change. Thus, it is argued, the image of a school regarding the promotion of student learning should be one where all teachers and students are invested with leadership capacity.

In this chapter we elaborate on the position outlined so far. First, we contextualise it by detailing a number of background considerations on leadership in education. A brief overview of a typology that indicates some of the various positions on leadership which have impacted on education, including student, teacher and organisational learning, over the last 20 years is presented. We go on to consider the basic ideas within the concept of 'distributed leadership' which has much to commend it for improving the quality of student learning. In line with the incremental approach to change advocated in Chapter 1, this leads us to argue that what is realistic is the promotion of one major facet of distributed leadership, namely, teacher leadership.

Background considerations on leadership in education

An early classical typology of leaders was proposed by Max Weber (1984). He identified three types: (1) traditional, (2) rational and (3) charismatic. Traditional leaders, like monarchs, come to their role, he argued, through social conventions. Rational leaders, on the other hand, are appointed on the basis of their technical, professional and bureaucratic expertise. The third type, charismatic leaders, possess a forceful or magnetic personality, or intrinsic spiritual endowment elusively identified as charisma. The source of their power is derived from the unconscious desires of their followers, and they are provided with the sense of meaning, purpose, vocation and fulfillment that they seek (Foster, 1989).

The study of leadership developed alongside the study of leaders. This field, particularly in its relation to education, has generated an enormous amount of interest among researchers and practitioners. Yet, despite the large research base, the search for a singular theory of leadership has proved futile (Harris, 2003a). Some have bewailed this situation. As early as 1959, Bennis (1959, p. 259), taking an extremely negative view, concluded that "probably more has been [said] and less is known about leadership than any other topic in the behavioural sciences". Over 30 years later, Sergiovanni (1992, p. 2), in a less cynical tone, noted that "after fifty years of steady research social science can tell us little about leadership". Fullan (1998), however, takes a more realistic view. While he argues that many new theories fail to provide robust examples, insights and powerful concepts of leadership, he also argues that more research needs to be undertaken to develop a meaningful action-based theory of leadership; a situation evident in the works of the likes of Day *et al.* (2000) and Leithwood *et al.* (1999).

Hallinger (2003), who has studied leadership for three decades, also draws attention to the situation whereby today's favourite leadership brand in education is soon replaced by another. This requires that we develop an understanding of what some of these 'brands' are. Doing so can also help in trying to deal with the problem outlined by MacBeath (2004), namely, that leadership is a term full of ambiguity and subject to a range of interpretations. A useful starting point in this regard is to consider briefly what Foster (1989) identifies as the two main traditions which have influenced the social scientific definition of leadership, that which comes from the political historical disciplines and that which comes from the world of business management and public administration.

The study of leadership through the political historical model highlights the role of significant individuals in shaping the course of history. Leadership in this sense is the story of events, actions and ideas of how individuals have transformed their social milieu (Foster, 1989). Leaders are individuals who make history through the use of power and resources.

In response to the criticism that inadequate distinctions were drawn between the concepts of leadership and power, Burns (1978) retorted that leadership involves a moral dimension while power, as demonstrated by the example of Hitler, does not. He also insisted that power-wielding is not leadership at all. Tucker (1981), by contrast, argued that an evil leader is still a leader. He then provided an alternative definition of leadership; "leadership is politics". In his views leaders, rather than being transformational, are 'goal-setters and mobilisers' dealing with the politics of group management.

While much debate focused on the tensions between the positions of Burns and Tucker, many have been happy to accept both contributions as valid; Tucker's contribution highlights the political and group dimension of leadership, while Burns' contribution stresses its moral and value base. Both also consider leadership as an individualistic ability that leaders use in various circumstances. At the same time, both views also neglect two crucial aspects. First, leadership is always context bound; it always occurs within a social community and is perhaps less the result of individual greatness than the result of human interactions and negotiations. Second, leadership cannot occur without followers and often the two roles are interchangeable, with leaders becoming followers and followers becoming leaders.

A more influential leadership model traditionally has been the bureaucratic-managerial one. It describes the views of scholars and business personnel on leadership. Here leaders are persons of superior rank in an organisation, leadership is goal-centred and goals are driven by organisational needs. The reason for exerting leadership is achieving organisational goals. The productive function legitimises the exercise of leadership. Leaders exercise their power within the environment bounded by tasks and responsibilities. The assumption is that leadership occurs only as a result of position. Top executives control the organisation and make individuals perform tasks at their level of competency. Their bureaucratic managerial leadership is tied with performance, goal achievement and productivity. Its failure to exercise control over the organisation and its membership is an assurance of failed organisation where nobody wins.

Rost (1985), refuting the latter position, has provided a useful departure point for considering a typology of contemporary theories of leadership in education. He insisted that while leadership is not organisational management, neither should it be equated with managerial effectiveness. Yet, he argued, the lack of distinction between management and leadership had by 1985 become a common feature of our language. The confusion, as he saw it, was evident when one recognised effective leadership in a leader who was unorganised, was little concerned with production, and displayed uncaring feelings, yet valued the commanding power of ideas.

A typology of leadership in education

The nature of educational leadership has changed drastically over the last decades. In the past it was the domain of politicians and senior government officers who, along with school principals, constituted the professional mouthpiece on educational matters. The enormous transformation brought about by information technology, socio-political structures, arts and sciences, global education and competition, created the need for educational leaders with vision who could command public respect, could articulate what education is becoming, and could express national or international views which transcend politics (Beare, 1998).

The study of leadership has also progressed apace. Leadership traits have been drawn from the study of personality, competencies, intelligence and neuropsychology. The phenomenon has been examined using the sociological lens of structure and relationship and the anthropological lens of culture. Furthermore, it is recognised that leadership is often situational and imbued with ethical, religious and historical influences. Also, MacBeath's (2004) observation that politics and economics are shaping leaders as they exercise micro-political skills, should not be overlooked. Consequently, it is not surprising that there is currently a great range of definitions of leadership types. A brief outline of seven types of leadership is now discussed.

Managerial leadership

Bush and Glover's (2003) explanation of managerial leadership focuses on functions, tasks and the behaviours of people. It assumes that the behaviour of the organisational members is largely rational. Also, influence on people is exercised through positions of authority within the organisational hierarchy.

Leithwood *et al.* (1999) observe that managerial leadership is similar to other leadership types found in classical management literature. Dressler (2001, p. 176), however, argues differently. Traditionally, as he sees it, "the principal's role has been clearly focused on management responsibilities". Now, however, "global and societal influence has increased the span of responsibility". Thus, it has come to include interpersonal relationships, sensitivity and communication skills, contextual factors, including philosophical and cultural values, and policy and political influence.

Instructional leadership

Bush and Glover's (2003) interpretation of instructional leadership focuses on teaching and learning, and on the behaviour of teachers in working with students. Student learning via teachers has become the target of the leader's influence. The emphasis is on the direction and impact of influence rather than on the process of influence.

For Leithwood *et al.* (1999) instructional leadership is the behaviour and attention teachers adopt while engaging in activities directly affecting the growth of students. In this regard, Southworth (2002) observes that instructional leadership is strongly concerned with teaching as well as with learning. Gelten and Shelton (1991) agree, stating that effective instructional leadership is characterised by a strategy to deploy all the resources available at school to achieve its instructional mission and goal. In a similar vein, Leithwood *et al.* (1999) state that instructional leaders possess the expert knowledge and the formal authority to exert influence on teachers. Furthermore, Hallinger and Murphy (1985) affirm that instructional leaders define the school mission, manage the instructional programme, and promote school climate.

The views of such commentators are echoed in the findings of Blase and Blase (1998) who carried out research with an investigation of 800 principals in various American schools. Their findings highlight that effective instructional leadership necessitates talking with teachers, promoting teachers' professional growth and fostering teacher reflection. Yet, some considered that Leithwood's (1994) warning still needed heeding, namely, that instructional leadership images that are heavily classroom focused are no longer adequate to face impelling educational challenges.

Transactional leadership

Transactional leadership is based on exchange relationships between leader and follower. Much of political leadership is viewed as being transactional. In exchange for the voters' support, the leader adopts a programme designed to help particular groups. Transactional leadership in schools is seen, as US observers put it, as being exercised by the superintendent relationship with unions, teachers and parents. The support of the leaders is worked out through the manipulations of various social forces guiding concessions, negotiations and accommodations of needs (Foster, 1989).

Transformational leadership

Transformational leadership is generally defined as the ability of a leader to envisage a new social condition and to communicate this vision to the followers. The leader inspires and transforms individual followers from higher levels of morality that make the promise of reward unnecessary. Bush and Glover's (2003) interpretation of transformational leadership describes the influence and the increased commitment of followers to organisational goals. Leaders seek to support teachers for their vision of the school and to enhance their capabilities to contribute to goal achievement. The focus is on the transformation process rather than on particular types of outcomes.

Transformational approaches are often contrasted with transactional leadership. Sergiovanni distinguishes between them as follows:

In transactional leadership, leaders and followers exchange needs and services in order to accomplish independent objectives . . . This bargaining process can be viewed metaphorically as a form of leadership by bartering. The wants and needs of followers and the wants and needs of the leader are traded and a bargain is struck. Positive reinforcement is given for good work and for increased performance. In transformational leadership, by contrast, leaders and followers are united in pursuit of higher-level goals that are common to both. Both want to become the best, both want to lead the school to a new direction.

(1991, pp. 125–26)

Sergiovanni concludes that when transformative leadership is practised successfully, purposes that might have started out being separated become fused.

Leithwood *et al.* (1999) observe that transformational leadership is the model that provides the most comprehensive approach. Harris *et al.* (2003a), however, point to appropriateness for context. They hold that during the last decade the debate between transactional and transformational leadership has dominated both policies and practices in various countries. Transactional leadership, they observe, flourishes where the system of commands and control is in place, while transformational leadership and more democratic leadership approaches have been adopted where decentralisation has occurred.

Moral leadership

Moral leadership is based on the values and beliefs of leaders and provides the school with a clear sense of purpose (Bush and Glover, 2003). It is similar to the transformational model, but with a stronger value base. Sergiovanni comments on this upholding of the importance of values as follows:

Excellent schools have central zones composed of values and beliefs that take on sacred or cultural characteristics. The school must move beyond concern for goals and roles to the task of building purposes into the structure and embodying these purposes in everything that it does with the effect of transforming school members from neutral participant to committed followers.

(1991, pp. 322–23)

The embodiment of purpose and the development of followers, he concluded, are inescapably moral.

For West-Burnham (1997) there are two types of moral leadership. On the one hand, there is 'spiritual leadership', which is the high order set of principles that many leaders possess. On the other hand, there is 'moral confidence'. This is the leader's capacity to act in a way that is consistent with the ethical system upheld over time. The morally confident leader demonstrates consistency between principle and practice, explains and justifies decisions in moral terms, and sustains them over time.

Taking up the notion of moral leadership, Sergiovanni (1991) argues that in the principalship the challenge of leadership is to make peace with two competing imperatives: the managerial and the moral. He goes on:

> The two imperatives are unavoidable and the neglect of either creates problems. Schools must be run effectively if they are to survive . . . But for the school to transform itself into an institution, a learning community must emerge . . . This is the moral imperative that the principals face.
>
> (1991, p. 329)

In similar fashion, Grace (2000) contends that moral leadership is the *sine qua non* attribute that all school principals, in particular, should possess. He concludes that "the discourse and undertaking of management must be matched by a discourse and understanding of ethics, morality and spirituality" (Grace, 2000, p. 244).

Invitational leadership

Bennis and Nanus (1985) propose a more practical, holistic and dynamic model of leadership – one that encourages leaders to pursue more joyful and more meaningful personal and professional lives, and invites others to do the same. Leaders, they (Bennis and Nanus, 1985, p. 39) argue, "articulate and define what has previously remained implicit or unsaid. Then they invent images, metaphors and models that provide a focus for new attention." Thus, they are led to the notion of invitational leadership.

Invitational leadership is based on unleashing the intrinsic energy people possess and summoning them cordially to see themselves as capable of tackling challenges, overcoming obstacles and accomplishing great things. It acknowledges the integrity, potential and interdependence of the teachers and their responsibility to work for the common good. This, Bennis and Nanus (1985) state, involves a generous and genuine turning toward others in empathy and respect, with the ultimate goal of collaborating with them on projects of mutual benefit. Thus, the emphasis shifts from command and control to cooperation and communication, from manipulation to cordial summons, from exclusiveness to inclusiveness, and from subordinate to associate.

Interpersonal leadership

Tuohy and Coghlan portray the 'normal' life of teachers as follows:

> Much of the teachers' day is taken up in an intensity of relationships . . . with their students; the changing context of their lives and developing

appropriate and effective responses to both their personal and academic needs requires constant reflection and adjustment.

(1997, p. 67)

Thus, they argue, attention to collaboration and interpersonal relationships is paramount. What is needed, in this view, are interpersonal leaders who focus on relationships with teachers, students and other members of the school community and adopt a collaborative leadership approach based on moral dimension. Such leaders should have advanced interpersonal skills to enable them to operate effectively with internal and external stakeholders (Bush and Glover, 2003).

An attempt to present other typologies of leadership would result in unnecessary repetition of concepts already discussed earlier. Also, a major lesson to be drawn from the account is that leadership diversity continues to evolve in response to new complexities in education. This lesson provides the stimulus for the exposition in the next section on leadership and learning.

Leadership and learning

Notwithstanding their association with some of the positions outlined so far, Fullan (2005), Lambert (1995) and MacBeath (2005), amongst others, also argue that there is no one single best leadership type. Consequently, they promote the notion of contingent leadership. This perspective aims at offering an alternative approach that requires leaders capable of adapting their leadership styles to particular situations. This is an attempt to respond to the wide variations of school contexts and the unique organisational circumstances, or problems, which schools face (Bush and Glover, 2003). It is when viewed within such a framework that we can see the value in the concept of distributed leadership, especially as it relates to teachers and their role in the improvement in the quality of student learning.

In our modern age, teachers have to demonstrate vision and provide leadership that appropriately involves the school community in the creation of shared beliefs and values. McNamara (2005, p. 6) argues that they have to understand the dynamic of change, be knowledgeable about it, be able to assess a school's readiness for it, and understand the dynamics of resistance and how it can be reduced. Fullan (2003) also insists that teachers offer the most suitable solution for the new complexities which schools are facing. If they are able to establish a framework for collaborative action and involve the school community in developing and supporting shared beliefs, values, mission and goals for the school, he argues, then change will last. What is needed are effective leaders who can combine different leadership skills to lead the school efficiently in different situations.

Elsewhere, Fullan (2001) argues that schools are being drawn in the correct direction by the recurrent multiple changes which are shifting the emphasis in education from individual to collective responsibility. Most schools, however, he believes, are currently not structured to facilitate the growth of distributed leadership or lateral capacity. Here, leadership is still predominantly locked into management structures. To achieve distributed leadership such schools need to redesign their internal 'architecture', normalise collaborative learning and adopt leadership for capacity creation and school sustainability.

The claims regarding the value of distributed leadership are attractive. Neuman and Simmons (2000) state that it can act to empower everyone in school to take responsibility for student achievement and to assume leadership roles in areas in which they are competent and skilled. Sergiovanni (1984) observes that it can act as a catalyst in bonding staff together and in easing the pressure on school principals. He foresees that the burden of leadership will be less if leadership functions and roles are shared. Copland (2002) goes a step further and contends that distributed leadership can unleash teachers' collective competency, ease the burden of the principal, lessen teachers' unrealistic expectations, and enable them to identify, support and assume aspects of leadership beyond those pertinent to the role of the principal. Similarly, Leithwood *et al.* (1999) foresee that distributed leadership will generate collegiality through the enhancement of teacher participation for school effectiveness. Through the sharing of greater democracy, they argue, teachers will become increasingly involved and empowered with leadership potential.

If this vision is to be realised, however, much needs to be done. Hargreaves and Fullan (1998) insist that the preparation of successful leaders is being dangerously ignored, yet the organisational skills of many leaders need to be harnessed. Schools need leaders at many levels who are able to deal with complex problems through their cumulative development of 'on the job' leadership. Teachers' commitment is necessary for sustainable improvement in schools and succession to leadership is also more likely if there are many leaders at many levels whose sights are set on continuous improvement. Also, as Collins (2001) sees it, the notion that a good leader is one who is able to build enduring greatness is a liability when it comes to sustained improvement. Rather, he argues 'great' leaders can be low profile teachers endowed with extreme personal humility and intense professionalism. It is these people who can be instrumental in bringing about remarkable, enduring achievement.

In distributed leadership, then, it is acknowledged that in most circumstances teams outperform individual attainment. It is the individual differences of team members that become the collective strength. Through collaborative efforts teams can shape common purpose, agree on performance goals, define a common working approach, develop high levels of complementary skills, and hold themselves mutually accountable for results.

Leithwood *et al.* (1999) recommend that leadership should be distributed among teachers as follows:

- Setting directions – vision building, goal consensus and the development of high performance expectations;

- Developing teachers – providing individualised support, intellectual stimulation and the modeling of values and practices important to the mission of the school;
- Organising and building a culture in which colleagues are motivated by moral imperatives and structuring, fostering shared decision-making processes and problem solving capacities;
- Building relationships with the whole school community;
- Promoting collaboration within and across the school through networking.

Such a view seriously challenges the traditional position of the principal within the school setting. The way has been paved somewhat because of the role becoming so packed with additional tasks and responsibilities during the last two decades of the twentieth century that the traditional parameters in which one functioned became increasingly obsolete, and in many cases beyond one's resources. For a while the answer was seen to reside in the idea of 'heroic principals'; those who, with their outstanding talents, could manage the largest and most complex of schools. Soon, however, it was superseded by the idea that leadership should and must be seen in our increasingly complex world of education, as distributed throughout a school rather than vested in one person.

In the latter regard, Elmore (2000) argues that the technical core of day-to-day instruction and decision-making has become detached from organisational policymaking resulting in an exponential increase in workload. It is this increased workload that has led principals to find ways to distribute leadership which also has a positive result of not only sharing the load, but also generating reform and instructional improvement. In a similar vein, Copland (2003) demonstrates the benefits of distributed leadership in establishing a more broad-based leadership in schools. However, it is arguable that it is the ideas of Spillane which have been the most influential in promoting understanding of what is involved.

Burch and Spillane (2003), Spillane (2005, 2006) and Spillane *et al.* (2001, 2004) developed a model of distributed leadership which provides a conceptual framework that incorporates leadership, instructional improvement and organisational change. Essentially, distributed leadership as they see it is not just a matter of giving away or delegating leadership, but weaving it into the fabric of the school. This notion is based on activity theory and theories of distributed cognition. From this a frame for studying leadership practice has been developed which, it is argued, is constituted in the interaction of school leaders, followers and the situation.

Spillane's account of distributed leadership is based on an investigation of school leadership undertaken by him and his colleagues at Northwestern University in the USA. It began in 1999 and involved studying 15 schools in the Chicago area over a period of five years. As a theory-building study, a number of research approaches were utilised to enhance understanding of distributed practice. It was also underpinned by recognition of what educators have long known, namely, that leadership can be practised by those who hold no formal administrative leadership position, such as classroom teachers.

Key to the theory generated is the notion that whether administrators intentionally share their leadership with others or not, distributed leadership is a fact of school life. This is a view that it would be very difficult, if not impossible, for one person to operate a school without a cadre of individuals to whom responsibility for various functions can be devolved. In any organisation, some will lead and some will follow, willingly or unwillingly. As Spillane explains:

> A distributed perspective is first and foremost about leadership practice. This practice is framed in a very particular way, as a product of the joint interactions of school *leaders, followers,* and aspects of their *situation* such as tools and routines.
>
> (2006, p. 3; italics original)

Thus, rather than view leadership practice as resulting from a leader's knowledge and skill, it is the interactions between people and their situation which defines distributed leadership (Spillane, 2006, p. 4).

Spillane has also developed the elements of distributed leadership to give an indication of how it would 'distribute' in practice. First, it would involve multiple leaders who would not necessarily have formal leadership roles. Second, it is not something that would be imposed on followers. Third, it is the actions of individuals that must be considered critical to leadership practice. The overall result of taking cognisance of these three elements would be a situation where individuals would interact with each other, "creating a reciprocal interdependency between their actions, which may be reciprocal, pooled or sequential" (Spillane, 2005, p. 146). Actions, thus, would acquire meaning and purpose "through critical interdependency resulting from a shifting mosaic of structure, routines and tools" (Spillane, 2005, p. 147). Spillane (2005, p. 149) also makes clear that "shared leadership, team leadership, and democratic leadership are not synonyms for distributed leadership", as the nature of distributed leadership depends on the situation. Neither does a team approach necessarily imply a distributed perspective unless the aforementioned three elements are present.

The work of Spillane provides important insights into how leadership responsibilities are distributed in schools. As he explains:

> The distribution of leadership among formally designated leaders and informal leaders differs according to the leadership routine, the school subject, the type of school, the school's size, and the school or school leadership team's developmental stage.
>
> (2006, p. 50)

His work also has important implications for students, teachers and the organisation generally. The indications are that through promoting greater involvement of staff in decision-making processes, the potential for enhanced teacher learning as well as student learning is increased.

It is clear from the work of Spillane that many opportunities exist for leadership to be developed among teachers in schools, whether or not they hold official leadership positions. Also, he contends that while leaders may seek differing ends, this does not necessarily mean that dysfunction will follow:

> Whether they [leaders] sought similar or different ends, the actions of one leader enabled or constrained the actions of another. In this way, leadership practice is stretched over leaders who seek different and even conflicting ends.
>
> (2006, p. 500)

Even when leaders seek differing outcomes, they can still function as a collective, moderating each other's position. Also, leaders do not function in a vacuum and followers play a significant role in defining leadership practice. Indeed, the effectiveness of a leader is largely dependent on the willingness of followers to agree, acquiesce or even disagree with leaders.

It is contended also that educational policymakers need to acknowledge that leadership in schools involves more than those who are formally appointed. In this regard, many opportunities exist to recognise and engage more teachers in leadership roles. As Spillane (2006, p. 202) explains, "district policymakers need to consider how their policies on issues from leadership preparation and development to accountability reflect and support this reality". If systems, schools, and those who are leaders and teachers within them are to progress, opportunities need to be provided for all to be empowered to improve leadership practice generally.

There is no doubt that the notion of distributed leadership has achieved considerable prominence (Timperley, 2008, p. 822). Gronn (2006, p. 1) has termed it "the new kid on the block", while Harris (2004, p. 13) has referred to it as being "in vogue". Such recognition, however, should not be taken as an indication that it is an idea that merits uncritical acceptance. For one thing, the enthusiasm of many should be tempered by some of the qualifying points made by those who are the principal advocates of the position. For example, Spillane does not regard distributed leadership as a cure for all that ails schools. Essentially, he states, it is "a conceptual or diagnostic tool for thinking about school leadership" and "is not a blueprint for effective leadership, nor a prescription for how school leadership should be practised" (2005, p. 149). For educators, it is not a matter of choosing the most appropriate model through which leadership may be exercised. Rather, the leader should actively seek out opportunities to enhance the organisation's outcomes by empowering others to assume, or develop, their leadership roles through formal and informal structures which might be either of a short or long duration in a distributed leadership setting.

Equally significant are the critiques of those not necessarily wedded to distributed leadership in the first instance. Amongst such theorists are Fitzgerald and Gunter (2006), who have analysed the notion of distributed leadership through the lens of the critical theorist. In doing so, they have raised the possibility that distributed leadership is put forward as a façade. It may be, they hold, that the concept has the potential to delude teachers that they are engaging in liberating practices, when in fact what is really happening is that standardisation practices are being reinforced in a new manner. Thus, they conclude, in promoting distributed leadership government policymakers may be deluding teachers that they are being encouraged to participate in a more democratic form of leadership, when the actual agenda is to steer them unwittingly towards the achievement of pre-set goals. To date there is little empirical evidence to substantiate such a view. This, however, does not mean that, if tested as hypotheses, they would not be upheld. Nevertheless, it highlights the need to investigate possible ways in which distributed leadership may operate to ensure the dominance of the status quo and the need to unmask associated practices of domination.

There are also critiques of distributed leadership on the grounds that those who espouse it do not make explicit the particular practices which it engenders and the principles which should guide them. Recognising this situation, Timperley (2008, p. 825) calls for research that helps us understand why different ways of distributing leadership may have differential consequences. Robinson (2008) takes up the same point in arguing for a shift from describing how leadership is distributed in particular contexts, and the antecedents and consequences of such distribution, to a "more normative stance that involves an implicit or explicit implication that how it is distributed is more or less effective" (Timperley, 2008, p. 825).

Other positions which seek to 'trouble' the current espousal of distributed leadership in schools as a relatively uncontested concept in the 'professional' as opposed to the 'academic' domain, also need to be highlighted. In particular, there is the need to take cognisance of those who, while seeing value in distributed leadership, do not see it as an 'either/or' situation in relation to other forms of leadership. Elmore (2004), for example, argues that effectively functioning schools need leadership along heroic lines to bring about major improvements, while they also need leadership to achieve well the more everyday tasks in which they are engaged. In making this distinction between tasks aimed at major improvements and everyday tasks, he is not arguing that the latter are unimportant. On the contrary, he recognises that one of the most important tasks of a school is the everyday one of contributing to student learning. Camburn *et al.* (2003) take up this same point specifically in relation to distributed leadership, arguing that schools with stronger distributed leadership will have more staff who are knowledgeable about and take responsibility for the outcomes of schooling, than schools not organised along such lines.

Here it is important to recall the point made in Chapter 1, that while those with the power and influence should be encouraged to acknowledge the ideas on distributed leadership as expounded by the likes of Spillane, they are not necessarily attractive to many. It is not just a matter of some being set in their ways and others fearing disruption. There is also fear of change because of the extent to which formal leaders are now held responsible for much of what goes on in schools. As Crawford (2005, p. 213) has commented, the head teacher in England and many other countries remains very accountable, through mechanisms such as inspection and league tables, for the success or failure of the school.

Harris (2003b, p. 319) has also drawn attention to this matter, pointing out that while distributed leadership requires those in formal leadership positions to relinquish power to others, "this potentially places the head or principal in a vulnerable position because of the lack of direct control over certain activities". The danger for such formal leaders is that should others take action which is considered to be undesirable by educational authorities it may not be of much use to plead innocence on grounds of having distributed leadership. In a similar vein, Timperley (2008, p. 831) argues that distributing leadership is a risky business "and may result in the greater distribution of incompetence".

Increasingly, however, state-prescribed policies are officially stating that the one area in which teachers are free, and even encouraged, to take a leadership role is in deciding on appropriate approaches to facilitating student learning. At least in this domain 'top-down' approaches no longer constitute significant impediments to the development of distributed leadership. Formal leaders need to take advantage of this situation and thus adopt an incremental approach to distributed leadership aimed primarily at trying to improve the quality of learning in the school. This is not to argue just for delegation. To take away requirements that teachers teach in one perceived correct manner and encourage them to use their professional knowledge and judgement in selecting appropriate pedagogical approaches is to set them on the road to becoming leaders of learning. As Harris (2008, p. 40) argues, those in formal leadership roles "need to create the cultural and structural conditions or spaces where distributed leadership can operate best and flourish". In making this point she also states that there is a need for strong and effective infrastructures within schools that allow teachers to be the best teachers they can be.

The point being made, then, is that while it may be unlikely that distributed leadership can be promoted in all of its facets at this juncture, one particular aspect of it, namely, teacher leadership both can and should be promoted. Timperley (2005, p. 397) is close to this line of argument when stating that it "is the development of instructional leadership, rather than other organisational functions, that has been shown to have the greatest leverage in effecting programmatic changes and instructional improvement". Crawford (2005) and Wasley (1991) argue similarly, and in a manner more consistent with the general thrust of this book, by placing the emphasis on student learning rather than on teacher instruction. Katzenmeyer and Moller (2001) add to this in indicating that one of the main aspects of teacher leaders is that they are leaders of students or other teachers, facilitators, coaches, mentors, trainers, curriculum specialists, and creators of new pedagogical approaches.

Finally, the indications are that developing teachers as leaders of learning can also contribute to the crucial matter of involving students in sharing leadership responsibilities, particularly in relation to their own learning. The United Nations' Charter on the rights of the child indicates the importance of giving students voice (United Nations, 2003). Ruddock (2004, p. 85) indicates a variety of ways in which teachers can take leadership to this end, including the establishment of school councils, the establishment of student working groups to explore a particular problem or idea and to report back with recommendations for action, the introduction of message boxes where students can post comments on their experiences and make suggestions, and the conducting of the occasional student referendum on key decisions for the school year-group, or class. Such action, she argues, is an effective way of recognising students' capabilities and of reducing the alienation that some feel "where their social maturity and their desire for greater autonomy and intellectual challenge and support are not recognised". There is also a certain amount of evidence which demonstrates that it can be effective. Aedo-Richmond and Richmond (1999, p. 206), for example, in reporting on a project in post-Pinochet Chile, note the presence of "community monitors, typically young people who offered extra assistance and personal attention to third and fourth grade students through after-school workshops". Similarly, Bentley (1998, p. 94) has described the Society of Innovators project in Sweden, aimed at tackling youth unemployment in under-populated rural areas. In a three-way partnership, young people created their own project, each guided by a slightly older peer mentor. The benefit was to the student, the monitors and the mentors in terms of increasing their social skills, personal confidence and knowledge.

Conclusion

In this chapter a number of background considerations on leadership in education were detailed. A brief overview of a typology that indicates some of the various positions on leadership which have been pertinent to education, including student, teacher and organisational learning, over the last 20 years was then provided. This led to an exposition on the basic ideas within the concept of 'distributed leadership'. The view of this form of leadership practice, particularly as expounded by Spillane, is one which moves beyond the principal, or head teacher, to consider other potential leaders. Essentially, it is about a very particular way of viewing leadership practice, one which is the product of joint interactions between school leaders, followers and aspects of the particular situations in which they work. It should not be seen as a panacea for all that ails schools, but as a model of leadership practices which has potential benefits for all concerned. Also, in line with the incremental approach to change advocated in Chapter 1, we concluded that what is realistic in the present educational environment is to seek to promote one major facet of distributed leadership, namely, teacher leadership. Much of the next three chapters of this book will now consider implications of this position for promoting learning at the level of the student, that of the teacher and that of the organisation.

5   Student learning

Introduction

So far the scene regarding broad developments in relation to student learning internationally has been set and the importance of adopting distributed leadership in associated initiatives has been emphasised. Also, it has been contended in the previous chapter that such a view is central in arguing for an orientation which is largely towards supporting students as flexible learners. This, in turn, of course, necessitates building the intellectual and professional capacity of individual teachers in the school, as well as promoting learning in the organisation itself. These are the concerns of the next two chapters. Before turning to such central matters, however, it is necessary to delineate more clearly what is being advocated in terms of promoting student learning. It is to this consideration we now turn.

The chapter commences with an outline of the understanding of learning to which we subscribe. Here, particular attention is paid to both the constructivist perspective on learning and to the concepts of 'surface and deep learning'. These embody ideas which we consider to be particularly helpful to educational leaders in shaping their thinking on the nature of student learning. We then go on to provide a broad outline of our views on enhancing student learning in the school. These are underpinned by a belief that there is no value in arguing for centrally-imposed approaches which can act as prescriptive blueprints since to do so would be to inhibit the fostering of the autonomy of teachers and students and, in turn, the fostering of lifelong learning.

The final section of the chapter is focused on one way of making sense of the great array of theoretical ideas, constructs and practical theories which serve to inform thinking on the promotion of flexible student learning. To this end, we offer and develop three propositions which serve to unify a significant number of related positions. These propositions are as follows: leadership for developing flexible learners should promote student self-regulated learning; leadership for developing flexible learners should promote learning in community; and leadership for developing flexible learners should promote learning which is problem-based. The assumption which underpins the desire to present them here is the same one that underpinned the work of

Entwistle and Ramsden (1983) 20 years ago in their Lancaster studies on approaches to learning, namely, that once teachers understand more about how to improve the quality of student learning then the better they will be at leading learning in the classroom.

What is learning?

Over the last 20 years there has been a certain amount of confusion in much of what has been written regarding learning-centred education. A central reason for much of this stems from the failure to distinguish between learning theory and the conditions that enhance learning. Barrow (1984, p. 98), in addressing this matter over 20 years ago, offered some very valuable points of clarification. He commenced by stating that learning theory "describes what happens when learning takes place, rather than why or how it takes place. It seeks to offer an explanation of what goes on in the process of learning." Then, after going on to state that "to learn is to acquire knowledge, not previously possessed, of propositions or skills", he elaborated as follows:

> So far as the meaning of 'learning' goes it does not matter whether this acquisition of knowledge is accidental, deliberately imposed from without, or sought after. Nor does the length of time one retains the knowledge cause any serious problem, though one would hope that what is learned is retained for some time, and might quibble about the case of somebody who forgot as soon as he [*sic*] had 'learned'.
>
> (1984, p. 98)

This is consistent with Fontana's (1981, p. 147) long-standing definition that "learning is a relatively persistent change in an individual's possible behaviour due to experience". Here, as Barrow (1984, p. 99) also pointed out, "reference to experience is designed to contrast with changes in behaviour that come about automatically through maturation and physical development."

Educational leaders, however, are primarily concerned with the conditions that enhance learning rather than with learning theory per se. This is not to say that theories of learning have been unhelpful. Gagne's (1970) theory, in particular, has been instructive over the years, especially in delineating qualitative differences in 'learning types'. On this, he classified eight types of learning: signal learning (making a conditioned response to a non-specific type of stimulus); stimulus response learning (a specific response is elicited by a stimulus); chaining (the ability to join two or more stimulus response connections together); verbal association (chaining in respect of verbal response connections); multiple discrimination (identifying different stimuli that resemble each other); concept learning (the ability to respond appropriately to a class of stimuli); rule learning and problem solving. Especially useful has been his notion that these types of learning are not just distinct, but also that they are hierarchical.

Equally useful has been the closely-related work of Bloom (1956) and his colleagues. Today educational leaders still find value in drawing upon his grouping of learning outcomes in three domains: the cognitive domain, the psychomotor domain and the affective domain. Regarding the cognitive domain, Bloom proposed that it could be classified into a hierarchy going from 'knowledge', 'comprehension' and 'application', to 'synthesis' and 'evaluation'. In a similar vein, Krathwohl, Bloom and Masia (1964) proposed a five-level classification of outcomes in the affective domain, while Harrow (1972) proposed a six-level classification of outcomes in the psychomotor domain. A more recent contribution, that of Anderson and Krathwohl (2001), entitled a *Taxonomy for Learning, Teaching and Assessing*, expanded Bloom's original taxonomy to reflect new ways of thinking about cognition and learning.

The work of Bruner also continues to be appreciated today. While Gagne, like Skinner (1969), adopted a behaviourist approach to learning, Bruner (1996) adopted a cognitivist one. His approach is that learning is not generally a matter of reflexive behaviour being reinforced by outside consequences. Rather, the importance of activity of mind is stressed. As he sees it, learning in many cases involves acquiring information, sorting it out, making sense of it, and testing it out in a variety of ways. This led him to state that learning is about 'internal model making'. Furthermore, his position that there are three modes of such model making, namely, the enactive mode (acting out), the iconic mode (making things) and the symbolic mode (representing, particularly using language), has been particularly enlightening. Another way of putting this is that certain things are learnt through repetition, others are understood in images, and others yet again result in one being able to give some kind of an account.

We see value in these and many other learning theories, notwithstanding their often different epistemological bases. This is to subscribe to a view of theory expounded by William James as far back as 1892, when he commented regarding the function of the study of psychology for educationalists:

> You make a great mistake if you think that psychology, being a science of the mind's law, is something from which you can deduce definite programmes and schemes and methods of instruction for immediate classroom use. Psychology is a science, and teaching is an art. An intermediary inventive mind must make the application, by using its originality. The science of logic never made a man reason rightly, the science of ethics never made a man behave rightly. The most such sciences can do is to help us catch ourselves up, check ourselves, if we start to reason or behave wrongly; and to criticise ourselves more articulately if we make mistakes. A science only lays down lines within which the rules of the art must fall, laws which the follower of the art must not transgress; but what particular thing he shall positively do within those lines is left exclusively to his own genius . . . and so while everywhere the teaching must

agree with the psychology, it may not necessarily be the only kind of teaching that would so agree; for many diverse methods of teaching may equally well agree with the psychological laws.

(1958, p. 15)

For many decades this position was overlooked as research in the professions, including education, became preoccupied with attempts aimed at the invention and discovery of sure-fired prescriptive models which would lead to easily generalisable solutions in each area (Hopkins, 1993).

Eisner (1983), however, one of the key players in breaking the mould, became instrumental in providing compelling arguments which enabled educational scholars and practitioners to question such a preoccupation. He made the case that because of the changing uniqueness of the practical situations that make up the educational domain, only a portion of professional practice can be usefully treated in the manner of a prescriptive science. The gap between general prescriptive frameworks and successful practice is, he held, dependent more on the reflective intuition, the craft, and the art of the professional practitioner than on any particular prescriptive theory, method or model. Recently, Bridges (2007) took up the same point when questioning some of the assumptions of the 'evidence-based practice' movement. In particular he called into question the view that the generalisations derived from large population studies can lead to recommendations at the national level for implementation at the local level. He went on:

> . . . you cannot logically derive lessons from a single specific instance from such generalizations. They always have to be linked to consideration of local conditions which might well point to a different recommendation . . . a teacher or school may test out different teaching strategies in their own environment and find out 'what works' for them. The fact that this enquiry was small scale and local does not invalidate it as a reliable basis for local practice even if it might be regarded as an unreliable basis for national policy without some further work.
>
> (2007, p. 2)

Thus, Bridges concluded, one cannot treat local and national decisions as if they have exactly the same requirements.

To summarise, the value to leaders of learning in the multitude of learning theories which accompany those outlined already, is not that they consist of 'true' accounts of learning. Rather, they constitute 'tools' for thinking intelligently about learning. In this regard, we now highlight two particular groups of theories which we currently find very helpful for informing our thinking on leadership for flexible student learning, namely, those on 'constructivism' and those on 'surface and deep learning'. In doing so, however, we wish to emphasise that we also recognise the importance of taking cognisance of various other positions, including that of socio-cultural theorists such as those summarised in James *et al.* (2007, pp. 18–20).

Constructivist theories of learning

Constructivists are concerned mainly with the mental models a learner utilises when responding to new problems, or new information. As they see it, learning always involves not only analysing, but also transforming, such new information. The transformation in turn, it is held, can only be achieved in light of what the learner already knows and understands. The proponents of a particular version of constructivism, namely, social constructivism, have extended this idea. They do so, as James *et al.* (2007, pp. 17–18) point out, "often with reference to the Russian psychologist, Vygotsky", who emphasised that another important characteristic of learning is that "it proceeds by interaction between the teacher (or more expert peer) and the learner, in a social context mediated by language and the social norms that value the search for understanding".

Social constructivism is only one of a number of versions of constructivist learning theory. Drawing attention to this back in 1991, Watts and Bentley defined constructivism as follows:

> Essentially, constructivism can be described as a theory of the limits of human knowledge, according to which all we can know is necessarily a product of our own cognition. We create our own conceptions of reality by channelling sensory data towards meditative reflections. Constructivism not only emphasises the central role of the construer but maintains that we are, at least partially, able to control constructive processes through conscious reflection.
>
> (1991, p. 4)

They concluded that beyond this core position there are innumerable views of constructivism.

Since then educationalists have come up with various common principles. Snowman and Biehler (2000), for example, give us the following four:

1   What a person 'knows' is not just received passively, but is actively constructed by the learner – meaningful learning is the active creation of knowledge structures from personal experience;
2   Because knowledge is the result of personal interpretation of experiences, one person's knowledge can never be *totally* transferred to another person;
3   The cultures and societies to which people belong influence their views of the world around them and, therefore, influence what they 'know'. In general, the understandings that people reach are largely consistent within a given culture;
4   Construction of ideas is aided by systematic open-ended discussions and debate.

Particularly useful also is the associated metaphor of 'scaffolding'. As Groundwater-Smith *et al.* (2007, p. 82) point out, it is helpful in trying to understand the teacher's role in the learning process. The notion is that scaffolding supports those parts of a building not yet ready to stand alone. Once one part of the building can stand alone, however, the scaffolding is removed to be erected in another part of the building in need of support. In similar fashion, it is held, the teacher can be seen as "a facilitator of a learning process rather than the transmitter of important knowledge that needs to be learnt". As the student learns a concept less support is needed and "the student becomes more independent" (Groundwater-Smith *et al.*, 2007, p. 82).

Theories of surface and deep learning

Another very helpful group of theories for informing thinking on leadership for flexible student learning is built around the concepts of surface and deep learning. Much of the thinking on these concepts originated in the mid-1970s in Sweden and found expression in the works of Laurillard (1979, 1993), Marton *et al.* (1984) and Marton and Saljo (1976a, 1976b). Bain summarised as follows the central argument running through these and related works:

> . . . if students approach their learning with the intention to reproduce facts and procedures (a 'surface' approach), then their learning will 'miss the point' of the material, it will be fragmented, its relevance to new circumstances will be missed, and misconceptions will remain intact. Alternatively, when students adopt a 'deep' approach, that is, when they seek the meaning of what they are learning and intentionally relate it to their existing knowledge, then quite different outcomes are likely to occur; the knowledge is relationally structured, it is integrated with the procedures required to put the knowledge into practice, it corrects misconceptions, and it can be applied adaptively to new circumstances.
>
> (1994, p. 1)

Bowring-Carr and West-Burnham (1997, p. 15) have expanded on this position in their model of levels of learning. At its most basic, they state, learning is "mere memorizing". Such learning takes place at the lower levels, or what they term "shallow learning". Here, they argue, learning involves "an increase of our knowledge about a topic, and then facts are acquired and retained so that they can be used when necessary". They are not, however, dismissive of learning at this level, far from it. Indeed, they see it as a "necessary precursor to other learning".

Bowring-Carr and West-Burnham then go on to posit three levels of deeper learning. This they do as follows:

The first [level of deep learning] is the abstraction of meaning from a series of related facts, after which there can be a move to an interpretative process aimed at understanding and ordering our reality. The third and most important level is reached when the learning changes the individual as a person. If what a person has 'learned' leaves him or her exactly the same as before, then the learning has been superficial, and will, sooner or later, be rejected, forgotten or ignored.

(1997, p. 15)

Deep learning, they conclude, means there is a change, the world is seen in a different way, and the perception of reality alters.

Enhancing the development of students as flexible learners

It is now apposite to return to the major point made at the beginning of the previous section, namely, that there is a need to distinguish between learning theory and the conditions that enhance learning. So far this chapter has concentrated on learning theories and the argument has been made that knowledge of a range of such theories is valuable to educational leaders as they constitute tools to facilitate thinking intelligently about student learning. Now, however, the attention will be turned to ways of enhancing the development of students as flexible learners.

Just as there is a wide array of learning theories, so is there a wide range of positions on enhancing the development of students as flexible learners. One could, for example, develop a whole exposition on Bruner's (1966) very powerful notion of the 'spiral curriculum'. This promotes the importance of continually introducing learners to the most powerful ideas that discipline our thinking in different kinds of enquiry. Furthermore, so the argument goes, this should not take place simply by adding new ideas. Rather, the challenge is to return time and again to the same fundamental ideas, but to do so in a different and more complex mode of representation.

One could also develop an exposition around various sets of principles assembled by educationalists interested in deducing classroom practices from constructivist learning theory. Killen (2003, p. 30), has come up with the following list which is very comprehensive in this regard:

1   Organise learning and instruction around important ideas (such as the primary concepts, generalisations and underlying themes of the content) rather than focusing on isolated facts;
2   Acknowledge the importance of prior knowledge by providing learners with a cognitive structure that they can use to make sense of new learning;
3   Challenge the adequacy of the learner's prior knowledge, often by creating some conceptual conflict;
4   Provide for ambiguity and uncertainty by presenting students with

problems that have ambiguity, complexity, uncertainty and multiple solutions;

5　Teach learners how to learn, how to regulate their learning skills and how to direct their own learning efforts;

6　View learning as a joint cognitive venture between learner, peers and teacher;

7　Assess learners' knowledge acquisition during a lesson so that they receive immediate feedback and so that they are able to see the connection between their learning and the testing of that learning.

Of equal interest would be an exposition on the constructivist notion of 'reciprocal teaching' where teachers provide students with guided practice in the asking for clarification questions around a text.

Given that it has not been mentioned so far, one might at this point also think we are being dismissive of direct instruction. This is not so. While our main emphasis is on the importance of using approaches other than direct instruction, it is considered that for some areas of learning direct instruction still has an important part to play. By direct instruction is meant whole-class expository teaching techniques. These include lectures and demonstrations, with the teacher delivering academic content, or 'formally' teaching some skills in a very structured manner. In other words, the emphasis is on directing the activities of learners.

Given the large body of evidence which indicates that many teachers tend to be influenced in their practice by the manner in which they have been taught themselves, the extent to which direct instruction has been utilised by succeeding generations of teachers should not be surprising. Thus, educational leaders often have to make a major effort and be very creative in order to find ways to break its dominance in the mental model of many teachers. In particular, they need to work against its attractiveness to teachers largely because it gives them great control over what, when and how students learn. Yet, it would be a mistake to argue for its total eradication.

The major case for not losing sight of the value in direct instruction and why its advocacy for certain situations does not contradict the main thrust of the learner-focused approach to education which we are arguing for is well summarised by Killen (2003). He draws attention to the work of Geddis (1996, p. 254) who highlighted the "incongruity of leaving children on their own to devise scientific perspectives that have taken the human race centuries to articulate". Accepting this point, Killen (2003) has put forward the 'common sense' argument that in some circumstances direct instruction is simply the most appropriate strategy to use. By way of illustration, he states that it may be useful to develop students' basic knowledge and skills through direct instruction techniques "before giving them a more active role in knowledge-seeking through strategies such as problem solving or experimentation" (2003, p. 63). He also points out that direct instruction does not have to be dull and boring. Rather, he contends, "the control and structure that characterise direct instruction can be achieved in interesting, warm, concerned and flexible ways so that a positive classroom climate is maintained and students enjoy learning"(2003, p. 63).

Nothwithstanding what has been said on direct instruction so far, it is necessary at this point to reintroduce a sense of balance and reiterate what has been implied regarding its place within the whole scheme of things, namely, that it should be used sensibly and only sparingly. Such a view has also been fundamental for some time to the position of a particular group of curriculum theorists. Eisner, (1969, np) for example, in his well-known exposition on 'instructional and expressive educational objectives' argued that education serves two functions. The first involves assisting students "to acquire those intellectual codes and skills which will make it possible for them to profit from the contributions of those who have gone before". Thus, they need to learn a range of such socially defined skills as reading, writing, and arithmetic provided for them by their culture. However, he also argued that students need to learn to make a contribution to their culture. Thus, teachers should be concerned with "providing opportunities for the individual to construe his own interpretation to the material he [*sic*] encounters or constructs" (1969, np). This, Eisner concludes, is essential, because a simple repetition of the past is the surest path to cultural *rigor mortis*.

More recently, a similar position has been articulated by Smith and Lovat (2003) in an exposition which builds on the work of the distinguished British curriculum theorist, Lawrence Stenhouse. All, they argue, need 'training' and 'instruction' in the technical processes necessary to acquire 'basic skills' and 'foundational information'. They also hold, however, that "other types of procedures are necessary for the fullness of education to occur" (Smith and Lovat, 2003, p. 129). They explain as follows:

> After all, being able to set up an easel, splash a little paint and recite certain facts and figures about Rembrandt's life does not constitute an artist. An artist is one who appreciates and understands the aesthetics of art and, ideally, is able to contribute to the world of art in a significant way. Only at these sorts of points can education be deemed to have truly happened. For Stenhouse, these levels of education are catered for through the processes termed 'initiation' and 'induction'. Initiation is the point of socialisation, at it were, into the culture associated with any area of knowledge. Initiation into the areas of knowledge is a subtle process. Also, Stenhouse asserts that induction is the point of true education. He argues that induction into knowledge is successful to the extent that it makes the behavioural outcomes of the students unpredictable.
>
> (Smith and Lovat, 2003, p. 129)

Here one finds an interesting case of the notion of surface and deep learning embedded in a prescriptive theory of curriculum. Furthermore, it is not difficult to recognise that if one subscribes to the adoption of such a position then teachers need a great repertoire of teaching and learning practices. In particular, this should include a range of practices aimed at enhancing the development of students as flexible learners.

Some core lenses for educational leaders engaged in the development of students as flexible learners

There was a time when one might have turned almost solely to educational psychology for guidance on how to go about enhancing the development of students as flexible learners. This, however, can no longer be the case. We now have at our disposal a great array of theoretical ideas, constructs and practical theories which serve to inform thinking on the promotion of flexible student learning. Amongst those with something to say on the matter are neuro-scientists, anthropologists, information technologists, curriculum theorists, and applied linguists, to name but a few. Consequently, educational leaders are in need of a set of core lenses through which they can make some sense of the wealth of material generated and the positions advocated.

One possible central lens is provided by the concept of 'student engagement'. Chapman (2003) has distinguished between two versions of this concept. The first refers to students' willingness to participate in routine school activities, such as attending classes, submitting required work, and following teachers' directions in class. Defined this way, school engagement overlaps considerably with compliance. The second version associates engagement levels with students' use of cognitive, metacognitive and self-regulatory strategies to monitor and guide their learning processes. In this view, student engagement is viewed as motivated behaviour that can be indexed by the kinds of cognitive strategies students choose to use.

It is in the second sense that the concept of 'student engagement' has come to be a very popular guiding position in curriculum documents in the last few years in a variety of states and countries. In Western Australia, for example, which witnessed the introduction of a new curriculum in 1998, there are references throughout the key document, *Curriculum Framework* (Curriculum Council of Western Australia, 1998) to the importance of students 'engaging' with education in eight learning areas. Specifically regarding mathematics, for example, it is stated:

> For students to become effective learners of mathematics, they must be actively engaged, and want to be able to take on the challenge, persistent effort and risks involved. This is most likely to occur when the student personally experiences an environment that is supportive but mathematically challenging and when processes that enhance sustained and robust learning are promoted.
>
> (Curriculum Council of Western Australia, 1998, p. 206)

It is further contended that "students should practise, (that is, 'do') mathematics, but doing mathematics involves much more than the repetition of facts and procedures; it also involves working mathematically" (Curriculum Council of Western Australia, 1998, p. 206). Also, in the section describing student action and reflection, it is stated that "mathematical learning is most successful when students actively engage in making sense of new information and ideas" (Curriculum Council of Western Australia, 1998, p. 207). Similar statements permeate the document in relation to the other seven prescribed learning areas. However, no single, comprehensive definition of engagement is provided. This, we hold, is reflective of the situation in various other states and countries. Also, the situation is not helped by the tendency for the concept to be used as a gravitational point for a range of ideas which is so extensive that it ceases both to have utility and to provide clarity of thinking for educational leaders.

Much more helpful is to take a less synoptic, yet still comprehensive approach. To this end three propositions are now offered which collectively can serve to unify a significant number of related positions. These are as follows: leadership for developing flexible learners should promote student self-regulated learning; leadership for developing flexible learners should promote learning in community; and leadership for developing flexible learners should promote learning which is problem-based. Each of these propositions will now be considered.

The promotion of student self-regulated learning

This sub-section outlines the first lens for making sense of the great array of theoretical ideas, constructs and practical theories which serve to inform thinking on the promotion of flexible student learning. It is centred on the proposition that leadership for developing flexible learners should promote student self-regulated learning. This is also what some (Field, 2000) are referring to when they talk about the development of the ability of students to 'learn how to learn', while for others the latter notion relates to learning how to gain access to knowledge and information through 'traditional' library searches as well as through computer-based systems.

The construct of student self-regulated learning is relatively recent in research on student performance and achievement in classroom settings. Its significance has been popularised in particular by Zimmerman and his now somewhat famous statement that "learning is not something that happens *to* students, it is something that happens *by* students" (Zimmerman and Risenberg, 1997, p. 110) (italics in original). His particular interest has been in learning how students become willing and able to assume responsibility for controlling, or self-regulating, their academic achievement. This, as Dembo and Eaton (2000, p. 474) point out, is important as research indicates that "learning self-regulatory skills can lead to greater academic achievement and an increased sense of efficacy".

Students, according to Pintrich (1995, p. 5), may regulate three different dimensions of their learning: their observable behaviour, their motivation and affect, and their cognition. Also, he states, there are three characteristics, or components, of self-regulated learning that function in relation to these dimensions. First, self-regulated learners attempt to control their behaviour, motivation and affect, and cognition. On this, he uses the analogy of a thermostat that regulates room temperature by monitoring the temperature and then turning on or off the heating or cooling unit to bring the actual temperature in line with the preset desired temperature. The second component of self-regulated learning is that there is some goal the student is attempting to accomplish. Like the preset desired temperature in the thermostat analogy, this goal provides the standard by which the student can monitor and judge his or her own performance and then make the appropriate adjustments. The third characteristic is that the individual student must be in control of his or her own actions. To illustrate what he means by this, Pintrich (1995, p. 5) states that a student changing behaviour in a classroom would not be an example of self-regulation if it was undertaken only in response to a requirement by teachers, and if one no longer engaged in the behaviour once the requirement was removed.

Zimmerman and Risenberg (1997) have identified the following dimensions of learning as providing direction for teachers in the promotion of self-regulated learning: motivation, methods of learning, use of time, physical environment and social environment. The following is a summary of Dembo and Eaton's (2000, pp. 476–86) outline of the sorts of activities in which teachers can engage in relation to each dimension:

1   Motivation: goal setting, self-talk; arranging or imagining rewards or punishments for success or failure at an academic task;
2   Methods of learning: rehearsal strategies, elaboration strategies, representation or mapping strategies;
3   Use of time: getting students to develop greater awareness of their current time usage, asking students how they want to use their time, asking students to make a short-term plan for their use of time, asking students to report on the success or failure of their new approach to time management;
4   Physical environment: asking students to identify different types of distractors in their study environments that interfere with attention and concentration;
5   Social environment: teaching students to interrupt their habitual non-productive thought processes that will guide them through problem situations (What is the problem? What is my plan? Am I using my plan? How did I do?).

They also highlight Zimmerman's cyclical approach to self-regulation (Zimmerman and Risenberg, 1997). This has the following components: self-observation and evaluation; goal setting and strategic planning; strategy implementation and monitoring; and strategic-outcome monitoring.

Zimmerman and Risenberg (1977) conclude that these four steps can be used to help students solve their own academic problems. They also argue that students should be given assignments whereby they are asked to identify a learning problem and conduct their own self-management study to develop and implement a plan to solve their problems. In time, they conclude, students can, as a result of regular engagement in assignments with such a focus, learn how to take responsibility for their own learning.

The promotion of learning in community

The second lens offered for making sense of the great array of theoretical ideas, constructs and practical theories which serve to inform thinking on the promotion of flexible student learning is captured in the proposition that leadership for developing flexible learners should promote learning in community. This is not to be confused with another laudable practice, namely, 'learning in the community'. In such a specific case what is involved is students spending some time in the workplace, often to get experience of the type of employment they wish to take up on leaving school. What is being referred to at present, however, is premised on Bowring-Carr and West-Burnham's (1997, p. 10) position that, by and large, we learn best in a community. Within a learning community, they argue, "the pleasures and uncertainties of learning are shared [and] tentative ideas are tested among trusted companions." Also, they point to the benefits which can be gained when "the first expressions of mastery of part of a topic are celebrated by the community together", and when some learning is stimulated by a group activity, and when that learning is demonstrated by the group. Within such a context, as Barth stresses in *Improving Schools from Within* (Barth, 1991, pp. 49–50), everyone is, and needs to be, a learner.

This also highlights the importance of cooperative learning, the focus of which is two-fold: it draws attention to the importance of discussion and language in sharing and clarifying ideas, and it provides a foundation for cooperative skills, processes and strategies essential to group functioning. It is through the group experience that individuals maximise their learning potential. In cooperative classrooms students and teachers are continually engaged in the process of observing, practising and giving feedback about the effectiveness of their cooperative skills. The benefits of such practices can include high achievement, deep understanding, learning being enjoyable, the development of self-esteem, the promotion of a sense of belonging, the development of skills for the future, and the acceptance of responsibility. Cooperative learning is consistent with the inclusive education movement and the empirically-based argument that institutions based on inclusive values create a 'win-win-situation' for all (Ainscow *et al.*, 2006).

Approaches to cooperative learning have been detailed for some time, particularly by Slavin (1983, 1995). In conjunction with these approaches teachers also need to draw upon what is known about the use of discussion in class

(Brookfield, 1990; Gooding and Stacey, 1993), a practice sometimes defined as the art of cooperative thinking aloud and the exchanging of ideas. Equally, attention needs to be given to the existing body of research on the value of small group work whose distinguishing feature is that students from time to time work together without direct intervention by the teacher. Here the learning environment is structured such that students can work productively together, under indirect guidance.

This is also an appropriate place to highlight how acutely aware we are of the importance of looking for ways to use information and communication technology (ICT) in the classroom so that students come to realise, as Bowring-Carr and West-Burnham (1997, p. 17) put it, "that learning is not an activity confined to a certain time and to a certain set of rooms". In making this same point Alden also points to the range of possibilities which ICT can provide for student engagement in active learning:

> They can interrupt the instruction whenever they wish, and reach out to the enormous wealth of information and resources available on the Web. They can produce products and participate in projects with other students and the instructor at the push of a button and receive individualised feedback.
>
> (1998, p. 4)

On this matter, it is important to pay attention to Smalley's (2003, p. 53) view that in bringing computers into the classroom, teachers must play a fundamental role in teaching and learning, in terms of both process and product. This is not a rejection of the notion of the teacher as a facilitator of learning. Rather, as Smalley (2003, p. 60) puts it, the teachers' role must be one of "knowledge-givers *and* enablers". He bases his position on Sternberg's (1998) five elements of learning – metacognition, selective attention, thinking, knowledge and motivation – concluding that the successful integration of ICT into the curriculum requires that teachers "equip learners with metacognitive skills, capture their attention, encourage them to think and use existing and new knowledge". All of this, he states, requires motivated learners who are able to communicate effectively.

One of the most comprehensive ways of promoting cooperative learning, and in a manner which extends learning beyond the confines of the school, is through service learning. Such learning has been an important part of American high schools and colleges since the early years of the twentieth century. In the last ten years various other countries have also come to realise its potential. Accordingly, many school cultures now value service learning as a key part of the curriculum and not an added extra. In its many forms it would appear to be one of the most important new developments linking schools and society in an increasingly technological and impersonal world. It cannot only be highly effective in developing a rich partnership between both the serving and the served, but also help to move young adolescents forward on the path of civic and moral identity and engagement. Also, it can enhance teaching in school by extending student learning into the community, as well as help to foster a sense of caring for others. Furthermore, as recent studies have highlighted it can play a part in increasing self-esteem, academic performance and social skills (Reinders and Youniss, 2006).

Strictly speaking service learning is not community service (Mooney and Edwards, 2001) since it must be linked to the curriculum, but it may include a community service component in a structured learning process. It systematically attempts to help students to use experiences in the community to better build upon, critique and evaluate knowledge already gained from educational experiences, messages from the mass media, influences of home and community, and readings they have done, and to then move them on to an intellectually 'higher ground'. Whatever the model (and there is quite a number of them) service learning involves leading students to ask real and relevant questions as they take responsibility for their own learning.

Cone and Harris (1996) developed a 'Lens Model for Service Learning Educators' which stresses the importance of students being intellectually challenged through pre-service training and through exposure to concepts which they will be expected to apply and understand in the community. The 'lens' is the service experience itself; an experience distinct from the student's everyday experiences and so allows for the broadening of perspectives. A holistic approach to reflection involving the student's intellectual and emotional capacities as well as written and oral skills then follows the experience. The model of Cone and Harris proceeds to introduce a vital component; that reflection is most effective when guided by an educator or mentor who can facilitate the student's learning. Students are invited to respond in writing to key questions, cite observations and explain their generalisations. The more frequently students use abstract concepts in observing, thinking about, describing and talking about the world, the more clearly the concepts become integrated into the thinking processes of the user. As these analytical methods and organisational concepts are acquired, they move students one step closer to being able to think critically and defend their point of view. Finally, the model returns to the learners as they integrate their experiences into new frameworks, attitudes and mindsets. Throughout all of this the process needs to be assisted and mediated by a mentor.

The promotion of learning which is problem-based

The third lens offered for making sense of the great array of theoretical ideas, constructs and practical theories which serve to inform thinking on the promotion of flexible student learning is captured in the proposition that leadership should promote learning which is problem-based. This again is to agree with Bowring-Carr and West-Burnham (1997, p. 13) when they claim that schools are faced with many problems as a consequence of the fragmentation of learning due to the imposition of national and state-wide curricula. This fragmentation they attribute to what they term "the factory model on which schools were created in the last century" and the associated notion of "breaking down to the smallest parts the work that children and teachers have to do in parallel with the breaking down of work on the assembly line".

Traditionally, the solution offered by many to such a situation is to promote problem solving as a unifying curricular ideal. The solution as we see it, however, is not in moving from a totally subject-based curriculum to one which is totally problem-based. Rather, a problem solving approach can be adopted in promoting learning, while the learning environment can also be structured so that students are regularly involved in inter-disciplinary and cross-disciplinary project work.

To advocate the regular adoption of a problem solving approach in promoting learning is to promote a strategy for "posing significant, contextualised, real world situations, and providing resources, guidance, and instruction to learners as they develop content knowledge and problem-solving skills" (Mayo *et al.*, 1993, p. 227). On this, Killen (2003, p. 175) states that problem solving *should* be effective as a mode of promoting learning since it is a basic human learning process. To make this point is also to draw attention to the fact that what we are talking about here is the use of problem solving as a deliberate strategy to teach *something*.

We also advocate another perspective on the promotion of learning which is problem-based, namely, one which is concerned with engaging students in project work so that their ability to solve problems can be enhanced. The most usual model upon which this perspective is based is Dewey's (1933) six step process of inquiry: encountering the problem; formulating a problem or question to be solved; gathering information which suggests solutions; generating hypotheses; testing hypotheses; making warranted assertions. Various approaches to engaging in project work have been suggested since the early decades of the twentieth century. In more recent times it has been popularised through the 'integrated education movement'. The work of Drake (1998) in particular stands out in this regard, not only because of the compelling case which she makes for the importance of students engaging in multidisciplinary-, interdisciplinary- and transdisciplinary-based work through engagement in projects aimed at developing students' problem solving capacities, but also because she has delineated various practical approaches to implementation.

Conclusion

This chapter commenced by outlining the particular understanding of learning to which we subscribe. We then went on to provide a broad outline of our views on enhancing student learning in the school. The final section took a more specific focus, outlining one way of making sense of the great array of theoretical ideas, constructs and practical theories which serve to inform thinking on the promotion of flexible student learning. To this end we offered three propositions which serve to unify a significant number of related positions. We also stated that we do not subscribe to centrally-imposed approaches for the promotion of flexible student learning since to do so would not only run counter to the notion itself, but also because of their potential to inhibit the fostering of the autonomy of teachers and students and, in turn, the fostering of lifelong learning. Equally, such a vision is not likely to be very productive unless time, energy and money is spent on building the intellectual and professional capacity of individual teachers in the school, as well as promoting learning in the organisation itself. It is to these matters we now turn in the next two chapters.

6   Teachers learning and teachers leading

Introduction

In the Introduction to the book we argued that students' learning is closely intertwined with teachers' learning. We also suggested that in accordance with the principles of adult learning (Szabo and Lambert, 2002) it is desirable for teachers to work collaboratively, to be reflective practitioners and to adopt a research stance in the classroom. In essence, these strategies equate to a constructivist approach to learning that enables teachers to construct meaning from interaction, discussion and professional dialogue (Harris and Muijs, 2005). In similar vein, Hargreaves (1997, p. 99) has observed that teachers' learning should be as constructivist as the learning of their students is meant to be. This chapter elaborates on such professional learning and describes the conditions within a school that are likely to stimulate and support it.

In defining powerful professional learning in this way it is important to stress that we are focusing on formal and informal activities that can occur within the school on a continuous basis and serve to promote the development of professional learning communities. In other words, the approach is one which has the capacity to promote and sustain the situated learning of all its members (Jackson and Tasker, 2003). We are not, therefore, as concerned with formal programmes of 'professional development' comprising activities such as one-off workshops, visits and external courses. We recognise that these activities can complement and enhance professional learning communities, but they have also been associated with teachers' learning that is "individualised, episodic and weakly connected to the priorities of the school" (Hargreaves, 1997, p. 98).

Reflective practice

Powerful professional learning for empowering teachers in contemporary school environments is embedded in the concept of reflective practice. This, however, is not a new notion. It has long been argued that a major precondition for improving the overall quality of education is that teachers be aware of their subjective beliefs about teaching and its contexts. In particular, there is, as Dewey (1933) put it, a need to develop teachers' capacities for reflective action and to move them away from a perception of the everyday reality as given, clearly defined and in need of no further verification beyond its simple presence. In contrast to 'routine' action, namely, action which is prompted by tradition, authority, official pronouncements and circumstances, 'reflective action' incorporates active, persistent and careful consideration of any belief or supposed form of knowledge in the light of the grounds that support it and the further consequences to which it leads (1933, p. 9). In addition, reflective thinking involves a state of doubt, hesitation, perplexity, mental difficulty, in which thinking originates and an act of searching, hunting and inquiring to find material that will resolve the doubt, and settle and dispose of the perplexity (1933, p. 12).

Insofar as it has been related to teachers' professional learning the concept of reflective practice has been heavily influenced by the seminal work of Agyris and Schon (1978), which developed important new insights into the possibilities of professional learning including that of teachers. They suggest that it is possible to explain people's behaviour by attributing to them 'theories of action' which determine practice. Within a person's theory of action, they distinguish between 'espoused theories' and 'theories in use'. Espoused theory is used to justify behaviour, while theory in use relates to how the espoused theory is enacted. It is quite possible for a teacher's theories in use as applied within the classroom to be based on assumptions about teaching and learning which may be incompatible with his/her espoused theories. It follows, therefore, that for teachers to learn about their theory of action and that of their colleagues, it is necessary to enquire into, and make explicit, espoused theories, or what is purported about teaching, and theories in use, or what actually occurs in the classroom. Establishing the connections between these two dimensions of theory in action, it is argued, will enhance professional learning and effectiveness.

In connection with professional learning, Agyris and Schon (1978) made an important distinction between 'single loop learning' and 'double loop learning'. In single loop learning, the focus is placed on considering actions. Small changes are made to specific practices, or behaviours, based on what has or has not worked in the past. This involves doing things better without necessarily examining or challenging underlying beliefs and assumptions; a limited response to change that allows traditional ways of working to be continued because theory in action remains unexamined. This kind of learning has been predominant in schools in which self and peer review of thinking, planning and practice have tended to be neglected (Harris and Muijs, 2005).

Double loop learning, however, engenders actions being considered in the framework of operating assumptions. In this approach to learning, people become observers of themselves. This is a form of critical scrutiny that changes the way in which decisions are made and deepens understanding of previously unchallenged assumptions. In this way, new theories in use may be constructed. Hence, the process of double loop learning entails teachers deliberately and systematically making explicit the taken-for-granted assumptions they bring to situations and subjecting them to scrutiny, a process which is at the heart of reflective practice.

Notwithstanding the position outlined so far, there has been some conflict in debates on the nature of the reflection in which teachers are expected to engage. One approach, for example, focuses largely on encouraging teachers to question the adequacy of their pedagogical and behavioural skills in all settings and on breaking down the notion that there is 'one correct way' of teaching. Then there are those who argue that the major focus of reflection should be a socially critical one. With respect to the work of teachers, it is seen as being concerned with how and why resistance should be shown to the increasing tendency on the part of system-level policymakers to take control of classroom content and processes from those inside the classroom and vest it in legislative and administrative bodies. However, it also involves focusing on such matters as the steady increase in inequality in the economy, in gender and race divisions in jobs, and on the classroom implications of such realities.

Because the aforementioned two positions have a worthwhile contribution to make to the development of the professionalism of teachers, it is helpful to note that the position proposed over 30 years ago by Van Manen (1977) is one in which they are not seen as being mutually exclusive. He suggested three levels of reflexivity. Level One is reflection at the level of 'technical rationality'. The primary emphasis in 'technical rationality' within the teaching context is on the efficient and effective application of educational knowledge for the purpose of attaining given ends. Reflection at this level is concerned with questioning the appropriateness of various courses of action in the classroom, but does not enquire about purposes.

Reflection at Level Two for Van Manen is that of 'practical reflection'. At this level what is involved is the clarification of the assumptions that are the basis of practical action. The interest is with the moral, ethical and value consideration of the educational enterprise. In engaging in reflection at this level the concern is with deciding the worth of competing educational goals and experiences, not just harnessing energies for their attainment. Finally, Level Three is the level of 'critical reflection'. This level focuses upon the way in which the goals and practices become systematically and ideologically distorted by structural forces and constraints at work in various aspects of society, including educational settings.

The promotion of such approaches to reflection on practice can be facilitated by taking heed of the principles of 'action enquiry'. Broadly speaking, this is concerned with enquiry into action in a field of practice. In this respect, Tripp's definition is helpful:

> Action [e]nquiry is an umbrella term for the deliberate use of any kind of a *plan, act, describe, review* cycle for inquiry into action in a field of

practice. Reflective practice, diagnostic practice, action learning, action research and researched action are all kinds of action inquiry.

(2003, np; italics original)

The cycle of enquiry specified by Tripp has the potential to enable teachers to make informed judgements about their own practice and bring about improvements. For example, action enquiry understood in this way can occur individually by teachers keeping reflective journals or compiling professional development portfolios. Nevertheless, there are limitations to reflecting alone (Harris and Muijs, 2005) and the potency of enquiry tends to be strengthened when others are involved.

Collaboration

It is a simple yet profound assertion that teachers are likely to learn through their interactions with other teachers. Little (1990), for example, identifies four kinds of collegial relations. Scanning and storytelling, help and assistance, and sharing, she considers to be relatively weak promoters of learning and improvement. Joint work, however, such as mentoring, action research, peer coaching, planning and mutual observation and feedback, she regards as powerful levers of interdependence, collective commitment, shared responsibility, review and critique. Hence, it can be argued that collaboration is a natural development of reflective dialogue (Seashore Louis and Leithwood, 1998). For collaboration to promote effective professional growth it must be based on mutual enquiry and sharing in order to lay the foundations of a professional learning community. It is when teachers engage in dialogue with each other as a matter of course that meaningful reflection and teacher learning occurs (Harris and Muijs, 2005).

Furthermore, collaborative effort augments the socio-emotional support within the school (Seashore Louis and Leithwood, 1998). As curriculum, pedagogy and assessment become increasingly complex, they also demand more intellectual rigour. Collaboration enables information and insights to be shared, common issues to be debated and innovative ideas tested. In doing so, these processes are likely to enhance teachers' confidence and agency both individually and collectively in responding critically to change (Fullan and Hargreaves, 1996).

Collaboration has taken on a particular meaning in schools of late with the current inclusive education movement. Within this context it involves joint communication and decision-making amongst educational professionals to create an optimal learning environment for students with exceptionalities. Kauchak and Eggen elaborate on this position as follows:

In collaboration, special and regular education teachers work closely to ensure that learning experiences are integrated into the regular classroom curriculum. For example, rather than pulling a student with special needs out of the classroom for supplementary instruction in math, a special education teacher coordinates instruction with the classroom teacher and then works with the student in the regular classroom on tasks linked to the standard math curriculum.

(2008, p. 105)

Within this paradigm, teachers are expected not only to aid in the process of identifying students with exceptionalities, but also collaborate in the creation of individual educational plans, seek out the help of special educators, and collaborate with parents and school administrators.

Notwithstanding the current preference for the notion of 'leadership' over that of 'management', and the espousal of such a position throughout this book, the 'collaborative school management' approach of Caldwell and Spinks (1988) also still has much to recommend it. In this model the school 'management team' is divided into a policy group and a project team. This is an attempt to provide a task-oriented focus with checks and balances to provide a certain amount of accountability. The policy group can consist of teachers, parents and students, and its task is to make decisions about goals, identify needs and policymaking guidelines, and share responsibility for evaluation activities. The project teams, by contrast, largely comprise teachers who collaborate in the undertaking of evaluation. The overall cycle consists of six phases: goal-setting and identification of needs, policy-making, planning of programmes, preparation and approval of programme budgets, implementing and evaluating. The important point with regard to present considerations is that collaboration runs right through the whole process.

As well as the advantages of collaborative activities within a school, similar benefits may also be derived from inter-school collaboration. Atkinson *et al.* (2007) have identified in the literature a number of inter-school collaborative activities, which have implications for the enrichment of teachers' learning. These activities include joint planning and school development projects sometimes entailing sharing of key staff, the sharing of curriculum facilities such as sports amenities and joint purchase of Information Technology equipment. Atkinson *et al.* (2007) go on to contend that such endeavours include opportunities to exchange ideas and good practice and to expanded avenues for professional learning which, in turn, refine teaching expertise. In addition, staff have outlets to share and voice any concerns with a larger number of colleagues. Within an enriched support network it follows that there are gains in staff confidence, motivation and morale. In similar vein, Jackson and Temperley (2007) argue persuasively in favour of 'networked learning communities', which they describe as comprising joint work, enabling effective practice to be examined in context by means of collaboration between institutions. These authors are convinced that this form of learning fosters professional learning, energises teachers and distributes and develops leadership.

The general sense of empowerment generated from collaboration suggests that teachers will benefit not just from engaging with a community of learners, but also from a community of leaders (Mitchell and Sackney, 2000). Accordingly, we now examine the ways in which teachers' learning that is collegial, job embedded, and evidence-based (Ball and Cohen, 1999) has an interdependent connection with leadership.

Teacher leadership

There is nothing novel in the observation that the forms of learning discussed earlier can also provide a platform for new forms of leadership for teachers (Darling-Hammond *et al.*, 1998). Indeed, it has been recognised for some time that teacher leadership is inextricably connected to teacher learning largely because of its ability to nurture professional learning communities. In order to portray how this connection is evident in the school environment it is worth devoting some attention to defining teacher leadership, explaining what teacher leaders do, and describing the conditions that have an impact on the exercising of teacher leadership.

As York-Barr and Duke (2004) have pointed out, teacher leadership is difficult to define because of the expansive territory it encompasses. Nevertheless, the way in which teachers' learning and leadership are mutually supportive and reinforcing has been captured by Fullan (cited in York-Barr and Duke, 2004, p. 261) in his comment that teacher leadership comprises a commitment to moral purpose, continuous learning and knowledge of teaching and learning, educational contexts, collegiality, and the change process. This conceptualisation of the term also seems to resonate with Katzenmeyer and Moller's (2001) insistence that teacher leaders are those who identify with and contribute to a community of teacher learners and leaders.

There are a number of ways acknowledged within the burgeoning literature on teacher leadership in which teacher leaders can identify with and contribute to a community of teacher learners and leaders. Harris and Muijs (2005, p. 65) have distilled from the literature six major activities of teacher leaders which require support and development. They are:

1   Continuing to teach and to improve individual teaching proficiency and skill;
2   Organising and leading peer review of teaching practices;
3   Providing curriculum development knowledge;
4   Participating in school-level decision-making;
5   Leading in-service training and staff development activities;
6   Engaging other teachers in collaborative action planning, reflection and research.

These six activities, although not exhaustive, provide a helpful framework for making the interrelationship between teachers' learning and teachers' leadership visible.

The first activity of teacher leadership identified by Harris and Muijs (2005) is continuing to teach and to improve individual teaching proficiency and skill which highlights the classroom orientation of the teacher leader as well as his/her disposition towards learning. If the craft of teaching is perceived as sophisticated and increasingly complex, rather than as a straightforward technical activity, it is axiomatic that continuous professional learning will be seen as imperative (Hargreaves, 1997). In this connection, Basicia and Hargreaves (2000, p. 7) also refer to an 'intellectual conception' of teaching, highlighting the need for professional judgement informed by knowledge, expertise, reflection, research and continuous learning. The challenges of being a practitioner according to this intellectual conception are considerable and necessitate that professional learning becomes integral to the job itself. From this perspective, the 'sheep dip' mentality of teachers who eschew professional learning because they have been 'done' on completion of their initial training is untenable.

Teachers, therefore, need to be powerful learners if they are to maintain a high level of professional performance in an occupation that has become increasingly difficult. They also need to be powerful learners so that they are able to present role models to their students as well as to the community as a whole. In this sense, a teacher's capacity to learn constitutes an important form of leadership in itself.

The second activity of teacher leaders extrapolated from the literature is organising and leading peer review of teaching practices. This engenders developing strategies for teachers to consult with one another, to discuss and share teaching practices, to observe one another's classrooms and to promote collegiality and support. These strategies, of course, are likely to facilitate professional learning through the fostering of reflection and analysis of teaching practice, providing formative feedback and encouraging collaborative ways of working across the institution.

As a result of these processes, multiple opportunities are created for teachers to exert leadership. These may include experienced teachers mentoring and coaching novice or struggling colleagues by providing instructive feedback and identifying strategies that enhance classroom practice. Informal guidance of this nature can occur through conversations in hallways, teachers' rooms and other school settings, or by means of more formal supervision. Another approach that could have application to the process of peer review of teaching practices is the use of the 'critical friend'. A critical friend in this context would be envisaged as someone who helps colleagues see their practice more clearly by enabling them to bring the familiar into new focus (Swaffield, 2002); in other words by supportively challenging assumptions. Normally, the role of the critical friend would be performed by an external agent, but could equally be undertaken by a colleague from a different section of the school. For example, a critical friend could be used to provide 'arm's length' advice to a colleague compiling a reflective professional portfolio as part of a formative appraisal process. Collectively, these strategies of peer reviewing classroom practice have the potential to create an environment in which teachers are engaging with a community of teacher learners and leaders.

The third activity of teacher leadership – providing curriculum development knowledge – is predicated on teachers' commitment to collegiality, continuous learning and knowledge of teaching and learning. One specific structure that is amenable for encouraging the provision of curriculum development knowledge is the support or study group (Fullan and Hargreaves, 1996). A study group will normally comprise like-minded teachers who are interested in collegial enquiry and taking action. A teachers' group may be convened for a range of purposes with the intention of examining issues, problems or phenomena occurring in practice, but certainly represents an appropriate forum for teachers to discuss and share their expertise in curriculum design and development. The impact of study groups can be strengthened if the members are encouraged to report regularly on their progress and challenges to the school as a whole. According to Fullan and Hargreaves (1996, p. 71), these kinds of groups are especially advantageous because they are developed by the teachers, with the teachers and for the teachers.

Teachers' groups have the potential for enabling teachers to participate in school-level decision-making, which constitutes the fourth substantial activity of teacher leadership. The participation of teachers in decision-making at the whole school level has traditionally been stifled by top-down, hierarchical approaches to school organisation more likely to foster the dependency of teachers than their initiative and responsibility. These circumstances generate 'glow-worm' teachers (Riley, 2003) who find it difficult to take responsibility for their professionalism and require a good deal of fanning for their teaching to glow once again (Early and Bubb, 2004).

An important means of restoring the glow in teachers of this ilk is by adopting a more extended understanding of leadership-engendering teachers and management working together. This inclusive approach to professional activities might embrace areas such as school vision-building, development planning, staff appraisal, professional development processes and cross-curricular initiatives. Bringing teachers in to whole-school policy planning and decision-making or the 'big picture' (Hargreaves, 2003, p. 192) can promote teachers' learning because involvement is likely to unleash their creative energies and encourage a risk-taking culture. Indeed, Barth (2001) goes further and asserts that the process of decision-making represents the best learning opportunity possible for teachers. It is also, of course, a significant acknowledgement and valuing by 'senior personnel' of teachers' professional expertise and judgement.

The fifth activity of teacher leadership is leading in-service training and staff development activities. If internal learning becomes an institutional norm, it appears to be a self-fulfilling prophecy that teachers will assume an instrumental role in leading staff development activities. Indeed, creating and participating in professional learning communities is in itself a "vibrant form of professional development" (Harris and Muijs, 2005, p. 56). Examples of collaborative practice already discussed in this chapter present rich and plentiful opportunities for teachers to lead their own learning and also embrace the sixth activity of Harris and Muijs (2005) that involves leaders of teachers engaging other teachers in collaborative action planning, reflection and research.

The sixth activity of teacher leadership is centred on the notion of the 'teacher researcher'. This notion is not new and may be interpreted in a number of ways. Stenhouse, for example, as long ago as 1975, argued that ideally the activities of research and development in relation to the classroom should belong to the teacher. In particular, he advocated that teachers should develop a capacity for autonomous professional self-development "through systematic self-study, through the study of the work of other teachers and through the testing of ideas by classroom research procedures" (Stenhouse, 1975, p. 144). In making this declaration, Stenhouse also recognised that if teachers were to acquire a capacity for autonomous professional self-development, a research tradition needed to be created, which would be accessible to teachers. Since 1975, of course, the notion of reflective practice has been advanced as an epistemology of professional creativity (Eraut, 1994), which refers to teacher researchers as those who reflect on and critique their practices (Handscomb, 2004). In accordance with the principles of action enquiry, teachers with a research stance to the classroom employ research and evidence to generate new ideas and approaches and then evaluate systematically the efficacy of any changes that have been implemented. In doing so, these processes sustain teacher learning and become a vehicle for teachers to teach other teachers. They encourage teachers to support each other's intellectual and professional growth, and increase the standing of teachers by demonstrating their ability to add to knowledge about teaching and effect evidence-informed change. These are the circumstances that highlight the extent to which teachers' learning and leading are interdependent.

So far, it has been argued in this chapter that teachers' learning is most effective when it is embedded in the life and work of the school (Hargreaves, 1997) and, in particular, is based on reflective practice constituting an integral dimension of teachers' work. It is teachers engaging in critical reflection that challenges tacit assumptions about practice and can lead to a reframing of theories-in-action through deliberation and heightened metacognitive awareness. Teachers' learning is also based on collaboration in reflection and enquiry which promotes shared purpose and develops teachers' sense of efficacy and agency. In this respect new forms of learning provide the conditions and opportunities for new forms of leadership for teachers.

Conditions that support teachers' learning

Attention is now turned to the conditions within a school that seem to be indispensable for creating and supporting the patterns of teacher learning and leadership which have been identified. It is, perhaps, a statement of the obvious that creating the foundation conditions for teacher learning and leadership in the ways described is closely connected with the concept of 'capacity building', or releasing the human potential available in an organisation (Harris and Muijs, 2005). Hopkins and Jackson (2003, p. 89) have identified four key dimensions of a school's capacity that are helpful in examining some of the implications for the organisation. The first dimension is the importance of all people in the organisation and the expansion of their contributions. In the context of this chapter it is clearly the expansion of teachers' contribution that is paramount. The second dimension of capacity relates to the synergies generated when internal arrangements and their interconnections are working optimally. Third, there are the organisational arrangements which support personal and interpersonal capacity development. The fourth dimension identified by Hopkins and Jackson impinges on the cultural territory of shared values, social cohesion, trust, well-being, moral purpose, involvement, care, valuing and being valued. Using this depiction of capacity as a reference point, it is possible to formulate some crucially important implications for the operation of schools, with particular reference to leadership, shared vision, relationships and support.

Leadership

As far as leadership is concerned, it is clear that capacity building is premised upon a re-distribution of power within the school, which moves from hierarchical control to peer control (Harris, 2003a) or, in other words, the distributed approach to leadership, which has already been examined in Chapter 3. Rather than leadership being understood in terms of the positional authority of an individual, distributed leadership is deemed to be created through the interaction of individuals and groups. Hence, distributed leadership results from the kind of collaborative activities already discussed in this chapter in which leadership is 'stretched' over the work of several individuals and the leadership task is accomplished through the interaction of multiple leaders (Spillane *et al.*, 2001).

Shared vision

A second key component of capacity building is the articulation of a shared vision that has been crafted with and among the school's stakeholders (Murphy *et al.*, 2006). A shared and inspiring vision which has a sharp focus on learning and consistently informs school policy planning and decision-making is likely to build norms of pedagogical practice that the staff supports. On this, Crowther *et al.* (2002, p. 40) refer to "a sense of shared purpose" that serves to align the school's stated vision with teachers' preferred approaches to teaching, learning and assessment and facilitates curriculum innovation. As they see it, a sense of shared purpose can often be manifested in a common language about teaching and learning and a school culture that is characterised by transparency and inclusiveness.

Relationships

Building a school culture of this nature is fundamental to the development of staff relationships that are conducive to teachers' growth. Social capital is built on trust (Hopkins and Jackson, 2003, p. 101) that allows open engagement and knowledge sharing. From this perspective, the facilitation of teachers' learning and leading according to the approach we have outlined might need to engender a shift from a culture of teaching characterised by individualism, isolation and privatism to one in which collective learning, continuous improvement and teacher leadership can take hold.

The close interdependence of organisational culture and the nurturing of staff relationships that foster teachers' learning and growth has been articulated well by Butt and Retallick (2002). Although these researchers focus on administrator/teacher relationships, it can be argued that their observations apply equally to positive professional relationships between teachers themselves. They contend that in situations where teachers perceive positive relationships with administrators there exists a 'positive climate' characterised by support, recognition, respect, trust and care. These modes of behaviour are buttressed by 'collegial communication', which is vertical in nature rather than horizontal and enables power and expertise to be shared across the staff. This combination of the context of positive climate and the process of collegial communication helps to provide favourable conditions for workplace learning and teachers' capacity building by promoting their self confidence, growth, problem solving and success.

Support

Another crucially important consideration for schools in developing the capacity of teachers is support. This may be divided into two main categories, namely, logistical support such as the timetable and resources, and social support, including plentiful opportunities for work placed professional learning and the leadership of the principal. In discussing logistical support, Harris and Muijs (2005) draw attention to the importance of such factors as providing time for teachers to meet and have professional conversations about teaching and learning, the importance of the physical proximity of the staff to encourage collaboration, well-developed communication structures and the operational discretion provided by school-based management.

The degree of logistical support for developing teachers' capacity will determine the scale and value of opportunities made available for professional learning. Ideally, as Muijs and Harris (2003) point out, these opportunities should not only serve to enhance teachers' skills and knowledge, but also their agency as leaders. In this connection, the kinds of collaborative work already highlighted, such as study groups, action research and mentoring, promote both leadership and learning. As such, 'leaderful' experiences can be transfused into teachers' work on a day-to-day basis.

Not surprisingly, in schools where leadership is embedded in collaborative processes of learning, the role of the symbolic leader or principal is crucial for "the leader is the critical change agent – the guardian and facilitator of transitions" (Hopkins and Jackson 2003, p. 101). Barth (2001) suggests, however, that it is not so much the role of the principal that is crucial in empowering teachers, but how the principal chooses to perform the job. From this point of view, if teachers are treated as semi-skilled workers who require to be technically trained, closely monitored and regulated, there will be a deleterious impact on developing teachers' capacity. If, on the other hand, teachers are treated as professionals who deserve continuous opportunities for learning, leadership and participation, they are more likely to experience a sense of instrumentality and commitment. It follows, therefore, that it is desirable for the principal to perform the job with the main intention of supporting others to be successful (Hopkins and Jackson, 2003). Crowther *et al.* (2002), for example, refer to the need for principals to 'step back' in order to encourage teacher colleagues to 'step forward' and take advantage of opportunities created for them to develop their leadership capabilities.

This observation again highlights the importance of the distributed approach to leadership for enhancing teachers' capacity (as well as that of others throughout the school community), which is becoming a dominant motif of schooling. On this matter, Senge *et al.* (2000, p. 495) refer to a principal of an innovative school who was asked how she defined her job. She responded by suggesting that her job, at its most fundamental level, was to create an environment where teachers can continually learn because teachers deeply engaged in their own learning would be able to create a learning environment for students.

The implications for principals of empowering teachers in such a way are considerable. Crowther *et al.* (2002), for example, assert that principals will need to become accustomed to unfamiliar approaches to power sharing and acquire skills and expertise in nurturing teacher leadership. There is, nonetheless, evidence to indicate that principals may lack the knowledge and experience required to promote this kind of leadership (York-Barr and Duke, 2004), in which case there are also significant implications for principals' selection, preparation and ongoing professional development (Blase and Blase, 1999).

Conclusion

In this chapter we have described approaches to teachers' learning that comprise formal and informal activities that can occur within the school on a continuous basis and serve to promote the development of professional learning communities. In keeping with the principles of adult learning (Szabo and

Lambert, 2002), the key elements of these activities are reflective practice and collaboration. We have also suggested that the forms of learning informed by reflective practice and collaboration present rich and diverse opportunities for teachers to experience new forms of leadership and develop their sense of agency, both individually and collectively. The chapter concluded by identifying the conditions within a school that seem to be indispensable for creating, supporting and sustaining appropriate patterns of teacher learning and leadership. These conditions are closely related to the level of organisational learning and it is to this theme we turn our attention in the next chapter.

7 Organisational learning and the intelligent school

Introduction

In Chapter 1, we introduced the concept of organisational learning, which constitutes the third level of learning within a school in combination with student learning and teacher learning. Each level is interconnected through the flow of opportunities across people, classrooms and school structures (MacBeath, 2006, p. 20). Student learning is dependent on teacher learning while teacher learning is enhanced by its receptiveness to students' learning needs. Organisational learning is, in turn, dependent on, and feeds into, teacher learning.

The concept of organisational learning has evolved from the recognition that organisations are increasingly facing changing, uncertain and ambiguous conditions which require the capacity for self-organisation, or the full use of the intellectual and emotional resources of its members. Engaging in organisational learning, therefore, pushes members beyond independent and individual learning to collective learning and interdependence to achieve shared aims (Collinson, 2008). From this perspective, organisations are conceptualised more in terms of processes and relationships than as structures and rules (Seashore Louis and Leithwood, 1998), for it is the inclination and capacity of individuals and groups within the organisation that create the potential for it to adapt to a changing environment (West-Burnham and O'Sullivan, 1998).

The idea of organisational learning has been familiar to the business and management world for some time, but has made a relatively recent appearance into the educational literature (Mitchell and Sackney, 1998). The education sector, however, is also subject to changing, uncertain and ambiguous conditions suggesting that the concept of organisational learning is equally applicable to schools. Indeed, it may be argued that organisational learning is fundamental to the creation of schools that are capable of providing the kind of education required for people to lead productive lives in the twenty-first century (Hargreaves, 2003).

In this chapter we elaborate on those learning processes in schools that bring to fruition the hidden capital of their staff and students, thus creating and sustaining the kind of organisations that learn. For this purpose, we pay particular attention to the notion of the 'intelligent school'. We also examine the implications that organisational learning has for leadership. Finally, we provide an overview of 'The IDEAS Project' in Australia, which is aimed at school revitalisation. While this project includes many of the notions outlined in this chapter it also goes beyond them in an exciting approach based on the view that teaching in a knowledge society will be a highly sophisticated, highly complex construct that can be viewed as three-dimensional.

The intelligent school

In our portrayal of schools as organisations that learn, we lean heavily on the literature that describes organisational learning in positive terms. From this perspective, a learning organisation presents a vision of a community which is characterised by humanistic values, enabling levels of cooperation and learning that will make the organisation more successful (Driver, 2002). From the outset, however, we wish to make clear how mindful we are of the existence of a more critical literature that is inclined to dismiss organisational learning as a thinly veiled form of control and manipulation (Burgoyne, 1999; Contu and Willmott, 2000; Fox, 2000). On this, Hartley notes the emergence in this critical literature of a new regard for issues of power, politics and trust; three fundamental dimensions of learning which, he states, "have been somewhat neglected in the past" (2007, p. 793). Thus, adopting the lens of the critical theorist can be useful in exposing possible distortions in what often goes on under the aegis of organisational learning.

On the other hand, we are cognisant that, with the exception of Ortenblad (2002), those who take a critical position have made hardly any efforts to show what a better and more radical perspective of organisational learning would imply. Equally, we recognise that much of the critique of organisational learning that has been in the ascendancy for many years relates mainly to organisations other than schools. The position we take in the remainder of this section is very much influenced by all of these considerations. Fundamentally, it is a stance which holds that since schools, more than the majority of organisations, are required to maintain a focus on learning as an activity, an alignment with the positive perspective on organisational learning is both understandable and justified.

A useful starting point in considering our position is the argument that a school defining itself as a learning organisation is required to possess and develop 'organisational intelligence' (Morrison, 2002). In similar vein, MacGilchrist *et al.* (1997) refer to the concept of the 'intelligent school', which draws on Gardner's (1983) notion of multiple intelligences as well as recent thinking about the nature of organisations to offer a new way of looking at schools. This enumeration of intelligences provides a strong foundation for building understandings on the somewhat elusive theme of organisational learning as it relates to the distinctive context of schools.

The first way in which schools learn, according to MacGilchrist's (n.d., p. 1) typology of intelligences, is through *contextual intelligence*. This form of intelligence refers to the capacity of a school to see itself in relationship to its wider community and the world of which it is a part, and its ability to respond to both the environment's positive and negative aspects. The idea of contextual intelligence, therefore, relates to the ways in which a school orients itself to its internal and external environment. In similar vein, Morrison (2002) identifies the constant scanning and sensing of the environment as a key characteristic of a school that engages in organisational learning. In this way, schools are cognisant of the pressures they face and how they should respond. These schools are also aware of how they can influence the environment. In this connection, Pedder and MacBeath (2008) have pointed out that schools are increasingly influenced by external environmental constraints, which highlights the need for them to be able to discern emerging trends so that they can link future possibilities to current school improvement priorities.

Morrison (2002, p. 136) identifies some of the strategies it would be desirable to adopt in leadership aimed at promoting the school's ability to relate to its environments. These include: communicating with their environments, gathering information, adapting their internal environments to meet the requirements of their external environments, developing networks with their communities, and conducting and acting on needs analyses. It can be argued, therefore, that a school's contextual intelligence equates to the fundamental *systems thinking* component of Senge's (1990) five disciplines, deemed crucial to the functioning of a learning organisation. Systems thinking, it will be recalled from the introduction, focuses on wholes rather than parts, goes beyond events to their underlying structure, and leads to experiencing the interconnectedness and inter-relationship of things. In simple terms, this perspective engenders an acute sensitivity to the 'big picture' (Senge, 2004). Voogt *et al.* (1998) have argued, however, that systems thinking can be particularly difficult to pursue in schools because of their tendency to be internally segmented. Furthermore, schools within a system are often loosely linked. This is a further factor that can compound a school's understanding of the interconnectedness of the parts and their contribution to the direction in which the school is heading.

A second way in which a school learns as identified by MacGilchrist (n.d., p. 2) is by means of *strategic intelligence*. She explains this form of intelligence by relating it to clarity about goals and the standards to be achieved, and ensuring that the aims and purposes of the school are shared by everyone. It is through the use of this type of intelligence, she argues, that a school is able to plan the action needed to achieve improvement and have the capacity to put vision into practice. As Voogt *et al.* (1998) point out, school leaders often have personal visions that fail to get translated into shared visions capable of galvanising colleagues. There is a need, therefore, to articulate a set of principles and guiding practices that facilitate the translation of individual vision into one that is evocative, inspiring and shared. In this connection, Morrison (2002) also refers to a need for "involved leadership", by which he means the necessity for school leaders to elicit views throughout the organisation and to synthesise them into an articulated and shared vision.

One systematic strategy which can be implemented to assist the planning of future action and change is school self-evaluation. According to MacBeath (2001, p. 4), self-evaluation can be defined most simply as "a process of reflection on practice, made systematic and transparent, with the aim of improving pupil, professional and organisational learning". A school that is adept in self-evaluation is able to draw on the synergy within the institution that has the capacity to become more intelligent than its individual members (MacBeath, 2001). The collective reflection and action engendered by a process of self-evaluation can be a precursor to a genuine shared vision because of its potential to reveal collective pictures of the future that enlist real commitment across the school community (Voogt *et al*, 1998). Likewise, Senge (1990) identifies *shared vision* as one of the five disciplines of the learning organisation that is manifested in common understandings and genuine commitment capable of unleashing people's aspirations and hopes so that they identify with the vision not out of compliance, but because they are motivated to do so.

MacGilchrist (n.d., p.2) describes a third form of organisational intelligence as *academic intelligence*, purporting that it represents the value attributed by the school to high-quality study and scholarship. This intelligence, she suggests, "incorporates the concept of 'value added' (what Harvey (2004) defines as enhancing students' knowledge, skills and abilities and empowering them as critical, reflective, life-long learners), the characteristics of effective learning and teaching, and the key importance of high expectations", which are collectively distinguished by an 'ethos' that encourages high achievement and performance. To this end, it is desirable that the ethos is manifested in a common language about teaching and learning, and by transparency and inclusiveness (Crowther *et al.*, 2002). Academic intelligence, therefore, is likely to be nurtured within a school if ways are found to bring to fruition the hidden capital of its students (MacBeath, 2006).

One way in which this hidden capital can be realised is by means of harnessing student voice. Proponents of this view hold that if student voice is to contribute to organisational learning, the challenge is to integrate it into school-wide policy that genuinely reflects a set of commonly held values within the school. This, however, will be dependent on teachers also having a voice. Taking account of this highlights the necessity for organisational learning to be attuned to different 'bandwidths' (MacBeath, 2006), as well as reiterating the interdependence of students' learning and teachers' learning. From this point of view, academic intelligence encourages the efficacy of both students and staff.

Closely intertwined with academic intelligence is *reflective intelligence* (MacGilchrist, n.d., p. 2), which refers to "the skills and processes of monitoring, reflecting upon and evaluating the effectiveness of the school in general and, in particular, the progress and achievement of the students". At the whole school level, the importance of self-evaluation for promoting reflective intelligence is once again highlighted. However, as Leithwood and Atkin (1995) are quick to point out, it is important that the evaluation is not conducted just to fine tune the school's operations according to accepted worldviews and assumptions. This approach will at best enhance a moderate degree of understanding, but will remain at a low level and be confined to single loop learning. Instead, it is far more desirable that double loop, or high level, learning should occur, which engenders schools taking a critical stance and reflecting on their experience as a way of learning collectively and individually about themselves (Pedder and MacBeath, 2008). Using the terminology of Agyris and Schon (1978), it is by means of double loop learning that any disjunction between 'espoused theories' and 'theories in use' can be revealed and dealt with by challenging previously accepted assumptions and developing a new worldview of the organisation. In the same vein, Senge's discipline (1990) of *mental models* refers to making explicit those deeply ingrained beliefs, values, mindsets and assumptions that determine the way people think and act.

Hence, a school's capacity for reflective intelligence can enable it to go beyond improvement to being transformative, insomuch as it can bring about substantial change in the understandings and behaviour of its staff. As an example of a change that could eventuate in this way, Leithwood and Atkin (1995, p.33) refer to the shift from teacher-directed whole-class approaches to student-directed group-based learning. A shift of this nature, it is argued, entails challenges to previously held and often deep-rooted assumptions about the nature of knowledge, the role of social interaction in learning and the basis of teachers' authority. To this end, double loop learning processes are involved which create new organisational knowledge and new norms that guide future actions and nurture new cultures (Scribner *et al.,*1999). The degree to which monitoring, reflecting upon and evaluating the effectiveness of the school in general and the progress and achievement of the students in particular are able to develop reflective intelligence will depend on acquiring data, turning it into useful information and ultimately into strategies for action (Leithwood and Atkin 1995). In MacGilchrist's (n.d.) terms, it is through collecting, analysing, interpreting and using a range of information that the school can judge effectiveness by drawing on its contextual intelligence and can plan improvements by drawing on its strategic intelligence.

Without embarking on a detailed examination of evidence-based practice, it is important to indicate that there are a number of data-gathering instruments that schools can utilise for monitoring, reflecting upon and evaluating the effectiveness of the school and the progress and achievement of its students. With reference to self-evaluation, MacBeath (1999, p. 7) argues that 'smart schools' are those that have access to, and know how to use "simple, economical and routine evaluation tools". These can include shadowing, photographs and videos, focus groups, diaries, interviews and surveys which help the [reflective] intelligence of the organisation expand because the processes are strongly embedded in the day-to-day life of school and class-rooms (James, 2007). Mulford (2005) focuses attention on more quantitative data-gathering instruments and suggests they can be applied to a broad range of areas within a school's overall operation which can assist the monitoring process. Such areas include planning and decision-making, teacher pedagogy, and student outcomes.

In relation to student outcomes, the shift to value-added assessment that measures the difference in students' learning achievement between entry to, and exit from, a school has become significant (Dimmock, 2000). Although Dimmock suggests, quite correctly, that this focus is mainly attributable to increased demands on schools for accountability, it can also be argued that value-added assessment may contribute to a school's reflective intelligence. MacGilchrist *et al.* (1997) argue that value-added data are most useful for enabling schools to identify areas of good practice as well as aspects of school life that need to be improved. Morrison (2002) goes further in his advocacy that a concern for measurement represents another key characteristic of a school that learns and that this, among other things, engenders identifying aspects of student performance that can and should be measured.

On a more cautionary note, Harvey (2004) stresses that it can be difficult to assess value-added assessments, especially if it relies on measurement of students' entry and exit grades, or abilities gained through the use of some-what crude indicators. This more circumspect perspective on using data to provide insights for school decision-making is a reminder that the utility of data is always dependent on human interpretation (Earl and Fullan, 2003). In other words, sense needs to be made of the data so that information and workable knowledge can be created, requiring considerable expertise from school leaders. There is some indication, however, that school leaders lack confidence in understanding and using data (Earl and Fullan, 2003), suggest-ing that they would benefit from more grounding in research and in data col-lection, management and interpretation. Indeed, the work of Shen and Cooley (2008) indicates that principals tend to use data mainly for accounta-bility purposes rather than for improving teaching and learning, and that they require greater knowledge and skills in facilitating data-informed decision making. Perhaps this observation on the need for school leaders to be 'data literate' also relates to the desirability of schools being able "to know them-selves, do it for themselves and [be able] to give their own account of their achievement" (MacBeath, 1999, p. 2). From this point of view, the school's reflective intelligence is contingent on its capacity to 'tell its own story', rather than have another version of it imposed, or manipulated, by a local educa-tional jurisdiction, or an assessment industry.

Closely associated with reflective intelligence is the notion of *pedagogical intelligence* (MacGilchrist, n.d., p. 2), described as ensuring that learning and teaching are regularly examined and developed so that they never become an orthodoxy. On the same lines, MacBeath (2005) advocates critical discourse on the learning/teaching interface, which can develop an understanding of 'fitness for purpose' when deciding the most appropriate strategies to use. Pedagogical intelligence corresponds closely with Senge's (1990) *personal mastery* discipline of the learning organisation insomuch as it engenders teachers reflecting on their work and evaluating it in relation to specific students' needs and research findings (Voogt *et al.*, 1998).

MacBeath (1999, p. 7) claims that teachers should be natural evaluators because they are involved regularly in reviewing their own work as well as their students' work and modifying their practice accordingly. These evaluative activities can be enriched when a culture exists among teachers (Ritchart and Perkins, 2008) which enables elements of effective learning and good teaching to be brought strategically to the surface of people's thinking. Likewise, James (2007) argues that teachers need to be stimulated to think about the principles that underpin their practical strategies in the classroom, making the development of beliefs and practices interrelated. Indeed, James goes on to assert that the teachers who had most success in the 'Learning How to Learn' project on which she reports were those who were able to apply learning principles to shape and regulate the learning processes of students in accordance with their needs. This capacity for strategic and reflective thinking seems to be at the core of a school's pedagogic intelligence.

If teachers are to be successful in regulating the learning processes of their students there will need to be continuous opportunities available for social exchange and interaction, an observation that draws attention to the fundamental function of a school's *collegial intelligence* (MacGilchrist, n.d., p. 3). This form of organisational intelligence is purported to be concerned with the capacity for staff to work together with the particular purpose of improving practice in the classroom. In this connection, Barth's (1991) portrayal of typical interactions that occur between teachers is instructive. According to him, teachers' interactions tend to be determined by a desire to maintain the norm of congeniality. Hence, teachers will not be inclined to confront each other about educational decisions that might not benefit the students if those conversations are construed as being potentially detrimental to maintaining congeniality.

Rather than promoting congenial conversations, Barth advocates that conversations occurring in schools should be determined by the norm of collegiality. Collegial conversations are defined as those that connect with what is happening in the school and the strategies required to enhance the quality of students' learning. From this perspective, collegial intelligence engenders teachers abandoning their preoccupation with 'getting along' and acting as professionals. A professional approach is more likely to result in differences between teachers and even conflict, because it invites voice and tests assumptions and attributions. Concurrently, however, it protects the dignity and self-respect of colleagues (Mitchell and Sackney, 2007).

Collegial intelligence also has a strong similarity with Senge's (1990) learning organisation discipline of *team learning*, which is created when teams share their experience, insights, knowledge and skills with each other about how to improve practice. In doing so, teams can develop their skills in reflection, inquiry and dialogue to form the basis for a shared vision of change and common commitments to action. It might be further argued that a school with a fully developed collegial intelligence extends its opportunities for teacher collegiality and collaboration beyond the organisation by means of networks. Jackson and Temperley (2007, p. 45), for example, have suggested that informed organisational learning is dependent on "permeability to external learning from other schools".

The efficacy of teachers' collaboration, of course, will be dependent on a climate of openness and trust. The existence of trusting collegial relationships provides the oxygen for teachers to engage in stimulating dialogue, to venture into informed risk taking and to encourage reasoned dissent (James, 2007). In the absence of trust it is axiomatic that conflict and disagreement are more difficult to control. In Louis' words (2007, p. 3), "trust is the basis of 'taken for granted' aspects of social interaction, a necessary ingredient for cooperative action and a foundation for social capital."

For this reason, it is desirable for a school to develop both its *emotional intelligence* and s*piritual intelligence* (MacGilchrist, n.d., pp. 3–4). Emotional intelligence relates to a school's capacity to allow the feelings of both students and staff to be owned, expressed and respected. Spiritual intelligence is characterised by a fundamental valuing of the lives and development of all members of a school community. Everyone is seen to matter and to have something to contribute. These intelligences are, of course, manifested in the overall 'culture' of the school, which may be defined as the informal expectations and values which shape how people think, feel and act (Deal and Peterson, 1998).

On a more prosaic note, perhaps, Southworth (2000) argues that a school culture is susceptible to being contaminated by 'toxins', or nourished by 'nutrients'. It stands to reason that a school's emotional and spiritual intelligences are likely to be debilitated when its culture is predominantly toxic. On the one hand, Southworth (2000) contends that a toxic culture is characterised by people within the school having ideas rejected or stolen, being subjected to constant carping criticism, being ignored, being judged, being over directed, not being listened to, and being misunderstood. At the risk of stating the obvious, these harmful behaviours detract from the level of trust and respect that is required for nurturing a school's emotional and spiritual intelligence or, in other words, its social capital. On the other hand, Southworth describes a nutrient-rich school culture as one in which people are valued, encouraged, noticed, trusted, listened to and respected. These are the behaviours that demonstrate high levels of emotional and spiritual intelligence across the school because they are motivating, inclusive, caring and empowering (Owen, 2001).

The last form of school intelligence in MacGilchrist's typology is the closely linked notion of *ethical intelligence*. This also has implications for the vigour of a school's culture. It is an intelligence that engenders a clear statement of values and beliefs enshrined in a school's statement of aims and, perhaps more importantly, concerns the way a school conveys its moral purpose and principles such as justice, equity and inclusivity.

The capacity of a school's vision and mission statements for contributing to its ethical intelligence cannot be taken for granted. Dawson (2007), for example, points out that a few school administrators can often develop these statements in a perfunctory manner for the main purpose of accommodating systemic requirements. It is hardly surprising that in these circumstances a vision and mission statement is unlikely to be meaningful because of its lack of connection to the day-to-day operation of the school. This situation might also result in a conflict between the 'hidden curriculum' – that which is learned alongside the formal curriculum (Hargreaves, 1978b) – and the school's official and espoused ideology.

Dawson (2007) goes on to argue that in order for vision and mission statements to be meaningful and enhance a school's ethical intelligence, it is necessary to establish 'value congruence'. Put simply, value congruence refers to the extent to which the values of individual members match the values of the organisation insofar as they meet social and psychological needs, contribute to personal dignity, develop relationships with others and conform with a school's mission.

The level of value congruence within the school will, in turn, determine the extent to which trust permeates the functioning of the organisation. Louis (2007, p. 3) describes two common forms of social trust. First, there is institutional trust, which is manifested in the expectation of appropriate behaviour in organised settings based on the norms of the school. Second, there is relational trust, which is the result of repeated interactions with others in modern organisations. Not surprisingly, minimal levels of both institutional trust and relational trust are required for an organisation to function effectively. Hence, a vision and mission statement that promotes value congruence in the school and is integral to a culture of trust can play a significant role in increasing the organisation's social capital through its ethical intelligence.

The IDEAS project in Australia

The IDEAS Project in Australia, which is aimed at school revitalisation, includes many of the notions already outlined in this chapter. It does, however, go well beyond them in its outline of an exciting approach based on the view that teaching in a knowledge society will be a highly sophisticated and complex construct where the net effect can be new knowledge that has the power to transform communities. This project is now outlined in order to promote thinking on how many of the ideas outlined in this chapter so far might be related to each other in a similar framework. The account constitutes an overview of the exposition provided by Andrews and Crowther (2002), two of its key architects.

IDEAS is the acronym for the 'Innovative Design for Enhancing Achievements in Schools' Project. It is an initiative of the University of Southern Queensland's Leadership Research Institute and the State Education Department in Queensland. It is designed primarily on the research base which exists on the links between professional learning communities and enhanced school outcomes. Andrews and Crowther (2003, p. 2) have described it as having three essential components, all of which "represent significant departures from mainstream educational reform literature of the past decade or more". Each of these components will now be outlined.

Component one

Central to the first component is the concept of organisational alignment. The notion here is that "schools that generate both depth and consistency across their major elements will engender a greater capacity to pursue high expectations for student achievement and to nurture a distinctive sense of identity" (Andrews and Crowther, 2003, p. 2). Based on this, the following five core elements of the school as an organisation have been identified:

- strategic foundations;
- cohesive community;
- infrastructural design;
- school-wide pedagogy (SWP);
- professional supports.

Andrews and Crowther hold that these differ significantly from the components of most organisational development models of the past. On this, they draw particular attention to the inclusion of SWP.

Component two

Component two of the IDEAS project is the implementation strategy. Four key theoretical concepts inform this strategy as it proceeds through five stages. These concepts are as follows:

- metastrategy;
- appreciative inquiry;
- action learning;
- capacity building.

Each of the five stages are now outlined.

Phase one

This 'initiating phase' normally requires the identification of one or more school-based facilitators and the institution of a school management team (ISMT) to work with a university support team.

Phase two

This is the 'discovery phase'. During this phase data are collected from teachers, students and community members about the existing level of organisational alignment of the school. The aim is to identify what are the most successful aspects of the school as well as the major challenges they are facing. This process, as it is put, "facilitates learning across the school community, but is centred on the work of teachers, particularly the identification and exploration of instances of pedagogical excellence" (Andrews and Crowther, 2003, p. 3).

Phase three

The third phase is termed 'the envisioning phase'. It involves the envisioning of the school community's aspirations.

Phase four

This is the 'actioning phase'. The actioning takes place within the school and involves teacher leaders and administrators working together. Andrews and Crowther elaborate on this as follows:

> Principals focus on community building and the coordination of within-school developmental efforts while teachers (either as individuals or as self-selecting small cohorts) are encouraged to trial aspects of their SWP, with a view to creating school-based definitions and meanings of these various aspects. Action research, action learning, peer mentoring, dialogue groups, phenomenological writing and group presentations have all been used successfully to explore the meaning of SWP in individual classrooms.
>
> (2003, p. 4)

Within this phase teachers are also encouraged to "cross-refer to authoritative theories of learning and teaching" and to reflect on their personal styles, values and personalities in relation to particular pedagogical approaches.

Phase five

The fifth phase is entitled "the sustaining phase". The focus here is on "sustaining the school's enhanced level of alignment, particularly in relation to its distinctive SWP" (Anderson and Crowther, 2003, p. 5). In this phase teachers are usually engaged in exploring the relationship between systemic pedagogical and curricular initiatives and their SWP. Great importance is attached to the position that any infrastructural changes decided upon should come only after the school's vision and pedagogical approaches have been agreed.

Component three

Component three of the IDEAS project is focused on leadership. The particular approach to leadership which is advocated is termed 'parallel leadership'. Parallelism, it is argued, embodies:

> . . . mutual respect, shared purpose and allowance for individual expression and recognises forms of leadership potential within the profession of practising teachers that have been obscured, and frequently denied, in the past. In IDEAS, the metastrategic leadership function of principals is asserted unequivocally. But equally important is bona fide leadership on the part of teachers.
>
> (Andrews and Crowther, 2003, p. 5)

The following 'teachers as leaders framework' is also offered:
  Teacher leaders convey convictions about a better world by:

- articulating a positive future for students;
- showing a genuine interest in students' lives;
- contributing to an image of teachers as 'professionals who make a difference';
- gaining respect and trust in the broader community;
- demonstrating tolerance and reasonableness in difficult situations.

Teacher leaders strive for authenticity in their teaching, learning and assessment practices by:

- creating learning experiences out of students' needs;
- connecting teaching, learning and assessment to students' futures;
- seeking deep understanding of tacit teaching and learning processes;
- valuing teaching as a key profession in shaping meaning systems.

Teacher leaders facilitate communities of learning through organisation-wide processes by:

- encouraging a shared, schoolwide approach to pedagogy (teaching, learning and assessment);
- approaching professional learning as consciousness raising about complex issues;

- facilitating understanding across diverse groups while also respecting individual differences;
- organising new ideas out of colleagues' dialogue and activities.

Teacher leaders confront barriers in the school's culture and structures by:

- 'testing the boundaries', not necessarily accepting the status quo;
- engaging administrators as potential sources of assistance and advocacy;
- accessing political processes in and out of the school;
- standing up for children, especially disadvantaged individuals and groups.

Teacher leaders translate ideas into systems of action by:

- organising complex tasks effectively;
- maintaining focus on issues of importance;
- nurturing networks of support;
- managing issues of time and pressure through priority setting.

Teacher leaders nurture a culture of success by:

- acting on opportunities for others to gain success and recognition;
- adopting a 'no blame' attitude when things go wrong;
- creating a sense of community identity and pride.

Andrews and Crowther (2003) conclude that schools that have engaged systematically in the IDEAS Project for around two years or more have frequently found that they have undergone significant change in their sense of identity, their level of organisational alignment and their pedagogical practices. Taken together, they state, "the three components – the Research-based Framework for Enhancing School Outcomes, the IDEAS process, and parallel leadership – represent a new conceptualisation of processes of successful school reform and a new conceptualisation of teachers as leaders in a knowledge society" (Andrews and Crowther, 2003, p. 5).

Conclusion

In this chapter we have considered the somewhat elusive concept of organisational learning. The concept is rendered more elusive because the related literature draws from an array of disciplinary perspectives making it virtually impossible to develop a comprehensive theory (Easterby-Smith, 1997). We also provided an overview of 'The IDEAS Project' in Australia which is aimed at school revitalisation, pointing out that while it includes many of the notions already outlined in this chapter it also goes well beyond them.

In order to capture the essence of organisational learning, we have suggested that it is closely related to the process of harnessing fully the intellectual and emotional resources of its members. We have also attempted to portray an ideal school, which provides an environment in which learning is more likely to be maximised. For this purpose, and in line with MacGilchrist *et al.* (2004), we have argued that an organisation capable of learning is required to possess and develop 'organisational intelligence'. These authors contend that it is the ethical and spiritual intelligences that comprise the vision of the school, while the others that have been discussed in this chapter constitute action intelligences. The efficacy of organisational learning as a whole, therefore, is dependent on the extent to which the vision intelligences connect to action intelligences, and vice versa.

As MacGilchrist (n.d.) emphasises, it is especially important for school leaders to recognise the interdependence of these intelligences because they have maximum impact when used in combination. She also draws attention to the need for leaders to acknowledge the potential that each type of intelligence has for development and improvement. In order to develop the school's intelligences it must be a priority for leadership to share vision, enrich culture, build relationships and create collective knowledge.

Before concluding, however, we wish to return to the point made at the beginning of the chapter that the notion of organisational learning is a contested one. Indeed, one would be remiss in not considering some of the positions advocated by various theorists who engage in such contestation before moving to adopt the various approaches we have advocated. Certain interpretivists, including those like Greenfield (1986) who also displayed a leaning towards sociological phenomenology, have, since the 1970s, criticised those who adopt models based on the assumption that human life is determined from without. Rather, they argue, "social life springs from within – because everyone does not interpret life in the same way we cannot presume uniformity in organisations" (Ryan, 2002, p. 987). On the other hand, the retort of other interpretivists is that while this is the case, groups can go on to form shared perspectives with shared values which can remain relatively stable over periods of time (O'Donoghue, 2007, pp. 26–28). This position provides a social-theory basis for Louis' (1994) argument that collective knowledge creation is possible in organisational learning, and distinguishes such learning from individual learning.

One should also not overlook the views of those who point out inconsistencies in the position of theorists like Greenfield who, on the one hand, criticise "technical forms of leadership for attempting to eliminate values from inquiry", while also taking "critical theorists to task for adopting explicit value positions" (Ryan, 2002, p. 989). We also see value in engaging with more critical perspectives on the grounds that they can inform and strengthen the development of organisational learning theory. In particular, Driver's (2002) argument that we should refrain from accepting the 'Utopian sunshine' of the proponents of organisational learning without question and instead be mindful of organisational learning perceived as 'Foucauldian gloom', is worthy of attention.

There are also practical issues which cannot be overlooked. MacBeath and Mortimore (2001), for example, in their studies on school effectiveness in Scotland, indicate that achieving shared values and collective learning is often problematic, especially in large secondary schools. The argument is that the system and culture of schools can separate people and prevent them from working coherently and collegially. The ways in which this happens, however, such as through the differentiation of stages of learning as prescribed by governments, and the separation of grades and subjects (Stoll *et al.*, 2002, p. 54), need to be considered as obstacles to be overcome, rather than as being insurmountable. Another practical consideration is highlighted by Hargreaves (2003, p. 186) where he observes that schools that exhibit the characteristics of organisational learning tend "to exert their effects slowly but sustainably over time". This is because organisational learning is a normal, albeit a complicated process rather than a "managerial lever that can be pulled by senior executives at their behest" (Easterby-Smith, 1997, p. 1109). This, of course, is not to say that we should refrain from inspiring teachers to have a lofty vision for pedagogical reform at the level of students, of teachers themselves and of the school as an organisation. The next chapter now focuses on this theme.

8 Inspirational developments in leading learning

Introduction

The focus of the last three chapters has been on student learning, teacher learning and organisational learning. At this point it is valuable to recall a point made in Chapter 1, namely, that we consider our position on each of these three areas to be a pragmatic one. In other words, while it constitutes a challenge to those charged with leading learning at the school's level, the realisation of what is being advocated is achievable. We also hold that one way of enthusing leaders of learning in the classroom to espouse the position is to expose them to inspirational developments which have taken place in different parts of the world. Consequently, this chapter outlines six such developments, two in relation to teacher learning and four in relation to student learning. These extend in scale from a macro-level set of projects to a single micro-level project. In keeping with the international focus of the book they relate to developments in Singapore, the USA, Ireland and East Africa.

The North Carolina Center for the Advancement of Teaching

So far considerations have centred on student learning. However, previous chapters in this book have also emphasised the importance of learning in other domains, including teacher learning. This section is now concerned with a very significant and long-standing initiative in the latter domain, the North Carolina Center for the Advancement of Teaching (NCCAT). The centre, which is a unit of the University of North Carolina, was established in 1985 to serve school teachers in order to enhance the learning of the children of the State. Its current stated mission is as follows:

> to provide a dynamic environment, in an atmosphere of respect and dignity, where North Carolina teachers engage in scholarly activities structured to stimulate intellectual curiosity, create thinking, inquiry, and discussion; examine and challenge ideas; have time for reflection,

inspiration, and professional networking; and develop renewed enthusiasm for teaching.

(http://www.nccat.org/about_history.html [Accessed on 1 March, 2009])

The official planning for this multi-million dollar NCCAT was initiated in October 1984. Hoffbauer (1992, p. 25) has pointed out that in an era of budget cuts and standardised curriculum this was somewhat unusual. Added to this was the fact that the State was traditionally recognised for low graduation and literacy rates, below average test scores, and poor teacher morale.

While a number of educational, social and political circumstances set the scene for the establishment of the NCCAT, the leadership shown by the governor of North Carolina at that time, James B. Hunt, Jr, was crucial. At the same time as the national education reform movement was underway, he headed up the North Carolina Commission on Education for Economic Growth to engage in research on the status of public education to ensure the future prosperity and well-being of the State's children and the development of a sound economy. J. Hunt (Hoffbauer, 1992, p. 25) was directly involved in supporting a number of important educational programmes. He also came to see that improving schools was especially critical. The concept of a teacher centre emerged as one of a number of strategies for expressing a high regard for teachers and teaching. On this, the ideas of Ms Jean Powell, who was North Carolina's Teacher of the Year at the time, were seminal. She encouraged the Commission to create a place where teachers could go to become enthusiastic about learning once again in their lives so that they could then pass on this enthusiasm to their students. Such a place, she argued, should be developed in order to enhance the self-worth, pride of accomplishment and enthusiasm of teachers in order to attract and retain the best.

In 1985, the State government officially established NCCAT as part of the University of North Carolina. Full-time operations began in the Fall of 1986 on the campus of Western Carolina University. In 1990, NCCAT moved to its own facilities on a hillside campus in Cullowhee. The main conference building on the NCCAT 30-acre campus includes several meeting rooms, dining and reception areas, kitchen, amphitheatre, technology lab, exercise room, library resources, staff offices, an outdoor patio and parking. Two residence halls are located a short walking distance from the main conference building. Each building has 24 rooms for overnight lodging along with commons areas. The NCCAT also has its own art collection.

When it was established the NCCAT was the first state-funded centre of its kind in the USA. Its main function, as Greene (1992, p. viii) has put it, was to allow practising teachers to take time out for friendship and reflection, thus transforming themselves into eager learners; a function which continues now. In justifying the initiative back in 1992, Greene stated:

Many of us spend our lives challenging fixity, apathy, passivity, imposition. . . . we know that the teacher who is treated transitively – reformed from the outside, supervised from above – is likely to become a functionary or a transmission belt. Bypassed as a person, someone with a sense of agency, such a teacher is altogether likely to rely on the predefined, the discrete, the fixed. We realise how frequently teacher reform movements have ignored the teacher as questioner, as beginner, someone caught in the wonderment and uncertainty, reaching beyond to choose and to know.

(1992, p. viii)

Shea (1992, p. 2) put it similarly. He commenced by stating that the term 'teacher renewal' has tended in the contemporary literature to refer to teacher recertification programmes. Such a usage, he argued, might be better termed 'teacher reform'. To explain what he had in mind he outlined the following distinction made by McPherson:

Reform too often assumes blame, while renewal starts with faith. . . . Because reform focuses on all of the members of the group (e.g., a school district, a school), it allows little variability in allegiances or practices. . . . But renewal is by its nature personal, and the restoration of confidence and skill and commitment and energy varies dramatically from teacher to teacher.

(1990, pp. 16–17)

Shea rejected the notion of teachers as pawns to be manipulated and controlled in order to achieve larger social goals and the situation whereby each educational crisis was thought to be caused by teachers. The process involved in the latter he termed "teacher scapegoating" and described it as one whereby teachers are identified as "lacking some essential human attribute thought necessary to the educational endeavor – deficient traits of moral character, inadequate technical skills and behaviors, or dysfunctional emotional personality structures" (Shea, 1992, p. 3).

The Center, by contrast, was established to provide primary and secondary school teachers with the opportunity to take charge of their own growth and development. Thus, from its inception it has provided multiple avenues for teachers to pursue their intellectual and creative interests, free from the structures of tests, grades, or follow-up classroom checks. The 'good teacher-renewal philosophy' which underpins the work of the Center has been outlined as consisting of:

1 A process for articulating a reliable understanding of the nature of reality (i.e., the realm of the empirical sciences and analytic philosophy);
2 A process for articulating the human significance of this reality (i.e., the realm of cultural sociology);

3   An ethical schema for generating common social ideals (i.e., the realm of ethics and politics);
4   A personal dialogical praxis for overcoming or minimising the identified discrepancies between the common social ideals and the actual state of affairs (i.e., the realm of personal aesthetic praxis).

It is also part of this philosophy that teacher renewal programmes should help a teacher resolve his or her day-to-day problems "through practical solutions that are both emotionally satisfying and aesthetically pleasing to the individual" (Shea, 1992, p. 13).

The core of the Center's activities are week-long seminars designed so that teacher participants can re-examine, refine, and in some cases reconstruct their existing world views. It is recognised that this requires time and probing self-examination. "By helping teachers to confront and manage the enduring problems of human existence, and by providing a conceptual framework for judging the adequacy of these solutions", it is held, "philosophy gives us the means of mastery over our environments in ways that are true, morally justifiable, socially acceptable, and aesthetically pleasing" (Shea, p. 14). At the same time, technical skills are not ignored; it is argued that this aspect of teacher education rests on three assumptions – that discrete pedagogical skills can be identified; that the skills can be transmitted to prospective practitioners; and that they can be appropriately drawn upon in practice to improve teacher performance (Shea, 1992, p. 17).

Overall, then, the NCCAT promotes a notion of education for practising teachers as being about 'renewal' rather than 'reform'. Griffin (1992) has provided an outsider's view on its activities. He was impressed by the conception of teachers as thoughtful members of an extended collegium, extolled the movement away from what he termed the trivialisation of teaching activity, and could not speak highly enough of enlightened decisions of those policymakers responsible for the Center's maintenance and development. The commitment to the Center's future is also indicated by the fact that a second campus is now in the construction phase and when it opens it will make NCCAT programmes more accessible to teachers who live and work in the eastern part of the State. We give the last word to the teachers themselves; the 2008 promotional material for NCCAT gives voice to some of the latest group of teachers to benefit from its seminars as follows:

> "Not only did we recharge our tired teacher bodies, we renewed our excitement for our classrooms. My students will richly benefit from the experience I had."
> "I am excited about what lies ahead. I have a group of new friends who will help me along, and I have a clear vision of what I want to accomplish."
> "I am back at school with a renewed zeal, energy, and love of teaching."
> (North Carolina Center for the Advancement of Teaching, 2008, p. 2)

The Agha Khan Foundation Projects in East Africa

This account of an inspirational development aimed at improving the quality of student learning is also concerned with teacher learning. It consists of a brief overview of the school improvement projects (in which teacher development is central) carried out under the Agha Khan Foundation in East Africa, and is based on a lengthy exposition by Anderson (2002). The Foundation is a private nondenominational development agency established by His Highness, the Agha Khan, in Switzerland in 1967. This, in turn, is a member of the Agha Khan development network. This consists of a group of institutions working together for social, economic and cultural development in specific regions in the developing world in order to improve the living conditions and opportunities of poor people. The ultimate aim is to achieve a level of self-reliance amongst the poor such that they can plan their own livelihoods and help each other.

The Foundation concentrates its work on resource-poor areas. Its priorities include education, health and rural development, with an emphasis on community participation, gender, the environment, and human resource development. The education program is concentrated in East Africa, and South and Central Asia, where the focus is on school improvement to attain a quality education for all by increasing access, retention and completion rates. Great emphasis in this task is placed on ensuring active student participation in the learning process. Grants for funding are made to the Foundation's sister organisation, Agha Khan Education Services, as well as to the Agha Khan University Institute for Educational Development, and to governments and nongovernmental and private-sector institutions that share the Foundation's goals. The Foundation's programmes also receive funding from more than 60 national and international development agencies, along with many individual and corporate donors.

The Foundation has been particularly active over the last two decades in the East African countries of Tanzania, Kenya and Uganda in undertakings aimed at creating effective, sustainable, field-based support systems for continuous school and teacher development. This initiative is noteworthy in terms of the extended period of time devoted to its activities, with each project having a life of between three and ten years. Also, it has been organised such that the knowledge from each project has fed into the planning and implementation of successive projects across the region. A major underlying assumption outlined by Anderson has been that the possibilities for improving the quality of student learning is enhanced when:

> improvement efforts are school-based, involve the whole school as the unit of change, attend to school management and other organisational conditions affecting the capacity of teachers to implement change at the school level, prepare for the institutionalisation of organisational structures and processes that enable continuous school development beyond

the school improvement project phase, and evolve through genuine partnerships among relevant education stakeholders.

(2002, p. 2)

Teacher development activities are central to this vision. While the nature of the activities vary across the projects, they generally include the following: enhancing access to school-based workshops; the provision of in-class assistance by consultants, supervisors, and peers; the organisation of team planning and problem solving by collegial work groups within the school; engagement in action research; facilitating teacher visits within and between schools; and the establishment of professional study groups. Most projects have also been aimed at developing local leadership for teacher and school development. Furthermore, there has been much investment in the development and improvement of teacher resource centres at the district, school cluster, or school level so that teachers' professional learning needs can be enhanced through access to professional reading and to quality teaching materials.

The projects deliberately eschew strategies that emphasise the provision of 'in-service training' for the delivery of 'pre-packaged' teaching and learning materials, lessons and teaching guides. The belief is that the latter approach would create a mindset amongst teachers that what is learnt relates only to the specific areas addressed, thus limiting the possibility of developing flexibility in the adoption of teaching methods. Instead, the approach is one aimed at developing teachers' understanding and skill in lesson planning and facilitating the acquisition of a broad repertoire of teaching strategies, with the expectation that they will gain the capacity to decide independently how to plan and apply these strategies across a broad range of curriculum subject matter to address various objectives and student needs. In order to try to make a real contribution to helping teachers master a wide repertoire of pedagogical skills some projects involved external consultants in in-school mentoring for periods of up to 6 to 12 months. This involved teachers not only in learning a variety of teaching methods, but also engaging in action research.

The overall evaluations of the projects are very positive, even though it is recognised that there is still great room for improvement. In particular, there is much still to be done by way of providing peer support and networking among teachers and across schools. Also, there is a long way to go before teachers become totally comfortable with letting children initiate discussion with each other in the classroom. Nevertheless, teachers, in general, are very enthusiastic about grouping students in class and recognise that much more can be done in this area. Also, teachers are coming to recognise the value in using a variety of pedagogical approaches and that group work which facilitates engagement in peer support and tutoring is advantageous.

Service learning in the International Baccalaureate

In Chapter 5 of this book the point was made that one of various productive ways of promoting student learning beyond the confines of the school, is through service learning. Such learning is considered to be valuable in the contemporary era for a number of reasons. For example, Conrad and Hedin (1991, p. 743) point to its liberating capacity when they state that "the greatest power of service is that it reveals that one is not powerless, that a contribution can be given, a difference made: I can do something, I am significant." Amongst other claims made is that service learning can connect learning to life, give meaning to an interdisciplinary curriculum, promote creative and critical thinking skills, and provide opportunities for introspection and reflection.

Conrad and Hedin (1991), pioneers in the field, also concluded that service learning can have positive effects on students' social and personal responsibility, including improvement in self-esteem, self-motivation, risk-taking and ability to solve real-life problems, improvement in one's taking of responsibility for one's own learning and improvement in one's concern for others. Evidence of student growth in critical thinking, motivation, engagement, curiosity and citizenship has also been noted (Eyler and Giles, 1999). Furthermore, research to date in the USA indicates that when service learning is explicitly connected to the curriculum by teachers who help students process and draw meaning from their experiences, the effects on cognitive, affective and behavioural development are positive (Billig, 2000, pp. 660–62).

This linking of service with academic goals is not new in the USA, of course, with progressives like John Dewey arguing back in the 1930s that the role of education is to transform society. Nevertheless, the incorporation of service learning into the curriculum more generally only started off in earnest in the early 1970s (Skinner and Chapman, 1999, p. 2), thanks largely to the foundation of the National Center for Service-learning which provided assistance to schools initiating service learning programmes (Alt and Medrich, 1994). Growth in the last two decades has been impressive: the National Center for Education Statistics found that 64 per cent of all public schools had students participating in service, with almost half of all American high schools incorporating service learning within the curriculum (Skinner and Chapman, 1999, p. 1); a 2002 report from the National Commission on Service Learning estimated that more than 13 million students participated in service, or service-learning, activities in the 2000–01 school year; while in 2005 it was noted that almost three-quarters of the states in the USA had some form of policy addressing service-learning, and one, Maryland, even made it a graduation requirement (Piscatelli, 2005, p. 59).

At the same time, as Silcox and Leek (1997) have emphasised, one must not allow the extent to which developments have taken place in the USA to overlook what is taking place in other parts of the world. They list an impressive array of initiatives in this regard. Through service learning programmes, students at a school in Slovenia brought the English language to their school as part of the curriculum after the fall of Communism, high school students in Tanzania built toilets and set up schools for the use of local villagers, while students at the Roehampton University in England studying for a Master's degree in 'international service learning' are placed in the Czech Republic, Ecuador, England, France, India, Israel, Jamaica, Mexico and the Philippines. These and many other initiatives are, as Silcox and Leek (1997, p. 1) put it, helping students develop critical thinking skills and are bringing to the field of service learning "new and invigorating ideas about how young people can express themselves more creatively".

One of the most comprehensive service learning initiatives is that which has been integral to the International Baccalaureat curriculum and which over 30 years ago was leading the field in stressing the importance of community service as part of the formal curriculum (Kulundu and Hayden, 2002, p. 30). The International Baccalaureate (IB) Diploma programme was originally designed to meet the needs of globally mobile students between the ages of 16 and 19 in international schools to gain access to universities worldwide. It was developed as a deliberate compromise between the specialisation required in some national systems and the breadth preferred in others (International Baccalaureate Organisation, 2004). From the outset the emphasis was laid on the development of the general powers of the mind to operate in a variety of ways of thinking rather than on the acquisition of general knowledge. At the same time, it is an academically demanding programme. Students study six subjects across six subject groups: first language, second language, individuals and society, experimental sciences, mathematics and computer science, and the arts. At least three, and not more than four, of the six subjects selected are taken at a higher level, and the others are taken at standard level, with the former providing depth of study and the latter providing breadth.

On top of the academic subjects which they have to study, students enrolled in the IB must complete three other core elements of the programme. The first of these is a course in the 'theory of knowledge', which is based on reflection on 'the main modes of thinking' and the relationship between disciplines. The second requirement is that students must write a 4,000 word extended essay, which requires the development of skills associated with independent research. The third requirement is student participation in what is known as 'creativity, action, service' (CAS) activities This particular requirement, which emphasises compulsory involvement in service, was described in 1994 as "one of the remarkable requirements which placed the IB ahead of its time" (Jenkins, 1994).

CAS is based on a framework such that students are exposed to experiential learning and reflection about that learning. In the course of two years they are expected to participate for 150 hours in the three areas of creativity, action and service. 'Creativity' is seen as covering a wide range of arts, hobbies and interests; 'activity' consists of physical activities where some form of physical training is involved on either a team or individual basis; and 'service' is undertaken in relation to such groups as the local community, the disadvantaged, and peer groups. While it is expected that around 50 hours should be spent on each strand, it is equally acceptable for the three strands to be treated separately, or for them to be integrated into a single project (Kulundu and Hayden, 2002, p. 31). Regardless of the approach, however, it is prescribed that "a preponderance of passive pursuits, e.g. films, viewing art, piano lessons, tennis and so forth, should be minimised" (International Baccalaureate, 1996). Rather, what is emphasised is the development of new skills, not simply practising those already acquired. Also, it is seen that the three strands offer favourable situations for involvement and enjoyment, and provide opportunities for students to develop on a personal level. In the process they also develop a social conscience to improve society through service.

Through CAS, thousands of students have benefited over the years. Those who have participated contend that it lives up to its major emphasis as follows:

> CAS should aim to challenge and extend the individual student; to develop a spirit of discovery and self-reliance; to encourage personal skills and interests; to inspire an awareness, concern and responsibility to serve the community, in general, and its disadvantaged, in particular.
> (International Baccalaureate Organisation, 1991, np)

It constitutes an outstanding example to leaders of learning of what can be achieved in curriculum design for flexible learning as well as an example to those in various parts of the world who are once again seeking models for the promotion of citizenship education. An additional benefit is the contribution to the greater good of the community. In this regard, it is an exemplar of Dovey and De Jong's (1990) vision of a curriculum which reflects a dialectical relationship between individual and social development, where each has the potential power to have an impact on the other.

'Project Work' in Singapore

A second inspirational development aimed at improving student learning is the 'project work' programme introduced in schools in Singapore. By way of background it is instructive to keep in mind that students in Singapore have for a long time had a high reputation for being strong in subject content knowledge and being well trained in the art of passing examinations. However, along with various governments around the world, the government of Singapore became increasingly concerned towards the end of the twentieth century that this would not be sufficient to ensure economic success for the future. Particular concern was raised over what was perceived to be students' lack of ability to generate and solve problems through application of knowledge and skills, weakness in oral communication and lack of exposure to collaborative work. Mr Wee Heng Tin, the then Director of Education, took the initiative in December 1997, by issuing an open letter in which he stated that the school curriculum required a major re-think so that improved teaching could be effected in order to prepare students for the knowledge-based economy of the twenty-first century. The result of a number of taskforces established to pursue this aim was a Ministry of Education policy document entitled *The Desired Outcomes of Education* (Ministry of Education, Singapore, 2000).

Several steps were taken to improve the curriculum so that students would be provided with skills to enable them to handle real-life situations. One such step was the introduction of problem-based learning approaches. Equally noteworthy was the introduction of what is termed 'project work'. This initiative represented a change in the dominant approach towards teaching and learning in Singapore, not just in its emphasis on interdisciplinary studies, but also through indicating that there was some room for departure within the curriculum for a view that students should be concerned almost solely with soaking up large doses of preordained subject content. The policy leaders also demonstrated insight in ensuring that project work was specifically timetabled in secondary schools to be conducted during regular curriculum time. Furthermore, curriculum content in certain other learning areas was reduced by 30 per cent. Overall, these developments were in harmony with a more general cross-curricular initiative nationally which came to be known popularly as the 'teach less, learn more' educational policy.

Emphasis within project work in the curriculum for Singapore's schools is placed on both individual work and teamwork, as well as on compulsory oral presentation and self-monitoring of learning (Ministry of Education, Singapore, 2003). It is considered to be a valuable approach for helping students to see links between and across subject disciplines and to apply their specific knowledge. Furthermore, in 1999 the Committee on University Admissions revised the admission criteria for entrance into the nation's universities to include not only 'A' level results, but also project work. This loosening of traditional parameters indicated a recognition on the part of leaders for learning in Singapore that if university entry requirements cannot be modified to accommodate major curriculum and pedagogical initiatives then acceptance and persistence of associated innovations are unlikely to be successful.

There is no body of knowledge to be reproduced in the project-work syllabus. Students have to draw on their existing knowledge from across subject disciplines, seek out new knowledge, and then apply it to the task they have chosen. The fact that they are assigned to groups randomly and thus cannot choose their group members indicates the extent to which importance is placed on the development of collaborative skills for later life in the work place. Working as a group, they cooperate to complete the task and, in doing so, have the opportunity to learn from each other. In reflecting on their individual learning and taking action to improve it, the expectation is that they will develop the metacognitive skills considered necessary for lifelong learning.

One of the main reasons for project work being conducted during regular curriculum time is to enable teachers to monitor students' progress regularly and provide feedback. The teacher's role is that of facilitator. He or she is expected to raise awareness and generate a sense of accountability in the students. Teachers are also expected to demonstrate leadership to ensure that students receive mentoring from lecturers in higher education institutions, including universities and polytechnics. Furthermore, they are challenged to let go of some of their traditional authority to create a more conducive learning environment that facilitates the development of creativity and breaks down rigidity.

There are four domains in project work: knowledge application, communication, collaboration, and independent learning. Although project work is often in the form of group work, students must track their learning curve and be responsible for their work. Responsibility for one's knowledge is placed in one's own hands. The outcome, it is argued, should be students who seek knowledge and answers for themselves.

Project work has become very popular in schools in Singapore and a wide variety of projects continue to be disseminated and reported publicly. One example of an initiative taken by the Project Work Unit in the Ministry of Education was the organisation of workshops on the 'storyline approach' for primary school teachers. This pedagogical approach, which has some correspondence with the well-known curriculum, teaching and learning position of Egan (O'Donoghue and Saville, 1996), as well as being based on constructivist notions of learning, has been described by Lien and May as follows:

> The 'storyline method' is an innovative approach to curriculum integration. It creates a context for curriculum linkage and active learning. The essential elements of a 'storyline' are the place or setting, the time, the characters and problems to solve. Working in groups, pupils create and design their own settings and characters. They give their own characters personalities. Following this, they discuss and plan their stories based on the settings and characters. The unfolding narrative provides structure and logic to curricular connections. Different subjects like English, mathematics, music and art come into play. The teacher asks key questions at appropriate stages and pupils learn by constructing their own knowledge. In addition, apart from the process of activity, reflection is also incorporated. Pupils learn to think for themselves and refine and extend their work and skills.
>
> (2002, p. 4)

Amongst the many other reports which have been published are those of teachers helping students in primary schools to move away from viewing project work in science as a form of assessment to seeing it as "an adventure, a journey of discovery of the mysteries and marvels of the natural world around them" (Kwen and Cwee, 2002, p. 15) and of lower secondary school students being involved in problem-based learning approaches, with teachers serving as mentors, resource personnel and assessors (Swee and Lan, 2002, pp. 9–14). Clearly, there is a certain movement away from the 'drill and kill' style of teaching which has long characterised Singapore's education system, to the adoption of more flexible approaches where the emphasis is more on student learning. It is too early to know the extent to which this has resulted in a major paradigm shift, if any, within the nation, but so far the indications are that such a change may well be on the way.

Brewster Academy, New Hampshire, USA

Brewster Academy, New Hampshire, USA, is a lighthouse school in terms of the embedding of technology to serve student learning. This is a co-educational, independent (private) secondary school (grades 9 to 13) of 350 students. Two-thirds of the students board at the school and enroll from 28 states and 16 countries. Over the last 10 years, Brewster has engaged in a comprehensive school reform effort that has resulted in the reform of all aspects of the school's programmes.

Dimmock (2000, pp. 175–76) has provided a comprehensive overview of the technology-oriented nature of the school. He details the school's campus-wide network, which involves 1,766 ports covering every classroom and dormitory and which gives access to both the Internet and the campus Intranet. This situation means that whether students are in class, in the school library, or in their dormitories, there is always a port to which they can connect. This is facilitated by the fact that every student and every staff member has a laptop computer. These are carried by all as they move between classes. Also, through the Intranet the students can call up a resident tutor and request help if they are having difficulty with their homework. Completed homework is sent via e-mail to a tutor who grades it, provides comments and then returns it via e-mail.

Dimmock, in reflecting on this situation, notes that such a system which allows universal access empowers teachers to change their ways. He goes on:

> For example, when teachers know that they can assign homework activity that involves spreadsheeting data from a science experiment, given that students have access to the necessary hardware and software, technology becomes a key factor in teachers' rethinking their pedagogy inside and outside the classroom. Similarly, when teachers can develop computer-based presentations at home with the certainty that the facilities exist in the classroom for all students to gain access, there is an incentive for them to do so. Technology-prepared lessons are more likely to become part of the day-to-day practice.
>
> (2000, p. 176)

All of the lessons take place within classrooms with appropriate architecture and lay-out of desks. Cables rise from the floor to desk height in technology posts. Four desks are organised around each post, thus allowing students to attend individually to whole-class instruction, to work in pairs, or to work in fours. Teachers also are grouped in teams of seven, with each team having responsibility for the whole curriculum of a group of students. Within the particular working space shared by each team the members meet regularly to discuss student progress, as well as disciplinary, welfare and counseling issues. In this setting access to each student's progress is available through the campus Intranet.

Bain (2004), the architect behind the holistic re-design of the school since 1992, has given a detailed exposition on the underpinning tenets of what has taken place. These are encapsulated within what he has termed the 'school design model' (SDM), the target of which is the acceleration of the growth of students academically and socially. It comprises eight research-based school-design elements. A summary of these is as follows:

- Learning statement: This documents the school's values and beliefs as they relate to how the school can best serve its students.
- Body of practice: This outlines a set of practices and approaches that the school believes, based upon its learning statement, will best serve its students. The intention is that all teachers will master them over time. At the same time, it is accepted that at no time will it constitute an absolute body of practice.
- Curriculum: This is seen in the SDM "to be an interaction of well supported pedagogy, content frameworks, and classroom interaction techniques that allows for the teaching of multiple groups in the same classroom, the adaptation of instruction to deal with individual differences, and the integration of instructional technology" (Bain, 2004, p. 155). Furthermore, it includes the notion that students should be actively engaged in the learning process. Also, within Brewster Academy there is deep study of fewer subjects than is normal in similar school in a four-year mastery curriculum "that focuses on demonstrable, authentic assessment outcomes" (Bain, 2004, p. 155).
- Training institute: The SDM includes a pre-service training programme to provide teachers with the skills necessary to work in the school. It is of six weeks duration, "is the entry point to the SDM process for faculty" and is the beginning of a process of formal mentoring by department heads "through team based collaborative decision making and feedback from students, peers, and supervisors with an opportunity for self evaluation" (Bain, 2004, p. 157).
- Human resource model: The elements of this model include a set of position descriptions for the roles of teachers and administrators in the school. These serve as the basis for a career path, beginning with Graduate Teacher and leading to the role of Senior Master teacher in

graduated steps. As Bain details, the transition through each step in the process is based on the submission of an electronic teaching portfolio employed by teachers to demonstrate mastery of each of the areas in the position description.

- Collaborative teaming: The SDM promotes a devolved collaborative decision-making model. To this end, the school is divided into teams that function as small schools, with, as already described, each team of teachers being responsible for the educational experience of a particular group of students.

- Feedback, reflection and evaluation: The SDM promotes the need for powerful mechanisms for gathering and sharing information, with feedback and evidence on the growth of the school, a student and a teacher being available all of the time.

- Technology: The considerations on the use of technology in the SDM focuses on the creation of a school operating system "that integrates the key transactions associated with the admission of students, the design and implementation of curriculum, the management and implementation of program, the management of human resources, and feedback" (Bain, 2004, p. 159).

This constitutes only a rudimentary outline of what is a very impressive and very sophisticated model for embedding technology to serve student learning. Nevertheless, it provides a general sense of those operations within a school dedicated to such a development.

'The Pres Girls' Club', Limerick, Ireland

Returning again to student learning, the example about to be outlined should be considered within the context of the current tendency in some quarters to argue that any initiatives aimed at improving the quality of student learning need to take cognisance of students' views on their situation. This is not to argue that it is a widespread tendency. On the contrary, as Smyth (2006, p. 279) has recently pointed out, the question of "how to pursue forms of leadership that listen to, and attend to, the voices of the most informed, yet marginalised witnesses of schooling, young people", has largely been kept off the official agenda in educational circles. Alongside this, he argues, we have the situation where 30–40 per cent of students in most Western countries are not completing high school. Various observers agree with Jones (1996) that this is due to a lack of human connections in schools. In a similar vein, Osterman (2000, p. 361) argues that discussions "seldom focus on students' need for belongingness, or the role of the school in meeting these belongingness needs".

Smyth (2006, p. 282) goes on to outline as follows what he regards as being "the minimalist scaffolding around which a view of leadership that takes cognizance of such a view" should be constructed:

- Giving students significant ownership of their learning in other than tokenistic ways;
- Supporting teachers and schools in giving up some control and handing it over to students;
- Fostering an environment in which people are treated with respect and trust rather than fear and threats of retribution;
- Pursuing a curriculum that is relevant and that connects to young lives;
- Endorsing forms of reporting and assessment that are authentic to learning;
- Cultivating an atmosphere of care built around relationships;
- Promoting flexible pedagogy that understands the complexity of students' lives; and,
- Celebrating school cultures that are open to and welcoming of students' lives regardless of their problems or where they come from.

There has been quite a lively debate in the academic literature on various aspects of some of these and related principles (Brooker and Macdonald, 1999; Cook-Sather, 2002; Fielding, 2004). This, however, as has already been pointed out, has not been accompanied by a great number of associated projects. At the same time, amongst the small group of those projects that have taken place are some which are quite inspirational. One of the best known of these is the ESRC-funded project in the UK entitled 'Consulting Pupils about Teaching and Learning' (MacBeath, Myers and Demetriou, 2001). Also, Raymond (2001) has reported on her 'students as researchers' project in Bedfordshire, England, which in four years has grown from a highly innovative initiative involving 15 students and 3 staff, to a ground-breaking approach to curriculum and school renewal involving in the region of 90 students and 14 staff. Similarly, Bullock and Wikeley (2001) have reported on a 'personal learning planning' initiative that set out to enhance students' understanding of, and confidence in, learning, the cornerstone of which was one-to-one, or small group discussions between tutors and pupils that focused on the latter's personal skills and abilities and then developing strategies to improve them.

A very small-scale, yet particularly inspiring initiative taken in Ireland is that of 'The Pres Girls' Club', an after-school physical activity club designed, coordinated and evaluated by teenage girls for teenage girls attending the Presentation School, a designated disadvantaged, city-centre, post-primary school in the city of Limerick. The participating girls are aged 15–18 years and their activities are facilitated by the PE PAYS (Physical Education, Physical Activity and Youth Sport) Research Centre at the University of Limerick. The club is a partnership initiative funded through the Limerick City Sports Partnership, with additional support from the authorities of the school, the local Southhill School Completion Programme and Limerick Youth Service. Prior to the establishment of the club most of the participants had disengaged from physical education and physical activity generally.

Their physical education teacher had identified their lack of engagement as her greatest challenge. She also sought support in understanding and in attempting to address the situation.

The club is phase two of a project which targeted the disengaged students and aimed to facilitate the design and delivery of a physical education curriculum which would be relevant and educationally meaningful to them and their context. Phase one sought to engage the students as decision-makers by involving them in the design, implementation and evaluation of a context-specific physical education curriculum through a 'participatory action research' methodology. The success of phase one (Enright and O'Sullivan, in press), together with an acknowledgement by the girls that physical activity provision in their community did not meet their needs, or facilitate their out-of-school physical activity engagement, inspired phase two. Particularly influential in this regard was the involvement of a number of the girls in research projects, facilitated by their PE teachers, which looked at the activity preferences of their peers, how they spent their leisure time and what sort of experiences would promote their engagement in physical activity.

The findings of the student research informed their decision-making relating to the focus and organisation of The Pres Girls' Club and provided a practical agenda for change. The girls decided that the aim of the club would be to help them enjoy and engage more in exercise, lose weight, get fit and be with their friends. It was also decided that:

1   The club would be called 'The Pres Girls' Club';
2   The club colours would be black and pink;
3   The club members would meet every Wednesday after school;
4   The club base would be located somewhere in the city rather than in their school;
5   The club members would choose their own activities;
6   The club members would be able to change activities when they wished;
7   The club members would work with leaders who would listen to them;
8   The club members would choose the music to be used when participating in their activities.

Having made these decisions as a foundation to designing the club, the students also became involved in reviewing, developing and promoting the club, and in maintaining relevance and interest.

At a number of stages during the first term of the club the girls held debriefing and planning meetings, where they reviewed how the club was developing and discussed and planned for future sessions. Many of the girls also took up advocacy roles in support of greater student involvement in decision-making in relation to matters which affected them. They spoke at the club launch, sharing their conviction that in order to create more engaging youth sport and physical activity experiences, physical education and physical activity professionals needed to "listen to young people and really hear them", and they presented evidence from their experiences in the club to support this position. The club members also produced a poster on their experience of designing and participating in the club, which they presented at a national conference attended by physical education, physical activity and health promotion professionals.

As well as developing basic academic skills many of the girls explicitly acknowledged the impact which their engagement with the project had on their learning. Typical of students' comments outlined by Enright and O'Sullivan (in press) are the following which highlight the amount and diversity of learning that occurred over the term:

> We have learned loads of things from the club: that it can be good fun being active and staying fit; how to use all the machines in the gyms; how to box; how to do aerobics and loads more.

Also, learning was not limited just to content. In particular, the girls recognised that their involvement in the project had made them aware of themselves as change agents, a matter on which one of them commented, "We learned that we can make a difference . . . Like we wanted some stuff to happen and then it happened. . . . we said what we wanted. You helped us get it and now we have it."

Because the club respected the girls' agency by allowing them opportunities to engage in decision-making, they respected it and were determined to make it work. In particular, they actively recruited new members and promoted their club in their school and community. One member commented with pride on this:

> I think we've convinced everyone it's a good idea. The school, our parents, even some of our lazy friends, and the guards [police]. They're all happy we're off the streets and doing something good and healthy and learning too.

Because they shared leadership and responsibility the girls consequently came to share ownership of the club.

The girls in the Pres Girls' Club were empowered by a positive and meaningful learning environment that recognised their capacities as competent social agents. Consequently, it continues to operate as an effective and engaging place of learning for its participants. It is fitting to close this overview with a recommendation made by the girls themselves:

> If you want to get more girls active you just need to listen to us and help us to make our own clubs. We know what we like and we'll work hard to make decent clubs that we want to go to and that we'll get our mates to go to, if we're listened to. The Pres Girls' Club works like that and we think it's great.

Conclusion

The intention of this chapter, as was outlined at the beginning, is to expose leaders of learning in the classroom to inspirational developments which have taken place in different parts of the world in the hope they might be enthused to espouse the position being advocated throughout the book. While the examples chosen have related to developments in quite different parts of the world and range from a macro set of projects to a single one operating at the micro level, it is also held that they are realistic in the sense that they indicate what can be achieved. The final example offered, however, which highlights the importance of taking account of students' own views on their situation, also leads on to the considerations of the next chapter. Here the latter position is taken a stage further. It is based on the argument that leaders of change ignore at their peril the views of those operating at the level of the school when it comes to promoting innovations aimed at improving the quality of learning.

9 The importance of leaders of learning giving voice to key stakeholders

Introduction

A fundamental notion underpinning considerations in previous chapters is that leadership needs to be exercised by students, teachers and other members of the school organisation in order to promote the enhancement of the quality of learning which takes place. However, unless it is also exercised across all levels of the educational sector then such enhancement is unlikely to eventuate. In the last chapter a number of cases were outlined indicating various possibilities in this regard both in terms of the construction of realistic, yet exciting, curriculum innovations, and the implementation of innovative pedagogical practices. It is very valuable to deliberate on cases of such a nature in order to promote inspiration amongst leaders for learning. However, the facilitation of this deliberation needs to be accompanied by the promotion of the argument that it is vital to give voice to the key stakeholders involved in the educational enterprise, especially those at the school level. This is to say that those educational leaders who are charged with developing and implementing policy aimed at enhancing student learning need to take cognisance of how potential leaders of learning lower down the bureaucratic chain, particularly teachers and students, as well as parents and other community members, make sense of their educational world. The present chapter considers this matter. It opens with an elaboration on the argument offered earlier. Six cases are then offered which illustrate how failure to take account of the central proposition of this argument have resulted time and again in the failure of theoretically sound projects with great potential to enhance student learning.

Why the concern about giving voice to key stakeholders?

Our argument that leadership needs to be exercised across all levels of the educational system in order to enhance the quality of learning which takes place is associated with the recognition over the last couple of decades that all students have unique needs, with differing abilities and interests and preferred styles of learning, and that not everyone learns at the same rate, or to the same level. The general thrust of related thinking as it manifested itself over 10 years ago, was summarised by Logan and Sachs as follows:

> The traditional view of the child as a receptive learner, didactic teaching styles, repressive forms of behaviour control and the validity of subject-based learning experiences have been challenged. They have been followed by a catalogue of experimentation in pedagogical styles aimed at getting the right mix for each child.
>
> (1998, p. 6)

The movement captured in this observation continues apace at present and is very much in line with the broad philosophy adopted throughout this book.

Notwithstanding our commitment to this philosophy, however, we are also acutely aware that successful take-up of associated practices requires much more than advocacy and dissemination through works like this and through professional development. On this, we are particularly sensitised to Mohammed and Harlech-Jones's (2008) point that teachers are frequently quite set in their practices, have their own ways of doing things, and are not easily manipulable. It is becoming increasingly apparent that the same can be said of students regarding their approach to learning, and also of parents when it comes to their expectations of the educational system. Yet, without the wholehearted cooperation of these and other key stakeholders, little is likely to be achieved.

Broadly speaking, this is to state a position long made by curriculum theorists, namely, that without engaging in adequate situational analysis and taking account of its results, the best thought-out plans are likely to be stymied from the outset. In other words, it is inadvisable not to examine and be mindful of the particular school context in which leadership and learning occur. Clearly this involves taking account of such material conditions as existing facilities and equipment. It is arguable, however, that all but the most naive now engage routinely in such a practice as it has become part of the culture of innovation and change across educational systems. For whatever reason, however, the same cannot be said in relation to the proposition that educational leaders, particularly those higher up the educational chain, ignore at their peril the views of those potential leaders lower down, especially teachers, students, parents and the 'general community', when it comes to promoting innovations aimed at improving the quality of student learning.

The argument being stated here is the now well-established one that the first step for any educationalist concerned with innovation and change is to become thoroughly familiar with the cultural environment within which what is proposed is expected to take place. The challenge, as Hawes (1979, p. 10) put it over 30 years ago, is to recognise the need to engage in "something in common with planning a journey". This, he says, is because "unless the traveler has some idea of where he [*sic*] is starting from and the conditions he may meet along the way, he is unlikely to be able to decide upon a satisfactory route". In later years Hargreaves (1993) made the same point more colour-fully when he contended that many social policies fail and nowhere is this more evident than in education where, he held, innovations frequently fail quite disastrously. The one common reason for this, Hargreaves argued, is:

> in grafting new ideas onto schools, we do it with so little knowledge about the nature of the everyday world of teachers, pupils and schools that our attempted grafts (and various forms of major and minor sur-gery) merely arouse the 'anti-bodies' of the host which undermine our attempts to play doctor to an educational patient.
>
> (1993, pp. 149–50)

It is only, he concluded, "when we understand the precise nature of the host body can we design our innovatory grafts with any confidence that they will prove to be acceptable". In agreeing with Hargreaves we hold that while gen-erating such understanding requires involvement in an intensive, laborious and time-consuming process, the consequences of neglecting it are almost inevitably negative, far-reaching and severe.

In the next sections of this chapter we seek to impress further the vital importance of this matter. However, rather than continuing to argue our position, we attempt to make our point by highlighting a disparate range of learning-focused innovations which floundered because of failure to proceed along these lines. The approach taken is very much a historical one in that the examples are selected from different periods over the last 40 years, rather than relating to just the last 10 years. Through proceeding in this manner we hope that the adage that those who fail to learn from the past are doomed to repeat it, will resonate both with leaders of learning and leaders for learning. Also, our examples are chosen from various parts of the world. Thus, we have also taken seriously a pedagogical principle of the major theorist, Jerome Bruner, the focus of the exposition on the first learning-focused innovation outlined in this chapter, namely, the importance of contrast in order to promote understanding of one's own situation.

Exposition on learning-focused innovation no. 1: MACOS in Queensland Australia

'Man: A Course of Study' (MACOS), a social studies curriculum designed in the USA in the 1960s for middle and upper grades of primary school, was very much influenced by the thinking of its major adviser, the eminent child psy-chologist Jerome Bruner (1966). The content of the course was the nature of humans as a species, and the forces that shaped and continue to shape our humanity. The design strongly reflected Bruner's rejection of an outcomes approach to curriculum and pedagogy in the sense of specifying clearly observable behaviours. Rather, what he promoted was based on five main ideals:

1   To give pupils respect for and confidence in the powers of their own mind;
2   To extend that respect and confidence to their power to think about the human condition, man's [*sic*] plight and his social life;
3   To provide a set of workable models that make it simpler to analyse the nature of the social world;
4   To impart a sense of respect for the capacities and humanity of man as a species;
5   To leave the student with a sense of the unfinished business of man's evolution.

Thus, he committed to a broad humanistic framework.

Working within such parameters, Bruner sought to provide an integrated approach to the teaching of social studies. This he did by arguing that, fundamentally, all of the social science disciplines have been built upon three main questions: What is human about human beings? How did they get that way? How can they be made more so? These questions recur time and again through MACOS as great organising devices. The other great organising devices were the following central concepts that were seen as providing the answers to these questions: values; world view; communication and language; technology; organisation of groups. Students were also to be introduced to such concepts as life cycle (including sexual reproduction), adaptation and aggression.

Bruner saw the development of all of these concepts within oneself as a process of 'internal model making'. This is a view that students should be introduced to the most powerful ideas that discipline our thinking in different areas of enquiry (in this case social studies). Also, he argued that this should take place not just through simply adding on new ideas, but rather by regularly increasing the complexity of what is presented. Hence, his notion of 'the spiral curriculum', with students revisiting the central concepts of the area of enquiry again and again. Furthermore, each time they are revisited it should be at a greater level of sophistication than previously.

Drawing upon the wealth of literature on teaching and learning available to him, Bruner also argued that materials for promoting the learning of concepts are richer if they allow for three modes of internal model making. These are the enactive mode (acting out), the iconic mode (the making of things), and the symbolic mode (representing, particularly using language). Furthermore, because of his awareness that there is a problem in rescuing the phenomenon of social life from familiarity so that it might be seen as 'primitive' or 'bizarre', and thus better facilitate learning, he advocated the use of contrast, games, the heightening of critical faculties, and the stimulation of self-consciousness as pedagogical tools.

MACOS was adopted widely throughout the USA, in the United Kingdom, and in various parts of Continental Europe and Asia. Evaluation studies were also very positive. Indeed, the success of the programme internationally led in

1975 to Bruner being given an award for his role in its development by the American Educational Research Association and the American Educational Publishers' Institute. Consequently, few outside of the State of Queensland in Australia could have anticipated the nature and depth of the resistance which emerged with regard to the programme when it was introduced in that particular part of the world. What is surprising, however, is that the local educational authorities who had taken the initiative to have it implemented in the State's schools did not foresee trouble. With the aid of hindsight it is arguable that if they had conducted a situational analysis the results would have prompted them to pay more attention to leadership issues than they did, particularly through providing detailed explanations of what was involved to teachers, parents and the wider community.

Marsh and Stafford (1988) and Smith and Knight (1981) have already offered comprehensive analyses of subsequent events which facilitate the provision of an overview both of what eventuated and why. They have drawn attention in particular to the deep-seated conservatism which existed within Queensland, a State of vast distances, where primary production was for long the mainstay of the economy and where over half of the population lived outside of metropolitan areas. It was against such a background that MACOS was introduced on a pilot basis in 15 schools in 1973. Significantly, parents and teachers at these schools were involved from the very beginning in trialling and adopting the programme's materials, including through discussion groups, and the outcome was a very high level of support from them.

By now, however, under pressure from a variety of interest groups, including Fundamentalist Christians, MACOS had been rejected by several States in the USA, commencing with Arizona in 1975. Some of the objections centred on the appropriateness of teaching values to primary school children from a social science perspective because of the assumption within the related disciplines that values are relative and that it is only factual details which can be accurately observed and measured about persons and things. The concern of the objectors was that children would not be able to hold such a view while at the same time develop a commitment to the perennial values of the Christian tradition which, it was stated, have been revealed by God and are central to the work of the school. Also, there was a negative reaction to children studying such topics as natural selection, infanticide and the survival of the fittest. The MACOS advocates, in their defence, quite legitimately pointed out that such practices were certainly not being advocated. Rather, they argued, it was valuable from a learning point of view to provide students with scenarios depicting such practices as they contrasted radically with the social practices with which they were familiar. Through such contrast it was held they could better come to appreciate their own situations as unique to their society.

Such objections were not, however, foreshadowed by educational leaders in Queensland and there seemed to be no realisation on the part of those leaders given the task of introducing MACOS in the State that the wider parent body and general community should be educated regarding its pedagogical principles. Problems began to emerge in earnest when, in July 1977, Mrs Mel Gabler, an activist in the anti-MACOS campaign in the USA, came to Queensland, where she received wide coverage in the press. Her presence was welcomed by a variety of very active pressure groups in the State with conservative, regional and fundamentalist orientations. During 1977–78 a number of them came into prominence, particularly the Society to Outlaw Pornography (STOP) and the Committee Against Regressive Education (CARE). Other groups included the Campaign for Responsible Education, the Community Standards Organisation, the Association of Catholic Parents, and the Women's Action Group. These groups had already tasted success in the 1970s in getting what they termed 'objectionable' books banned from the State's secondary school libraries. Now they harnessed the strategies and tactics communicated to them by Mrs Gabler as having been successful in the USA in a campaign which led to the banning of MACOS in various States there.

Soon Queensland members of parliament were lobbied, the local and daily press received regular media releases, the editors of regional and daily papers received a steady stream of letters for publication, and interviews on radio and television were organised. The overall message was that MACOS was part of a push on the part of an influential group of people within the State's Education Department who were promoting an anti-Christian, anti-family and socialist agenda. Also, rigorous censorship was advocated to counteract a movement which was portrayed as part of a political conspiracy and which was also seeking to promote sexual permissiveness. The fact that this was not remotely in the minds of the designers of the MACOS programme was irrelevant; their well-intentioned approaches to fostering student learning were easily distorted to suit the cause of the protestors.

It was not long before doubts and fears were sown in the minds of concerned parents. They became particularly worried that perhaps undesirable values and attitudes might develop in their children because of the cultural relativism of MACOS. So successful were the pressure groups that the Cabinet, as Marsh and Stafford (1988, p. 193) put it, "came down on the side of moral protection of minors, of upholding standards and of stamping out purported incursions by humanists, socialists and libertarians". In January 1978, while Parliament was in recess, the Minister of Education announced that MACOS would be withdrawn from all Queensland schools. The following month the programme was banned from all schools and a Select Committee of Inquiry into the State's education system was established. Within a little over a year it recommended that MACOS remain banned from the State's schools. Thus came to an end in Queensland the teaching of one of the most influential curriculum programmes on the international stage in the twentieth century, which was based on powerful pedagogical principles. One cannot help but conclude that the outcome could have been radically different if those entrusted with leading the policy initiative had consulted children on their likely reactions to the topics, parents on the appropriateness of the topics in the first instance, and teachers on likely community interest.

Exposition on learning-focused innovation no. 2: Target-Oriented Curriculum in Hong Kong

In 1989, a government report (Carless, 1997, p. 354) highlighted a range of problems in the education provided in Hong Kong schools. These focused on many of the issues we have emphasised in earlier chapters as being crucial to attend to in the provision of quality student learning: an overcrowded and fragmented curriculum, an overemphasis on rote learning, lack of awareness of the role of language in education, little catering for individual differences, and assessment methods focused mainly on ranking students (Carless, 1997, p. 354). Two years later reforms were introduced which, as Morris (2002, pp. 13–24) has pointed out, sought to achieve the following changes: a move away from a focus on subject specific goals to a focus on generic skills (problem solving, reasoning, inquiry, communication and conceptualisation); a move away from teacher-centred and whole-class approaches to teaching and learning to one stressing pupil activity, task-based learning, interaction, and catering for individual differences; and a move away from a reliance on norm-referenced selective testing "towards forms of assessment which identify progressive targets, provide feedback for learning and are criterion referenced". Morris (2002, p. 14) went on to say that the 'reform' was notable in the following respects:

- It was a single reform which was designed to radically change all of the basic elements of the school curriculum;
- It was strongly influenced by a range of reforms that have been termed outcomes-based education (OBE), most notably the National Curriculum in England and Wales, and the Curriculum Frameworks in Australia;
- It was initiated and introduced by the departing colonial government during a transition period that was dominated by the anticipation of the handover of sovereignty in 1997 and so was intensely politicised;
- It shared with other reform efforts in Hong Kong a reliance on a top-down system of decision-making in which superordinate groups made key decisions to be carried out by subordinate groups.

The framework for implementing the associated activities was drawn up by four experienced expatriate curriculum officers commissioned by the Education Department.

The general primary school context against which the associated debates and initiatives were formulated has been outlined by Carless (1997, pp. 353–54). Most primary schools, because of lack of space, operated two shifts a day, with one group of students in attendance up to mid-day and the other commencing at 1.00 pm. This situation also meant that there was a shortage of space for textbooks and teaching resources. Class sizes tended to be between 35 and 40, and classrooms tended to be cramped. The situation was exacerbated by pollution and noise from traffic and construction work, while air-conditioned rooms were not the norm.

Despite these adverse conditions, Hong Kong had a reputation for having well-disciplined students willing to learn. Parents had high expectations of schools, including that a high level of academic content would be taught and that large amounts of homework would be set. They also had a reputation for sometimes bringing pressure on school principals to ensure that their wishes were attended to in this regard and to produce high results in examinations. Primary school teachers often felt this pressure. Also they were, in the main, non-graduates who had qualified through a three-year pre-service teacher preparation programme. Nevertheless, they were known for being hard working and dedicated to teaching their students.

The reform developed against this background was initially termed 'Target and Target Related Assessment' (TTRA) and it was accepted as government policy. It was planned to be introduced into Primary 4 classes from 1995, and a system of criterion-referenced assessment was to be developed to replace the practice of assessing pupils' academic achievement at Level 6. Also, the results of this assessment were to be used to stream students into different secondary schools. Very early on, however, there was a hostile reaction from both the educational and the political community. The accusations were that the reform was poorly thought through, rushed and impractical. This led to the simplification of documents and a change of name to the 'Target-Oriented Curriculum' (TOC). Also, once implementation was recommended greater emphasis came to be placed on teaching and learning than on assessment.

By 1999, however, the initiative was so problematic there was a perception that it had been abandoned. This perception was reinforced by the withdrawal of extra funding to support the dissemination and resourcing of TOC "on the grounds that it was no longer a distinct policy initiative" (Morris, 2002, p. 16). Reference to TOC was now avoided in the public speeches of the educational policymaking community, while a new policy initiative, described as a 'Holistic Review of the Hong Kong School System' emerged. In addition, Morris (2002, p. 23) claims that TOC had little or no effect on teaching and learning in many schools despite its formal adoption. He adds that "the decision to adopt the initiative was taken solely by school principals and their motives were not primarily linked to the intrinsic features of the reform *per se*". Rather, they tended to see the TOC as a vehicle for achieving one or more of the following: "Legitimating existing programmes of school improvement generally; improving the school's capacity to compete with other local schools for pupil intake; and increasing the input of resources" (Morris, 2002, p. 23).

The demise of the TOC was not helped by the changing political scene in Hong Kong, especially the change of sovereignty and the associated change in government. Also, the prevailing economic climate was not conducive. Nevertheless, one cannot escape the conclusion once again that a range of issues which proved to be problematic could have been overcome if the views of teachers, in particular, had been sought in the first instance and if appropriate leadership had been provided to address the issues which they would have highlighted. Also, it would have helped to have taken account of research which indicates that previous pedagogically-driven initiatives in Hong Kong such as the 'activity approach' and the 'cross-curricular themes approach', while "symbolically adopted by schools" (Morris, 2002, p. 23), had little impact on the classrooms. Carless (1997, p. 358) indicates how one possible reason for this situation is tied to the practice of 'top-down' decision-making in Hong Kong. The problem with the latter situation, he points out, is that if successful curriculum and pedagogical implementation is to take place, it is necessary to engender a feeling of ownership amongst the teachers who will be involved in putting the associated ideas into practice (MacDonald, 1991, p. 3). The opposite, however, was the experience, at least in the government-run schools in Hong Kong, with principals being placed under strong pressure to adopt the TOC.

Poor leadership was also evident in that sufficient attention was not paid to overcoming certain structural features. For example, the primary school curriculum organised around discrete subjects (Chinese, English, mathematics and general studies) was maintained, yet the TOC was premised on the need for pupils to learn through involvement in task-based learning and that they should develop their generic skills, or what were termed 'the five fundamental ways of learning'. Thus, Morris (2002, p. 20) concludes, the capacity for integration was "strongly constrained by the boundaries that operated".

Morris also points out that while the need for more formative school-based systems of assessment were advocated, and that while the TOC also stressed the value of a broad range of knowledge, skills and attitudes, what was introduced was in addition to, rather than instead of, the continuation of the traditional systems of grades, marks and rank orders. While this was viewed as necessary, it created what appeared to be unresolvable tensions in schools. Consequently, it is not difficult to accept the claim that TOC had little or no effect on teaching and learning in many schools despite its formal adoption (Morris, 2002, p. 23). This cannot be attributed only to lack of consultation with teachers and not giving them a voice. Nevertheless, the indications are that it was a significant factor. Lam (2003, p. 651), for example, has made it clear that only a very small number of school teachers were consulted when the associated assessment framework was developed. Overall, he states, there was not enough effort made by policy developers to familiarise themselves with the culture of the schools, to understand the preferences of teachers, and to try to empathise with how they understood their practical world (Lam, 2003, p. 653). Finally, taking up the same point, Morris and Lo (2000, p. 182) concluded that teachers were "bemused and concerned as to the complexity and lack of clarity of the TOC", but that when they began to express their concerns "their voices were soon silenced".

Exposition on learning-focused innovation no. 3: The education Action Zone initiative in Britain

The fate of the Education Action Zone (EAZ) initiative in Britain, established by New Labour in 1998, was a little different from that of the preceding cases in at least two ways. For one thing, it was short lived. Second, it would not be correct to label it a failure. However, it is likely that much more could have been achieved if the host situations had been thoroughly analysed and if heed had been taken of the analysis by those in leadership positions. In this regard, it is another example again which is valuable by way of illustrating the importance of leaders giving voice to key stakeholders.

Franklin (2005) has provided a very valuable overview of the EAZ programme. He indicates that its origin was that of a variety of related initiatives, including the desire of the British Conservative Party which came to power in 1979, to limit the power of the Local Education Authorities (LEAs) which, traditionally, played a major part in regulating schools in England and Wales. Later, New Labour, when it took over the reins of government, also shared this desire and the associated view that LEAs were not the best vehicle for increasing academic standards. The EAZ concept for dealing with this situation involved bringing together clusters of usually 15 to 25 low-achieving rural and urban schools in socially and economically distressed areas. The administrative unit for each zone, its Action Forum, normally comprised representatives of individual schools, parents, business, community organisations and the voluntary sector, and it was charged with raising academic standards through partnerships. These partners, according to the plan, would play an important part in the management of the zones and in providing financial support.

To commence the initiative, the first 25 zones received £750,000 from the government annually for three years, while the prospect of extending support to five years was indicated if there was satisfactory performance. Each zone was also expected to supplement this funding by raising £250,000 in cash, or in kind, from the business and other sectors. Franklin (2005, p. 6) goes on to point out that, along with introducing schemes for financing and managing schools, an EAZ could also be allowed to introduce a number of other educational initiatives. These programmes, Franklin (2005, p. 6) has stated:

> included efforts to enhance the quality of teaching and learning, to provide support for families and students, to partner with external organisations, and to promote policies of social inclusion.

They could also introduce initiatives that would depart from the National Curriculum.

In November 2001, the New Labour government announced that the programme was being discontinued and that none of the existing zones would receive funding beyond the initial five-year commitment. Meanwhile another scheme, introduced in 1999, continued. This had led to the establishment of a number of smaller EAZs as part of the Excellence in Cities programme for addressing low achievement in inner city schools (Franklin, 2005, p. 7). They had similar targets to the original EAZs and also required the development of partnerships, but they were funded and administered through the LEAs.

It was claimed by the government that the original EAZs had been successful in raising academic standards, reducing gaps in levels of achievement, persuading business to finance the zones, and promoting governance partnerships between parents, the community and business. The reason for discontinuing them, so the argument went, was that they were never expected to have a long life anyway. Rather, they were considered, it was stated, to be a temporary initiative "that brought with them a number of important successes that would constitute the basis for further educational reform" (Franklin, 2005, p. 8). Such an approach was one which ignored findings like those of Tyack and Cuban (1995) which indicate that the more successful route to reform is one that aspires to changes that are less extensive, that occur slowly over time, and that allow the personnel within the schools to modify and adjust them to fit their existing practices. Even if one ignores such a shortcoming, however, it is arguable that much more could have been achieved if the conditions of the host situations had been seriously analysed beforehand, a conclusion which at least can be arrived at in relation to one zone studied in one of England's most disadvantaged areas.

The results of the aforementioned study on one especially problematic EAZ, which was conducted by Franklin (2005), indicate how lack of leadership resulted in a failure to address a number of crucial conditions prior to implementation. In particular, the LEA, which served as a mediating institution for enlisting schools, was one which had inadequate budgeting processes, a poorly designed education development section, and lack of success in introducing information technology in schools. While time and effort should clearly have been spent addressing this situation, a more positive path could also have been paved by conducting appropriate teacher preparation. From the outset many of those affiliated with the area's teachers association did not share the government's optimism regarding the innovation. Some were annoyed by the fact that only a few schools within a region could be involved. Others were wary because of a belief that the business partnerships which were integral to the initiative would lead to the privatisation of public education. Another concern was that if business came to control the schools a commercialised curriculum focused solely on preparing youth for work could eventuate. Others yet again feared the opportunity provided by the initiative to depart from provisions governing their pay and working conditions. The situation also was not helped by head teachers pushing their staff and governing bodies to approve participation, lured almost solely by the money that the programme would bring to their schools.

Much better leadership could also have been shown through the appropriate expending of time in preparing parents better for participation prior to the initiative being introduced. This is especially so since the policy was based on an assumption that the best way to enhance student learning and achievement is to ensure that parents are actively involved in both their children's and their own education. A lack of appropriate preparation, however, led to much misunderstanding. Some were afraid that joining the zone "would force them to share their resources with poorer and less well performing schools", or that "the children would be bussed out of their schools to schools elsewhere within the EAZ" (Franklin, 2005, p. 12). Parents also did not feel confident to participate in governance and they got little encouragement from head teachers. Indeed, some head teachers felt that such participation would create more problems than it would solve. Also, the multicultural character of the area made it very difficult for any one parent to be selected as a forum representative.

Around the same time as Franklin was conducting his study, Whitehead and Clough (2004) were engaged in research based on their observation that there was no role for students in the partnership model which was central to the EAZ policy. In order to highlight that certain possibilities were being overlooked they drew attention to Fullan's (1991, p. 170) question of over 15 years ago when he asked: "What would happen if we treated the student as someone whose opinion mattered?" Interestingly, in their investigation in two inner city zone schools they discovered that many of the 139 Year 8 students they interviewed not only had views on how they went about their learning, but also on what their learning needs might be and the steps that could be taken in response. Whitehead and Clough (2004) were not so naive as to suggest that students' ideas should serve as the final word on how approaches to learning need to change. What they did foreground, however, is Ruddock and Flutter's (2000, p. 86) argument that there is a need to move beyond much current practice and recognise students' social maturity and experience by giving them responsibilities and opportunities to share decision making. Clearly, the EAZ initiative was also one of missed opportunity in this regard and in terms of distributing leadership for learning to the level of the classroom teachers and the learners themselves.

As with the previous case outlined, the demise of the EAZs cannot be attributed only to lack of consultation with the key stakeholders and not giving them a voice. Again, however, the indications are that it was a significant factor. Theakston *et al.* (2001), for example, commenting on the findings of two research projects they conducted which were instigated by the National Union of Teachers, argued that a significant proportion of teachers working within EAZ schools felt they did not 'own' the initiative. They also noted that a common complaint was that classroom teachers did not know what was happening in their zone and that "there were limited opportunities to become involved in its development, if they chose to do so" (Theakston *et al.*, 2001, p. 196). Similarly, Simpson and Cieslik (2002) concluded from their research that within the EAZs, parents were viewed only as supporters of their children's learning at home and in the classroom and that they were not about "empowering parents to 'bring voice' to the overall approach" (Simpson and Cieslik, 2002, p. 124). Gewirtz *et al.* (2005, p. 651) summed up this major area of weakness on considering their own research in the area when they stated that the experience with EAZs exemplified the need "to pay closer attention to the real. . . . voices, choices and values of the people these policies are designed to help".

Exposition on learning-focused innovation no. 4: Transnational educational borrowing in the South Pacific nations

It is not just in Western and Western-oriented countries that educational leaders charged with developing and implementing policy have failed to take cognisance of how potential leaders of learning at the more 'grass roots' levels of the educational system make sense of their educational world, with consequent failure of potentially valuable pedagogically-based projects. The history of transnational educational borrowing in the South Pacific Island nations over the last 30 years is riddled with examples illustrative of this. In 1990, for example, LeSourd (1990) reported on a United Nations project begun in 1979, for the development of a social studies curriculum for nine nations in the South Pacific and demonstrated that what eventuated was incompatible with contextual assumptions about learning, a consequence of the expatriate curriculum developers proceeding without listening to the voices of the people. The following year, Thaman (1991, p. 4) drew attention to the problem in many of the same nations dealing "with new ideas enthusiastically championed by many education experts and consultants operating in, or passing through" the islands. In particular, he highlighted how a model of curriculum development lacking in cultural sensitivity had produced social studies curricula which emphasised individual achievement and competition while parents and teachers expected the school to emphasise social and moral training. Failure to consult with those at 'the front line' on how they understood their educational world and to consider ways to bridge the gap between such understanding and that of the curriculum implementers, resulted in, yet again, another set of valuable pedagogical ideas going awry.

There have also been situations where new curricula designed by overseas 'experts' emphasising teaching for understanding rather than rote learning, and stressing student participation rather than lecture methods, were not successful because of the fact that teachers were not engaged in efforts aimed at discovering their views on what they needed by way of preparation to facilitate successful implementation. Mangubhai (1984) noted that a situation of this nature was exacerbated in Fiji in the early 1980s because external examinations continued to dominate the educational system and teachers were reluctant to attempt new departures lest they might jeopardise students' chances of getting high scores. A similar experience has been recorded in the case of Western Samoa. Here attempts were made in the 1970s to fashion curricula to fit the Samoan setting. However, by the early 1980s the bulk of the course of study ignored this approach, partly because the New Zealand examinations continued to be used as criteria for determining the success of students at the close of the secondary school stages (Thomas, 1984, p. 227).

Equally disconcerting was a tendency in the educational sector of some of the South Pacific nations to prescribe uncritically developments which had already proven to be inappropriate in other parts of the developing world and also to do so without seeking the views of teachers, students, parents and the local community. Influenced by the arguments of international aid donors, countries like Western Samoa, Fiji and the Solomon Islands, for example, in the belief that it was the persistence of 'white-collar' aspirations by parents and students which accounted for many problems in education, embarked on a reform of school structure and curricula to try to ensure that the curriculum would be 'de-academicised' with a much stronger emphasis being placed on vocational subjects (Throsby and Gannicott, 1990, p. 39). In Papua New Guinea (PNG), where the largely expatriate-dominated National Department of Education's Curriculum Development Division espoused such thinking (Deutrom, 1990, p. 24), it was also strongly argued that the same road should be taken (Avalos, 1992, pp. 311–16), even though the balance of international evidence suggested that a vocational or diversified curriculum is unlikely to result in an improved quality of schooling (Psacharopoulos and Woodhall, 1985, p. 230; World Bank, 1980, p. 33; 1988, p. 64).

In the latter situation the voices of influential academics succeeded in persuading the educational authorities not to proceed. This, however, has not been the common experience in PNG, which gained its independence from Australia in 1975. Amongst the large number of unsuccessful projects was a mathematics programme inspired by the ideas of Zoltan Dienes. This introduced 'the new maths' through student-centred, individual discovery methods similar to those then being used at the time in South Australian schools. However, it assumed far too high a level of general knowledge and competency on the part of the teachers. Also, it was erroneously based on a premise that PNG children progress at roughly the same rate from cognitive to symbolic thinking as do Western children (McLaughlin, 1990, p. 26). Similarly, what was described as a "very well-designed and trialled" (Jones, 1974, p. 47) primary science programme was unsuccessful in PNG schools because there was a lack of equivalence with student conceptualisations and the concepts to which the programme had been aiming. Another innovation in the mid-1970s which failed was the 'General Teaching Programme' which attempted to provide an integrated multi-subject approach in the first two grades of high school. It failed not only because of its rapid and authoritarian introduction, but also because, in Beeby's (1966) terms, it demanded 'stage of meaning' teaching from teachers in 'the stage of formalism'. In other words, the level of both the general and professional education of the teachers was such that they could function largely only by being formal in their teaching style, by being authoritarian in their discipline, and by having syllabuses and textbooks prescribed. Yet the programme, in its efforts to make learning more meaningful, required classrooms that would be student-centred and schools that would be self-directed. A similar explanation has been offered for the difficulty which many teachers experienced with the school-based curriculum development component of the 'Secondary Schools Community Extension Project' (SSCEP) (Crossley, 1983).

In 2000, an outcomes-based education (OBE) programme for primary and secondary schools was introduced into PNG schools by the 'Curriculum Reform Implementation Project' (CRIP) sponsored by the Australian government aid agency, AUSAID. CRIP, as Hayes (2007) has put it, consists of a team of educational consultants from Australia, most of whom have never taught in a PNG classroom. They work with a team of counterparts in the PNG Department of Education, most of whom never heard of OBE before its introduction, did not become aware of its failures in other countries until very recently, and were not in a position to evaluate its suitability for PNG schools from the outset. Hayes has been particularly concerned about the position which holds that while the outcomes of the OBE curriculum are to be provided by national curriculum developers, it is to be left to the teachers in the schools to decide on the most appropriate content and teaching and learning approaches to be used. Regarding primary schools, for example, he has pointed out that the infrastructure, human resources and budget allocations are insufficient to sustain such an approach; most of the schools do not have a library, while in 90 per cent of them there is no electricity, no computers and no TV or video. Also, class sizes average about 50 and in many rural schools children still sit on the floor and have no desks.

Local input which could provide insights on how to deal with the situation have, however, been ignored by the consultants and their PNG counterparts. Overall, the leadership approach is very much a power-coercive one rather than a distributed one. Little attention is paid to the ideas of those who are experienced and working closely with those in the field, teachers are rarely consulted about their views, and parents and local communities are often treated as if they do not exist. It is little wonder that the project is turning into a fiasco.

Exposition on learning-focused innovation no. 5: A teacher-development programme in Pakistan

This example of how the failure of educational leaders charged with developing and implementing policy to listen to the voices of potential leaders of learning at the 'grass roots' level of the educational system, can result in failure in theoretically sound projects with great potential to enhance student learning, is from Pakistan. Specifically, it summarises the recent account of Mohammed and Harlech-Jones (2008) which describes the experience of teachers who attended a secondary mathematics teacher education pro-gramme at a university in Pakistan which has been at the forefront of efforts to improve the quality of education in the nation. At this university teachers of mathematics were offered in-service education aimed at developing them as education leaders in their schools. This development was part of a move nationally over the last 10 years, seeking to shift teachers from using traditional didactic approaches to teaching, to being facilitators of students' learning.

After completing the course the teachers gave a very positive impression of their experience. Before embarking on it they were, they claimed, operating within a paradigm where they saw their job as simply that of conveying infor-mation to students in a one-way process. As a result of participating in the course, however, they came to believe that students would learn better if they were given the opportunity to engage in practical activities and to relate mathematics to their daily lives. In particular, they came to appreciate the importance of a collaborative learning environment. Yet, there were no great changes in their classroom practices! Mohammed and Harlech-Jones (2008, p. 45) found that the teachers did not allow their students to express their views in class, did not listen to what students said, did not debrief students' answers, and did not encourage them to discuss mathematics amongst themselves.

This disappointing situation has not been attributed solely to failure to consult with the graduated teachers, to listen to their opinions and to encourage them to give voice to their views. For one thing, it was not possible to do anything about the physical conditions under which the teachers worked, including the poor conditions of the classrooms, lack of resources and large classes. Also, they still had to abide by the strict routines of the school system and return to their heavy teaching workloads since failure to work within system-level expectations could have resulted in poor annual appraisals and possibly affect adversely the level at which they were employed.

The teachers also became frustrated by the lack of follow-up support from the university. While they were in attendance there they were energised by the new ideas to which they were introduced, by participation in ongoing reflec-tion, and by social and professional interaction with peers. Soon after leaving this environment, however, and ending up back in their schools they began to feel isolated in their endeavours to bring about reforms. Consequently, not only did they fall back on old practices, they also became disillusioned as they began to question seriously how applicable interactive teaching and approaches to critical thinking were to the reality of schools.

Along with these influences, however, the teachers also ascribed the situa-tion in which they eventually found themselves to the lack of encouragement for their independent views from the senior leaders in their schools. They were not encouraged to discuss their own experiences and were not listened to when they sought to express them. They continued to experience the same lack of intellectual thinking amongst colleagues as before, were not facilitated in establishing a forum for professional dialogue about classroom issues, and were still expected to teach to the prescribed textbooks, complete preordained tasks and meet centrally-established standards. The only interest of the schools' authorities, as they saw it, was in celebrating that their staff members had completed a course at a prestigious university since it enhanced the schools' reputations.

Exposition on learning-focused innovation no. 6: An attempt to integrate information technology into a Thai educational setting

This final example of the failure of a theoretically sound educational innovation aimed at improving pedagogical practice at the school's level is based on an account by Gipson (1998). Again, it highlights the vital importance of leaders of learning taking account of a variety of influences when planning their approaches. The general background to the account is the educational reforms which commenced in Thailand in the final decades of the twentieth century. These were driven largely by the desire that the nation should remain economically competitive within the South East Asian region. A key argument associated with the movement was that the emergent workforce should be trained in the skills required for the information-based society. Thus, great emphasis was placed on the need for the development of fluency in the English language, of thinking critically and creatively, and of competence in information and communications technologies. At the same time, however, there was also concern that the country's cultural heritage should not be threatened by associated practices.

Such thinking provided the foundation for the conception and development of the Tridhos School Village as a model for educational reform. It has been described as "an innovative independent school in Thailand licensed by the Ministry of Education under a new category of Thai schools teaching in English" (Gipson, 1998, p. 2). The geographical setting chosen for its establishment is a rural area in the north of the country. The teachers to be chosen were expected to move away from traditional didactic approaches to teaching and utilise more student-centred, experiential approaches.

From the outset there was a commitment to Tridhos becoming a lighthouse school in its use of educational technologies. This presented particular challenges given the geographical remoteness of the school site, the great lack of services, and the intermittent power supply. A clear recognition of this situation meant that before any construction took place on the school site a US-based educational consulting company was commissioned to work with the architects and the curriculum designer to develop a technology plan. The key decision that arose as result of this plan centred, as Gipson has put it,

> on four interrelated issues: the choice of platform; the network and networking protocol and design considerations on the networking topology; choices on software – what would best deliver the educational program; and Internet service provision – what would be the link and how extensive would it be.
>
> (1998, np)

It was decided that what would be required of the company chosen to address these issues was not a supplier–purchaser arrangement. Rather, the underlying notion was that the best arrangement for both the school and the information technology providers would be one where the two established a mutually supportive, long-term partnership.

A comprehensive technology plan which took account of the school's curriculum design and desired pedagogical practices to be implemented before the school's opening in May 1997 was drawn up. In line with this plan a bidding process was developed to acquire a network installer, hardware and software suppliers, and Internet service provider. It was believed that those who bid would be attracted by the partnership model as a great deal of publicity would be focused on what was a radical innovation within the educational scene in Thailand. An added attraction, it was felt, was that if the project succeeded, replication across the nation would result in ongoing purchases over many years. Matters, however, did not eventuate as anticipated. The potential companies were unable to reorient their thinking away from notions of maximum profit and limited long-term support. Obstacles also presented themselves because of a culture of bribery in business. The consequence was that only two companies presented who were capable of responding to the demands of the RFP [request for proposal] and only one submitted an appropriate quotation for the networking and hardware and software solutions.

Problems also arose when it came to deciding on the most appropriate platform and in acquiring an effective Internet partner. On top of all of this it proved very difficult to recruit suitable personnel to take on the roles of technology coordinator, systems administrator and computer technician. Lack of individuals with experience in running a school network and non-competitive salaries were influential factors in this regard. Consequently, as Gipson (1998, np) put it, " the vision for the network was never realised". This, in turn, led to a loss of faith on the part of the teachers in the integrity of the Network and the support that they could get. The teaching staff also did not receive adequate professional development in the use of the technology. Moreover, the meager efforts made to address this matter were dogged, as Gipson (1998, np) has stated, by "problems in acquiring appropriate software and the general low levels of confidence and competence in the information technology". As a result, many teachers lacked appropriate understanding of, and experience in, the technology when the school opened. Also, once the school commenced teaching there was little follow-through and support, with the result that technology was not used in the classroom at anything approaching the level planned.

Gipson concludes his account of this failed pedagogical innovation by outlining some lessons to be learnt. He does not yield in his commitment to a comprehensive information technology plan directly woven into the fabric of a school's curriculum and teaching and learning model as constituting "a highly articulated vehicle for educational innovation and a reforming vision" (Gipson, 1998, np). As he puts it, "tightly coupled connections made between technology use, curriculum and pedagogy at an early stage of the school development" also means that the design of classrooms and technology infrastructure can reflect the demands of the teaching and learning programme. In addition, he remains firmly of the belief that the establishment of long-term partnerships with the major technology providers is vital. However, he highlights how "the move from design to implementation can provide many complex frustrations and engender many costly problems if it is not conducted with integrity to the original plan and if sight of the original vision is lost". In particular, he draws attention to how leaders of innovations such as that attempted at Tridhos need to ensure that there is adequate service and support for all aspects of the uses and applications of the educational technologies. This should involve ensuring an appropriate investment in expertise in technology personnel and technology team leadership, and in the provision of comprehensive preparation of teachers "to ensure that they become confident experts rather than diffident users" (Gipson, 1998, np). Not to act along such lines, he concludes, can result in poor utilisation, limited return of investment, "and ultimately a significant compromise of the original educational vision".

Conclusion

The core of this chapter presented six case studies aimed at illustrating how essential it is to give voice to the key stakeholders at the school level involved in providing leadership for innovations aimed at improving the quality of learning. Particular attention was given to teachers and students in this regard, but the need to consult parents and other community members was also emphasised. The assumption in providing the various cases is that while many of them may be unfamiliar to a host of readers, they are sufficiently engaging to help them to clarify their own situations and to recognise the folly of failing to understand the nature of the environments in which students learn. It is hoped that, collectively, they constitute one contribution to help halt the trend of reinventing the problems of the past when it comes to considering the most appropriate strategies to adopt in providing leadership for learning within the schools' context. Finally, we give the last word on this to

Mohammed and Harlech-Jones (2008, p. 39), where they point out that while many contemporary pedagogical initiatives advocate respect for the knowledge and experiences of children, reformers often ignore the accumulated knowledge of teachers and the contexts in which they have to work, and when the reforms fail "it is put down to failure in implementation rather than to failure on the part of leaders to understand the context".

10 Forging links between leadership and learning

Introduction

Schratz (2006, p. 41), with specific reference to Austrian schools, asserts that the terms leading and learning belong in different domains of pedagogical discourse and are associated with different protagonists in the process of education. In other words, it is deemed that school leaders should lead, teachers should teach and learners should learn. Schratz's observation, of course, is not confined to the Austrian context and highlights that traditionally the connections between leadership and learning have tended to be unacknowledged by schools. Nevertheless, one of the main motifs to have emerged from the previous chapters of this book is captured in the notion of the mutually supporting nature of leadership and learning. In this regard, West-Burnham and O'Sullivan (1998, p. 184) describe the relationship between leadership and learning as symbiotic in the sense that "one is not possible without the other and the success of one is determined by the extent to which the other is available".

It does seem, however, that advocating an explicit interrelationship between leadership and learning is more straightforward than demonstrating how complex connections between the two activities are made visible within the school environment. From this point of view it could be argued that the process of forging links between leadership and learning in the context of school has tended to be located at a normative level rather than being described in practice with the authority of empirical evidence. As MacBeath *et al.* (2005, p. 25) have pointed out, leadership and learning are concepts which appear to have acquired greater credence amongst policymakers in recent years, but the link between them has not been subjected to critical analysis.

The main objective of this chapter, therefore, is to illustrate ways in which leadership and learning are indispensable to each other, with a consideration of implications for practice and with reference to the three levels of learning within the school. For this purpose, particular cognisance is taken of the five principles of leadership for learning articulated by The Cambridge Network (http://www.leadershipforlearning.org.uk/index.php/lfl-principles

[1 February 2009]). These five principles constitute a significant outcome of the Carpe Vitam leadership for learning international research and development project that was directed from the University of Cambridge between 2002 and 2005. This enterprising project has been well-documented elsewhere (MacBeath, 2006; MacBeath *et al.*, 2005) and need not be described in detail here. Nevertheless, given this book's consideration of international perspectives towards leadership and learning, it is instructive to point out that the chief rationale was to clarify the two concepts of leadership and learning and examine how they are made meaningful within and between different cultural traditions and linguistic conventions. The principles, therefore, are the result of a rigorous and prolonged dialogue between researchers, principals, teachers and school board members across seven countries. Furthermore, as the principles were developing they were tested against practice and analysed with reference to the research literature.

Maintaining a focus on learning as an activity

The first principle of leadership for learning practice involves maintaining a focus on learning as an activity. This is the first of the Cambridge Network Principles. This principle is predicated on the belief that everyone is a learner, including students, teachers, principals, the school as a community and the wider educational system. As such, this principle highlights the value of conceptualising the learning agendas that occur throughout the school according to the three interrelated levels (Knapp *et al.*, 2003) explicated in previous chapters, namely, 'student learning', 'teacher learning' and 'organisational learning'. The principle is also a reminder that "visualising all three learning agendas, the opportunities for learning each entails, and the connections among them is an essential step in leading for learning" (Knapp *et al.*, 2003, p. 14).

The main priority of any school should be to enable the most powerful students' learning possible. We have argued that such learning engenders equipping students for survival, success and happiness in a rapidly changing society. We have also argued that this objective requires schools to support students as flexible learners. For this purpose, we suggested in Chapter 4 that there should be an emphasis on self-regulated learning, learning in community and learning which is problem-based. It is these approaches to learning which are most likely to nurture the knowledge, skills and dispositions that promote students' empowerment and a sense of agency that infuse learning with a 'leaderful' component.

We have frequently emphasised that students' learning along these lines can only be enabled if teachers too have the opportunity to construct meaning from interaction, discussion and professional dialogue (Harris and Muijs, 2005). In particular, this engenders regular engagement in collaborative reflective practice which can not only be professionally empowering, but also enables elements of effective learning and good teaching to be aligned and explicit.

In connection with the requirement of this leadership for learning principle to maintain a focus on learning as an activity, it is important to emphasise that the professional learning agenda needs to embrace not only teachers' learning, but also the learning of the school principal. MacGilchrist *et al.* (1997) draw attention to the importance of principals being able to model and convey implicit and explicit messages to students and staff which are amenable to a learning culture extending across the school. This notion of the head teacher acting as a 'head learner' presents a clear example of how leadership and learning are interdependent, but principals' inclination to acknowledge this connection will be dependent on their preparation and continuing development. Blase and Blase (1999, p. 138), for example, suggest that these processes should de-emphasise principals' control of teachers and focus instead on developing aspiring and practising principals' capacity to harness professional dialogue and collegiality among the teaching staff. From this perspective Blase and Blase argue that principals' learning should be grounded in group-development, theories of teaching and learning for adults and students, action research methods and reflective practice.

Creating conditions favourable to learning as an activity

The creation of a flourishing professional learning culture is, of course, a prerequisite for creating the organisational conditions for schools to become learning schools (Southworth, 2002). This observation is directly associated with the second principle of leadership for learning practice that involves creating conditions favourable to learning as an activity. This is the second of the Cambridge Network Principles. The principle highlights another theme that has featured strongly in the discussions in the previous chapters, that is, the influence of the school's culture on leadership and learning.

In his intriguing 'epidemiological' model of the change process, Gladwell (2000) suggests that for a change to become embedded within an organisation, the culture needs to be such that it allows people to grow. This observation seems to be particularly germane to leadership for learning. On this, MacGilchrist *et al.* (1997, p. 13) have identified three main ways in which the culture of a school serves to promote people's efficacy and agency is manifested in practice.

One way in which the culture of the school becomes evident is through professional relationships. The nature of relationships that exist, for example, between the principal and the staff, as well as those occurring between teachers themselves, will be indicative of the ways in which people within the school feel, think and act. Likewise, the attitudes that are held towards the students and other constituent groups associated with the school are suggestive of its underlying culture. In this connection, we have argued already that an indispensable component of this culture must be trust and openness, which are the levers of cooperative action and social capital (Louis, 2007) and lie at the heart of processes of leadership and learning.

A further manifestation of a school's culture will reside in its organisational arrangements (MacGilchrist *et al.*, 1997). In connection with leadership for learning, it is the ways in which responsibilities are distributed, the procedures used for making decisions and the means of communication, which present powerful insights into a school's level of engagement with leadership for learning.

A more tangible organisational arrangement emphasised by MacGilchrist and her colleagues (1997) concerns environmental management. It is generally considered, for example, that a school's culture can often be gauged by the extent of graffiti in the students' toilets, or the amount of rubbish strewn across the grounds. More pertinent to nurturing leadership for learning, perhaps, is the existence of the kinds of spaces that encourage learning. Space can have a significant impact on learning (Chism, 2006), but the way space is arranged in schools has tended to be taken for granted. It could be argued that traditionally, classrooms have been uninspiring for students' learning and designed more for a transmission style of teaching. In addition, there has been an assumption that learning does not occur outside the classroom so that the potential of informal learning spaces elsewhere in the school has been underutilised. For these reasons, Chism (2006, p. 10) argues that there needs to be more research conducted on the impact of existing and experimental spaces on learning. In particular, she suggests that basic research should be undertaken on the influence of the physical environment on creativity, attention and critical thinking. She also advocates applied research on the effect of different kinds of lighting and furniture on comfort, satisfaction and interaction. It seems reasonable to assume, therefore, that in order to foster leadership for learning practices in schools there needs to be a physical as well as an intellectual investment.

A third major way in which MacGilchrist *et al.* (1997) suggest that a school's culture is expressed is according to opportunities for learning for students as well as adults. In regard to students, these authors draw attention to the nature of the curriculum on offer, but there is no distinction made between the formal, or overt, curriculum, and the 'hidden curriculum'. The hidden curriculum, we would argue, is a key concept relating to learning that unfortunately seems to have gone out of fashion in the school improvement literature. Given that the hidden curriculum comprises "that which is learned and taught alongside the formal or official curriculum" (Hargreaves, 1978a, p. 97) it has profound implications for the exercise of leadership for learning. The hidden curriculum is conveyed by messages communicated by the school in its day-to-day operations apart from the official statements of school vision and mission. The medium, therefore, is a key source of messages which can influence attitudes, values, beliefs and behaviour of students and others associated with the school.

This is not the place to present a detailed analysis of the impact that the hidden curriculum is purported to have on students' (and teachers') learning. It should be emphasised, however, that the messages communicated through the hidden curriculum have been identified as being potentially debilitating for students and at odds with the official ideology of the school. For example, Hargreaves (1978a) suggests that the impact of the hidden curriculum on many "working class" students is one of "damaged dignity", the effect of which is so massive and pervasive that few students subsequently recover.

The primary value of the concept of the hidden curriculum, therefore, lies in its ability to draw attention to aspects of schooling that are rarely acknowledged and remain largely unexamined. Messages communicated by a school's culture and organisation can support or undermine stated purposes and official curricula. From this perspective, the second principle of leadership for learning practice focusing on the creation of conditions favourable to learning as an activity seems to depend to some extent on a school's aptitude for making the hidden curriculum visible so the learning experienced by students (and others in the school) is as intentional as possible, as well as empowering.

Creating a dialogue about the connections between leadership and learning

For a school to develop a critical awareness of the hidden curriculum and assist students to learn in ways that are conducive to leadership for learning, it is desirable that a dialogue be created about leadership for learning. This is the third of the Cambridge Network Principles. In the introduction to this book we have observed that in the original Greek sense of the word, *dia-logus* engenders a free flowing of meaning through the group that allows it to discover insights not attainable individually (Voogt *et al.*, 1998). More specifically, Morrison (2002, p. 140) describes dialogue as "suspending judgment, identifying assumptions, listening, enquiring and reflection". It is through these continuous processes that the principles guiding leadership for learning within the school's context can be clarified and can reveal what leadership for learning looks like in practice.

Engaging in dialogue around leadership for learning for these purposes is analogous to the notion of making thinking visible. Indeed, insofar as making thinking visible connects with making learning explicit, it must be considered integral to the practice of leadership for learning itself. Perkins (2003) suggests that a culture of visible thinking can be achieved by teachers and students using the language of thinking and by devising thinking routines to support and nurture thinking. A culture of visible thinking throughout the school, therefore, helps to bring learning to the surface in teacher–student dialogue as well as in the dialogue in which teachers share their understandings and enhance their practice.

Making learning explicit through real dialogue has implications for both teachers' learning and students' learning. James (2007, p. 217), for example, reporting on the main messages derived from a research project conducted on 'learning how to learn', emphasises that dialogue promotes the "collaborative, strategic and reflective thinking" found to be vital to teachers' learning. It is this kind of learning, she contends, that corresponds with the ways that are in mind when it is advocated that students' should be learning how to learn in the classroom. In other words, a continuous and rigorous dialogue around leadership for learning can enable students and teachers to take responsibility for their learning and thereby develop their agency.

Sharing leadership

The processes of taking responsibility for one's learning and to act on behalf of, and with, others in proactive forms of initiative-taking provide the main linkages between leadership and learning (MacBeath, 2006, p. 5). They are also fundamental to the fourth principle of leadership for learning practice articulated in the Cambridge Network that involves the sharing of leadership. According to Harris and Lambert (2003) the key notion engendered by shared leadership is learning together and constructing meaning and knowledge collectively and collaboratively. These authors are, in other words, highlighting the interdependence of leadership activity and learning activity. They (Harris and Lambert, 2003, p. 17) go on to comment that:

> Leadership involves opportunities to surface and mediate perceptions, values, beliefs, information and assumptions through continuing conversations. It means generating ideas together; to seek to reflect on and make sense of work in the light of shared beliefs and new information; and to create actions that grow out of these new understandings.

These are the processes, the authors argue, that are at the core of leadership, which they regard as being fundamentally 'about learning together'. These are also the processes that are amenable to a distributed model of leadership that is generated from the interactions and dynamics engendered by groups and teams learning together (Harris, 2003b).

It may be argued that the efficacy of distributed leadership will depend on the extent to which leadership is perceived to be invited and entails messages being communicated to people that promote their worth. According to Stoll and Fink (1996, p. 109), invitational leadership is anchored on four basic tenets. The first is referred to as optimism, or the assumption that people have untapped potential for growth and development. The second is respect, which is manifested in vigorous discussion and reasoned dissent. The third is trust in people to behave as though they are able, worthwhile and responsible. Finally, the fourth tenet requires leaders to be intentionally supportive, caring and encouraging. The combination of these tenets in use helps to create an environment in which the energy and creativity of others are released.

Fostering a shared sense of accountability

It could be argued that the demand for accountability is a factor that militates against the sustenance of distributed leadership in schools (Oduro, 2004) and yet the Cambridge Network's fifth principle of leadership for learning practice involves fostering a shared sense of accountability. This principle, therefore, is informed by a more positive interpretation of accountability than one of surveillance. In this connection, Earl's (2005b, p. 7) distinction between what she describes as 'real' accountability and accounting is instructive. According to Earl, accounting is "gathering, organising and reporting information that describes performance". Accountability, however, is "the conversation about what information means and how it fits with everything we know and about how to use it to make positive changes". Earl, in fact, goes further and suggests that accountability is intertwined with "a moral and professional responsibility to be knowledgeable and fair in teaching (and learning) and in interactions with students and their parents". She goes on to argue that real accountability "engenders respect, trust, shared understanding and mutual support".

In a similar vein, Stoll and Fink (1996) advise that although it is often perceived that accountability and empowerment are incompatible, this is not necessarily the case. These authors contend that the empowerment residing in accountability will be dependent on the existence of processes and support that facilitate and monitor change in the school – processes that develop confidence, risk taking and openness in people's engagement with accountability practices.

Forster (1999) suggests that the process of "rendering an account" presents the most empowering approach to school accountability because of its scope for affirming partnership and collective endeavour. The rendering of an account occupies the school in a process of self-evaluation, communication and renewal which involves staff, parents and students, and promotes an accountability relationship manifested in shared goals, mutual respect and trust (Forster, 1999). The notion of rendering an account resonates with MacBeath's exhortation (1999) that schools must have the ability to tell their own story with the aim of improving student, professional and organisational learning.

Conclusion

The main purpose of this chapter has been to illustrate ways in which leadership and learning are connected and to shed some light on how these connections can be forged in practice. There is no doubt that the Cambridge Network's five principles of leadership for learning present invaluable signposts for traveling along this complex and potentially hazardous route. They have assisted us in identifying ways in which some of the murkiness can be cleared for revealing the internal conditions within a school that are conducive to leadership for learning. In this connection, Bowring-Carr and West-Burnham's advice (1997, p. 122) based on the dictum that 'form must follow function' is helpful. These authors suggest that leadership for learning entails the school being led in a way that becomes a microcosm of learning process. Similarly, Frost (2006, p. 21) contends that leadership for learning must be premised on the belief that the capacity for leadership arises out of powerful learning experiences. Hence, it is advisable for a school that subscribes to leadership for learning to identify as clearly as possible that its core function is learning. In particular, there is a need to visualise with clarity all three learning agendas, the opportunities regarding each, and the connections among them as an essential step in leading for learning (Knapp *et al.*, 2003).

The opportunities for learning, Bowring-Carr and West-Burnham (1997) suggest, will be dependent on another core function of the school, which is the creation of an explicit culture that facilitates learning. In other words, the norms, values, incentives, skills and relationships which provide sustenance for learning to happen. In particular, it is desirable for trust and openness to permeate a school's culture because they are the levers of cooperative action and social capital (Louis, 2007) and lie at the heart of processes of leadership and learning. From this perspective, a process of getting the culture right may be envisaged as "laying the groundwork for new ways of doing things", or as "growing [leadership for learning] organically from emerging thinking and practice" (Swaffield and MacBeath, 2006, p. 203).

Bowring-Carr and West-Burnham (1997) go on to argue that following clarification of the school's core 'function' as learning, the 'form' of leadership can then be identified. In light of the preceding discussion, however, we believe that shared leadership represents a further dimension of the school's core function insofar as it engenders learning together and constructing meaning and knowledge collectively and collaboratively (Harris and Lambert, 2003), and exemplifies the interdependence of leadership activity and learning activity. The core function of learning, we would also suggest, is affirmed by the adoption of a shared language of learning throughout the school, enabling learning to be brought to the surface. As Bowring-Carr and West-Burnham remark (1997, p. 159):

> The overriding question to ask about the key words in [the school's] lexicon is whether they reflect an institution that is focused on teaching or on learning, on control or on enabling, on maintenance or on change. Does the language encourage investigation, doubt, research, or does it suggest that the rules are set and everyone needs to follow them.

The language that the school uses helps to give meaning to the pursuit of learning and can also assist in revealing the ways in which leadership for learning can be manifested in the structures of the school, a key consideration in relation to the dictum that 'form follows function'.

It follows, then, that to make leadership for learning integral to both the culture and structure of the school it is necessary to picture the implications for learning presented by every aspect of the organisation. For example, in relation to the agenda of students' learning, it seems self-evident that certain processes and structures will need to be scrutinised carefully to reveal the ways in which they reflect understandings and approaches to learning. In particular, it is helpful to examine the curriculum, as understood in its broadest sense for the messages – overt and covert – in terms of what it conveys about students' learning. Powerful messages about learning may be communicated across a range of structures and processes within the school, such as classrooms and allocation of classes, approaches to behaviour management, the extent to which student voice is encouraged, and the learning environment and school grounds.

Similarly, it is necessary for the school to picture the implications for teaching and learning presented by structures and processes such as professional development, performance management, the structure of meetings, and arrangements provided for induction. At the level of organisational learning, it is such facets of the school as policies and procedures, decision-making/taking processes, governance and community partnerships which will reflect and reify the stance adopted towards leadership for learning.

It is possible to argue that adopting the dictum of 'form follows function' as a strategy to operationalising leadership for learning is contiguous with a cultural approach to school improvement. MacBeath (2005, p. 11) describes this approach as "winning hearts and minds". It involves a process of galvanising support "premised on staff learning and schools learning through collaborative activity, through internal networking, informal conversations and a constant simmering of new ideas never far from people's thinking". Structural innovation, therefore, tends to arise "organically from need, initiative and inspiration" in a climate which encourages the principles of leadership for learning that have been enumerated in this chapter.

To conclude, we consider that it would be remiss of us not to draw attention to Bertolt Brecht's *In Praise of Learning* (Willett, 1992, pp. 110–11), which seems to be such a powerful evocation of leadership for learning. This is not the place to engage in a detailed interpretation of the poem's meaning. Rather, we would like to suggest that the poem is displayed widely and recited frequently as a constant reminder of the essential goodness of the leading learning agenda.

References

Aedo-Richmond, R. and Richmond, M. (1999). Recent curriculum change in post-Pinochet Chile. In B. Moon and P. Murphy (eds). *Curriculum in context*. London: Paul Chapman.

Agyris, C. and Schon, D. (1978). *Organisational learning: A theory of action perspective*. Reading, MA: Addison-Wesley.

Ainscow, M., Booth, T. and Dyson, A. (2006). *Improving schools, developing inclusion*. London: Routledge.

Alden, J. (1998). *A teacher's guide to web-based instruction: Getting started on intranet- and internet-based training*. Alexandria, VA: American Society for Training and Development.

Alt, M.N. and Medrich, E. A. (1994). *Student outcomes from participation in community service*. Berkeley, CA: U.S. Department of Education, Office of Research.

Anderson, L. and Krathwohl, D. (2001). *A taxonomy for learning, teaching and assessing: A revision of Bloom's taxonomy of educational objectives*. New York: Longman.

Anderson, S. E. (2002). *Improving schools through teacher development: Case studies of the Agha Khan Foundation projects*. Lisse, The Netherlands: Swets and Zeitlinger BV.

Andrews, D. and Crowther, F. (2002). Parallel leadership: a clue to the contents of the "black box" of school reform. *International Journal of Educational Management*, 16(4), pp. 152–59.

Atkinson, M., Springate, I., Johnson, F. and Halsey, K. (2007). *Inter-school collaboration: A literature review*. Slough: NFER.

Ausubel, D. P. (1968). *Educational psychology*. New York: Holt, Rinehart and Winston.

Avalos, B. (1992). The need for educational reform and the role of teacher training: The case of Papua New Guinea. *International Journal of Educational Development*, 12, pp. 309–18.

Bagnall, N. (2000). The balance between vocational secondary and general secondary schooling in France and Australia. *Comparative Education*, 36(4), pp. 459–75.

Bain, A. (2004). Secondary school reform and technology planning – Lessons learned from a ten year school reform initiative, *Australasian Journal of Educational Technology*, 20(2), pp. 149–70.

Bain, J. (1994). *Understanding by learning or learning by understanding: How shall we teach?* Brisbane: Griffith University.

Ball, D. L. and Cohen, D. K. (1999). Developing practice, developing practitioners:

Toward a practice-based theory of professional education. In L. Darling-Hammond and G. Sykes (eds). *Teaching as the learning profession: Handbook of policy and practice* (pp. 3–32). San Francisco: Jossey-Bass.

Barker, B. (2009). Public service reform in education: Why is progress so slow? *Journal of Educational Administration and History*, 41(1), pp. 57–72.

Barrow, R. (1984). *Giving teaching back to teachers: A critical introduction to curriculum theory*. Sussex: Wheatsheaf Books.

Barth, R. S. (1991). *Improving schools from within*. San Francisco: Jossey-Bass.

—— (2001). Teacher leader. *Phi Delta Kappan*, 82(6), pp. 443–49.

Bartlett, S. and Burton, D. (2007). *Introduction to education studies*. London: Sage.

Bascia, N. and Hargreaves, A. (2000). Teaching and leading on the sharp edge of change. In N. Bascia and A. Hargreaves (eds). *The sharp edge of educational change. Teaching, leading and the realities of reform* (pp. 3–26). London: RoutledgeFalmer.

Beare, H. (1997). *Designing a break-in-the-mould school for the future*. Keynote address presented at the ACEA Virtual Conference. Canberra. July.

—— (1998). *Leadership for a new millennium. The ACEA's William Walker Oration*. Melbourne 1998. Melbourne: The Australian Council for Educational Administration.

Beeby, C. (1966). *The quality of education in developing countries*. Cambridge, MA: Harvard University Press.

Bennett, M. E. (2001). Inspection: A catalyst in school improvement. Unpublished PhD Thesis. University of Strathclyde.

Bennis, W. (1959). Leadership theory and administrative behaviour: The problem of authority. *Administrative Science Quarterly*, 4(2), pp. 259–301.

Bennis, W. and Nanus, B. (1985). *The strategy for taking charge*. New York: Harper and Row.

Bentley, T. (1998). *Learning beyond the classroom: Education for a changing world*. London: Routledge.

Billig, S. (2000). Research on K-12 school-based service learning: The evidence builds. *Phi Delta Kappan*, 81(9), pp. 658–64.

Black, P. and Wiliam, D. (1998) 'Inside the black box': Raising standards through classroom assessment. *Phi Delta Kappan*, 80,(2), pp. 139–48.

—— (2005) Lessons from around the world: How policies, politics and culture constrain and afford assessment practices. *The Curriculum Journal*, 16(2), pp. 249–61.

Blackmore, J. (1999). *Framing the issues for educational re-design. Learning networks and professionalism activism*. Hawthorn, Victoria, Australia: Australian Council for Educational Administration.

Blase, J. and Blase, J. (1998). *Handbook of instructional leadership: How really good principals promote teaching and learning*. London: Sage.

—— (1999). Effective instructional leadership. Teachers' perspectives on how principals promote teaching and learning in schools. *Journal of Educational Administration*, 38(2), pp. 130–41.

Bloom, B. (ed.). (1956). *Taxonomy of educational objectives, handbook 1: Cognitive domain*. New York: David McKay Co.

Blunkett, D. (1998). Blunkett response. *Journal of Lifelong Learning Initiatives*, 7, np.

Bonnet, G. (1997). Country profile from France. *Assessment in Education*, 4(2), pp. 295–306.

Boston, K. (1999). The classroom: Let's get real. *Australian College of Education: Western Australian Chapter Newsletter*, pp. 2–4.

Bowles, S. and Gintis, H. (1976) *Schooling in Capitalist America: Educational reform and the contradictions of economic life*. New York: Basic Books.

Bowring-Carr, C. and West-Burnham, J. (1997). *Effective learning in schools. How to integrate learning and leadership for a successful school*. London: Financial Times Pitman Publishing.

Bridges, D. (2007). *Evidence-based reform in education: A response to Robert Slavin*. European Educational Research Association Annual Conference, Ghent. 19 September.

Broadfoot, P. (1996). *Education, assessment and society*. Buckingham, UK: Open University Press.

Broadfoot, P. and Black, P. (2004) Redefining assessment? The first ten years of assessment in education. *Assessment in Education*, 11(1), pp. 7–25.

Brooker, R. and MacDonald, D. (1999). Did we hear you? Issues of student voice in a curriculum innovation. *Journal of Curriculum Studies*, 31(1), pp. 83–97.

Brookfield, S. (1990). *The skillful teacher: On technique, trust, and responsiveness in the classroom*. San Francisco: Jossey-Bass.

Bruner, J. (1966). *Towards a theory of instruction*. New York: Norton.

—— (1996). *The culture of education*. Cambridge, MA: Harvard University Press.

Bryce, T. (2003). Could do better? Assessment in Scottish schools. In T. G. K. Bryce and W. M. Hume (eds). *Scottish education, second edition: Post devolution* (pp. 709–20). Edinburgh: Edinburgh University Press.

Bullock, K. and Wikeley, F. (2001). Personal learning planning: Strategies for personal learning. *Forum: For Promoting 3–19 Comprehensive Education*, 43(2), 67–9.

Burch, P. and Spillane, J. P. (2003). Elementary school leadership strategies and subject matter: Reforming mathematics and literacy instruction. *The Elementary School Journal*, 103(5), pp. 519–35.

Burgoyne, J. (1999). Design of the times. *People Management*, 5, pp. 38–44.

Burns, J. M. (1978). *Leadership*. New York: Harper and Row.

Bush, T. and Glover, D. (2003). *School leadership: Concepts of evidence*. Nottingham: National College for School Leadership.

Butt, R. and Retallick, J. (2002). Professional-wellbeing and learning: A study of administrator–teacher workplace relationships. *Journal of Educational Inquiry*, 3(1), pp. 17–33.

Caldwell, B. J. and Spinks, J. (1988). *The self-managing school*. London: Falmer Press.

Cambridge Primary Review (2009). Available on : http://www.primayreview.org.uk/index.html. (Accessed on 1 June, 2009)

Camburn, E., Rowan, B. and Taylor, J. E. (2003). Distributed leadership in schools: The case of elementary schools adopting comprehensive school reform models. *Educational Evaluation and Policy Analysis*, 25(4), pp. 347–73.

Carless, D. R. (1997). Managing systemic curriculum change: A critical analysis of Hong Kong's target-oriented curriculum initiative. *International Review of Education*, 43(4), pp. 349–66.

Carron, G. and Chau, T. N. (1996). *The quality of primary schools in different development contexts*. Paris: International Institute for Educational Planning, UNESCO Publishing.

Chapman, E. (2003). Alternative approaches to assessing student engagement rates. *Practical Assessment, Research and Evaluation*. Available on: http://PAREonline. net/getvn.asp?v = 8andn = 13. (Accessed on 2 February, 2009)

Chapman, J. (1995). Set the signals at green! The William Walker oration. *Journal of Educational Administration*, 33(1), pp. 4–21.

Chapman, J. and Aspin, D. (1997). *The school, the community and lifelong learning*. London: Cassell.

Chism, N. V. N. (2006). Challenging traditional assumptions and rethinking learning spaces. In D. G. Oblinger (ed.). *Learning spaces*. Available on: http://www.educause.edu\learningspaces. (Accessed on 6 March, 2008)

Cibulka, J., Coursey, S., Nakayama, M., Price, J. and Stewart, S. (2003). *Schools as learning organizations: A review of the literature*. National College for School Leadership. Available on: http://www.ncsl.org.uk/ncl. (Accessed on 2 February, 2009)

Collins, J. (2001). *Good to great*. New York: HarperCollins.

Collinson, V. (2008). Leading by learning: New directions in the twenty-first century. *Journal of Educational Administration*, 46(4), pp. 443–60.

Cone, D. and Harris, S. (1996). Service learning practice: Developing a theoretical framework. *Michican Journal of Community Service Learning*, 3, pp. 31–43.

Conrad, D. and Hedin, D. (1991) School based community service: What we know from research and theory. *Phi Delta Kappan*, 7(10), pp. 743–49.

Contu, A. and Willmott, H. (2000). Comment on Wenger and Yanow. Knowing in practice: A 'delicate flower' in the organizational learning field. *Organization*, 7, pp. 269–76.

Cook-Sather, A. (2002). Authorizing students' perspectives: Trust, dialogue, and change in education, *Educational Research*, 31(4), pp. 3–14.

Copland, M. A. (2002). The Bay Area school reform collaborative: Building the capacity to lead. In Murphy J. and Datnow, A. (eds). *Leadership lessons from comprehensive school reforms* (pp. 159–83). Thousand Oaks, California: Corwin Press.

—— (2003). Leadership of inquiry: Building and sustaining capacity for school improvement. *Educational Evaluation and Policy Analysis*, 25(4), pp. 375–95.

Cotgrove, B. (1997). Schools in the post-industrial culture. Paper presented at the Australian Council of Educational Administration Virtual Conference. Canberra. July.

Crawford, M. (2005). Distributed leadership and headship: A paradoxical relationship. *School Leadership and Management*, 25(3), pp. 213–15.

Crook, D. (2007). Missing. Presumed dead? What happened to the comprehensive school in England and Wales? In B. M. Franklin and G. McCulloch (eds). *The death of the comprehensive high school: Historical, contemporary, and comparative perspectives* (pp. 147–68). New York: Palgrave Macmillan.

Crossley, M. (1983). Strategies for curriculum change with special reference to the secondary Schools Community Extension Project in Papua New Guinea. Unpublished PhD Thesis, La Trobe University.

—— (1984). Strategies for curriculum change and the question of international transfer. *Journal of Curriculum Studies*, 16, pp. 75–88.

Crowther, F., Kaagan, S. S, Furgeson, M. and Hann, L. (2002). *Developing teacher leaders. How teacher leadership enhances school success*. Thousand Oaks, California: Corwin Press, Inc.

Cummings, W. (1990). Evaluation and examination. In R. Thomas (ed.). *International comparative education* (pp. 87–106). Oxford: Pergamon.

Curriculum Council of Western Australia (1998). *Curriculum framework*. Perth: Curriculum Council.

Darling-Hammond, L. (1997). *The right to learn: A blueprint for creating schools that work*. San Francisco: Jossey-Bass.

Darling-Hammond, L., Cobb, V. and Bullmaster, M. (1998). Professional development schools as contexts for teacher learning and leadership. In K. Leithwood and K. Seashore Louis (eds). *Organizational learning in schools: Contexts of learning* (pp. 149–76). Lisse, The Netherlands: Swets and Zeitlenger.

Dave, R. H. (1973). *Lifelong education and the school curriculum*. Hamburg: UNESCO Institute for Education.

—— (1975). *Reflections on lifelong education and the school*. Hamburg, Pergamon Press.

Dawson, M. (2007). *School vision and mission statements: What do they mean to the work of teachers?* Paper presented at the Australian Council of Educational Leaders (ACEL) Conference. Darling Harbour, Sydney, Australia. September.

Day, C. (1999). *Developing teachers: The challenges of lifelong learning*. London: The Falmer Press.

Day, C., Harris, A., Hadfield, M., Tolley, H. and Beresford, J. (2000). *Leading schools in times of change*. Milton Keynes: Open University Press.

Deal, T. E. and Peterson, K. D. (1998) *Shaping school culture. The heart of leadership*. San Francisco: Jossey-Bass.

Dehmell, A. (2006). Making a European area of lifelong learning a reality? Some critical reflections on the European Union lifelong learning policies. *Comparative Education*, 42(1), pp. 49–62.

Dembo, M. H. and Eaton, M. J. (2000). Self-regulation of academic learning of middle-level schools. *The Elementary School Journal*, 100(5), pp. 473–89.

Deutrom, B. (1990). *Relevant education for all: An inservice handbook*. Papua New Guinea: Department of Education.

Dewey, J. (1933). *How we think*. Boston DC: Heath.

Dimmock, C. (2000). *Designing the learning-centred school: A cross cultural perspective*. London: Routledge.

Dimmock, C. and Walker, A. (1997). Comparative educational administration: Developing a cross-cultural conceptual framework. *Educational Administration Quarterly*, 34(4), pp. 558–95.

Dove, L. A. (1982). *Lifelong teacher education and the community school*. Hamburg: UNESCO Institute for Education.

Dovey, K. and De Jong, T. (1990). *Developing people*. Grahamstown, South Africa: Rhodes University, The Institute for Social and Individual Development in Africa.

Drake, S. (1998). *Creating integrated curriculum: Proven ways to increase student learning*. Thousand Oaks, CA: Corwin Press.

Dressler, B. (2001). Charter school leadership. *Education and Urban Society*, 33(2), pp. 170–85.

Driver, M. (2002). The learning organization: Foucauldian gloom or Utopian sunshine? *Human Relations*, 55(1), pp. 33–53.

Dunn, R. and Dunn. K. (1975). *Educator's self-teaching guide to individualizing instructional programs*. West Nyack, NY: Parker.

Earl, L. (2005a). *Thinking about purpose in classroom assessment.* Australian Curriculum Studies Association: Canberra.

—— (2005b). *From accounting to accountability: Harnessing data for school improvement.* Paper presented at Australian Council for Educational Research Conference, 'Using data to support learning', Melbourne, 7–9 August.

Earl, L. and Fullan M. (2003). Using data in leadership for learning. *Cambridge Journal of Education,* 33(3), pp. 383–94.

Earl, L., Watson, N. and Torrance, N. (2002). Front row seats: What we've learned from the national literacy and numeracy strategies in England. *Journal of Educational Change,* 3, pp. 35–53.

Early, P. and Bubb, S. (2004). *Leading and managing continuing professional development. Developing people, developing schools.* London: Paul Chapman Publishing Ltd.

Easterby-Smith, M. (1997). Disciplines of organizational learning. Contributions and critiques. *Human Relations,* 50(9), pp. 1085–1113.

Eisner, E. (1969). Instructional and expressive educational objectives. Available on: http://eric.ed.gov:80/ERICWebPortal/custom/portlets/recordDetails/detailmini.jsp?_nfpb=trueand_andERICExtSearch_SearchValue_0=ED028838andERICExtSearch_SearchType_0=noandaccno=ED028838 (Accessed on 2 February, 2009)

—— (1983). The art and craft of teaching. *Educational Leadership,* January, 5–13.

Elmore, R. (2004). *School reform from the inside out: Policy, practice, and performance.* Cambridge, MA: Harvard University Press.

Elmore, R. F. (2000). *Building a new structure for school leadership.* Washington, DC: The Albert Shanker Institute.

Enright, E. and O'Sullivan, M. *The Pres girls.* Paper in preparation by E. Enright and M. O'Sullivan, PE PAYS Research Centre, Limerick: Ireland. University of Limerick.

Entwistle, N. and Ramsden, P. (1983). *Understanding student learning.* London: Croom Helm.

Eraut, M. (1994). *Developing professional knowledge and competence.* London: The Falmer Press.

European Lifelong Learning Initiative (1994). *Lifelong learning: Developing human potential.* Report from the first global conference on lifelong learning, Rome, Italy, December.

European Parliament – Commission of the European Communities (1995). *Amended proposal for a European Parliament and Council decision establishing a European year of lifelong learning.* Brussels: European Parliament.

European Round Table of Industrialists (1997). *Investing in knowledge.* Leuven: Katholieke Universiteit Leuven.

Eyler, J. and Giles, D. (1999). *Where's the learning in service learning?* San Francisco: Jossey-Bass.

Field, J. (2000). *Lifelong learning and the new educational order.* Stoke on Trent, UK: Trentham Books.

Fielding, M. (2004). 'New wave' student voice and the renewal of civic society. *London Review of Education,* 2(3), pp. 197–217.

Fitzgerald, T. (2003a). Interrogating orthodox voices: Gender, ethnicity and educational leadership. *School Leadership and Management,* 23(4), pp. 431–44.

—— (2003b). Changing the deafening silence of indigenous women's voices in educational leadership. *Journal of Educational Administration,* 41(1), pp. 9–23.

—— (2004). Powerful voices and powerful stories: Reflections on the challenges and dynamics of intercultural research. *Journal of Intercultural Studies*, 25(3), pp. 233–45.

Fitzgerald, T. and Gunter, H. (2006). Teacher leadership? A new form of managerialism. *New Zealand Journal of Educational Leadership*, 21(4), pp. 44–57.

Fontana, D. (1981). *Psychology for teachers.* London: Macmillan.

Forster, K. (1999). Accountability at the local school. *Educational Philosophy and Theory*, 31(2), pp. 175–87.

Foster, W. (1989). Towards a critical practice of leadership. In J. Smyth (ed.). *Critical perspective on educational leadership* (pp. 39–62). London: Falmer Press.

Fox, S. (2000). Communities of practice, Foucault and actor-network theory. *Journal of Management Studies*, 37, pp. 853–67.

Franklin, B. (2005). Gone before you know it: Urban school reform and the short life of the Education Action Zone initiative. *London Review of Education*, 3(1), pp. 3–27.

Fraser, B. (1989) An historical look at curriculum evaluation. In C. Kridel (ed.). *Curriculum history* (pp. 114–28). Landham, MD: University Press of America.

Fraser, S. E. and Brickman. W. W. (eds). (1968). *A history of international and comparative education: Nineteenth century documents.* Glenview, IL: Scott, Foreman.

Frost, D. (2006). The concept of 'agency' in leadership for learning. *Leading and Managing*, 12(2), pp. 19–28.

Fullan, M. (1982). *The meaning of educational change.* New York: Teachers College, Columbia University.

—— (1991). *The new meaning of educational change.* New York: Teachers College Press.

—— (1992). *Successful school improvement.* Buckingham: Open University Press.

—— (1998). Leadership for the twenty first century: Breaking the bonds of dependency. *Educational Leadership*, 55(7), pp. 6–10.

—— (2001). *Leading in a culture of change.* San Francisco: Jossey-Bass.

—— (2003). *The moral imperative of school leadership.* California: Corwin Press.

—— (2005). *Leadership and sustainability: System thinkers in action.* California: Corwin Press.

Fullan, M. and Hargreaves, A. (1996). *What's worth fighting for in your school?* Columbia University: Teachers College Press.

Gagne, R. M. (1970). *Conditions of learning.* London: Holt, Rinehart and Winston.

Gardner, H. (1983). *Frames of Mind. The theory of multiple intelligences.* New York: Basic Books.

—— (1991). *The unschooled mind: How children think and schools should think.* New York: Basic Books.

—— (1993). *Multiple intelligences: Theory and practice.* New York: Basic Books.

Garvin, D. A. (1993). Building a learning organization. *Harvard Business Review*, 1993, np.

Geddis, N. (1996). Science teaching and reflection: Incorporating new subject matter into teachers' classroom frames. *International Journal of Science Education,* 18(2), pp. 249–65.

Gelpi, E. (1984). Lifelong education: Opportunities and obstacles. *International Journal of Lifelong Education*, 3(2), pp. 79–87.

Gelten, B. and Shelton, M. (1991). Expanded notion of strategic instructional leadership: The principal's role with student support personnel. *Journal of School Leadership*, 1, pp. 338–50.

Gewirtz, S., Dickson, M., Power, S., Halpin, D. and Whitty, G. (2005). The development of social capital theory in educational policy and provision: The case of Education Action Zones in England. *British Educational Research Journal*, 31(6), pp. 651–73.

Gipps, C. (1998). Student assessment and learning for a changing society. *Prospects*, 28(1), pp. 32–44.

Gipson, S. (1998). The challenges of integrating information technology into a Thai educational setting: The story of Tridhos School Village, Chiang Mai. Available on: http://www.ascilite.org.au/asetarchives/confs/edtech98/pubs/articles/gipson2.html (Accessed on 6 Septmenber, 2008)

Giroux, H. A. (1994). Teachers, public life and curriculum reform. In A. C. Ornstein and L. S. Behar (eds). *Contemporary issues in curriculum* (pp. 41–49). Boston, MA: Allyn and Bacon.

Gladwell, M. (2000). *How little things can make a big difference*. London: Abacus.

Goad, L. H. (1984). *Preparing teachers for lifelong education*. Hamburg: UNESCO Institute for Education.

Goldstein, H. (2004). Education for all: The globalization of learning targets. *Comparative Education*, 40(1), pp. 7–14.

Gooding, A. and Stacey, K. (1993). Characteristics of small group discussion: Reducing misconceptions. *Mathematics Education Research Journal*, 5(1), pp. 60–73.

Goodson, I. F. (1987). *The making of curriculum. Collected essays*. New York: Falmer Press.

Grace, G. (2000). Research and the challenges of contemporary school leadership: The contribution of critical scholarship. *British Journal of Educational Studies*, 48(3), pp. 231–47.

Greany, T. (2000). Learning to learn: Key skills or utopian idea. *Journal of Lifelong Learning Initiatives*, 17, pp. 24–25.

Greene, M. (1992). Foreword. In A.G. Rud Jr. and W.R. Oldendorf (eds). *A place for teacher renewal: Challenging the intellect, creating educational reform* (pp. vii–ix). New York: Teachers College Press.

Greenfield, T. (1986). The decline and fall of science in educational administration. *Interchange*, 17(2), pp. 57–80.

Griffin, G.A. (1992). Learning from NCCAT: An outsider's view. In A.G. Rud Jr. and W.R. Oldendorf (eds). *A place for teacher renewal: Challenging the intellect, creating educational reform* (pp. 128–145). New York: Teachers College Press.

Gronn, P. (2006). The significance of distributed leadership. *BC Educational Leadership Research*, 7. Available on: http://slc.educ.ubc.ca/eJournal/Issue7/Articles/DistributedLeadership_%Peter%20Gronn.pdf (Accessed on 2 February 2009)

Groundwater-Smith, S., Ewing, R. and Le Cornu, R. (2007). *Teaching: Challenges and dilemmas*. Sydney: Thomson.

Hake, B. J. (1999). Lifelong learning policies in the European Union: Development and issues. *Compare*, 29(1), pp. 53–69.

Hallinger, P. (2003). Leading educational change: Reflection on the practice of institutional and transformational leadership. *Cambridge Journal of Education*, 33(3), pp. 329–53.

Hallinger, P. and Murphy, J. (1985). Assessing the instructional management behaviour of principals. *The Elementary School Journal*, 86(2), pp. 217–47.

Hameyer, U. (1979). *School curriculum in the context of lifelong learning*. Hamburg: UNESCO Institute for Education.

Hancock, V. (1997). *Creating tomorrow's learner: Information literate, technologically competent*. Paper presented at the Australian Council of Educational Administration Virtual Conference. Canberra. July.

Handscomb, G. (2004). Collaboration and enquiry: Sharing practice. In P. Early and S. Bubb. *Leading and managing continuing professional development. Developing people, developing schools* (pp. 89–99). London: Paul Chapman Publishing Ltd.

Hargreaves, A. (1997). The four ages of professionalism and professional learning. *Unicorn*, 23(2), pp. 86–114.

—— (2003). Professional learning communities and performance training cults: The emerging apartheid of school improvement. In A. Harris, C. Day, M. Hadfield, D. Hopkins, A. Hargreaves and C. Chapman (eds). *Effective leadership for school improvement* (pp. 180–95). New York: RoutledgeFalmer.

Hargreaves, A. and Fink, D. (2005). *Sustainable leadership*. San Francisco: Jossey-Bass.

Hargreaves, A. and Fullan, M. (1998). *What is worth fighting for out there?* New York: Teachers College Press.

Hargreaves, A., Earl, L. and Schmidt, M. (2002). Perspectives on alternative assessment reform. *American Educational Reform Journal*, 39(1), pp. 69–95.

Hargreaves, D. (1978). Power and the paracurriculum. In C. Richards (ed.). *Power and the paracurriculum: Issues in curriculum studies* (pp. 97–108). Driffield England: Nafforton Books.

—— (1993). Whatever happened to symbolic interactionism? In M. Hammersley (ed.). *Controversies in classroom research* (pp. 135–52). Buckingham: Open University Press.

Hargreaves, D. H. (1978a). Power and the paracurriculum. In C. Richards (ed.). *Power and the curriculum: Issues in curriculum studies* (pp. 97–108). Driffield, England: Nafforton Books.

——. (1978b). The two curricula and the community. *International Journal of Research in Education*, 1(1), pp. 31–41.

Harlen, W. (2005). Teachers' summative practices and 'assessment for learning' – tensions and synergies. *The Curriculum Journal*, 16(2), pp. 207–23.

Harris, A. (2002). *School improvement: What is in it for schools?* London: Routledge.

—— (2003a). Teacher leadership and school improvement. In A. Harris, C. Day, D. Hopkins, M. Hadfield, A. Hargreaves and C. Chapman (eds). *Effective leadership for school improvement* (pp. 72–83). London, RoutledgeFalmer.

—— (2003b). Teacher leadership as distributed leadership: Heresy, fantasy or possibility? *School Leadership and Management*, 23(3), pp. 313–24.

—— (2004). Distributed leadership and school improvement. *Educational Management Administration and Leadership*, 13(2), pp. 11–24.

—— (2008). *Distributed school leaders: Developing tomorrow's leaders*. London: Routledge.

Harris, A. and Lambert, L. (2003). *Building leadership capacity for school improvement*. Maidenhead, Berkshire: Open University Press.

Harris, A. and Mujis, D. (2004). *Improving schools through teacher leadership*. London: Open University Press.

——(2005). *Improving schools through teacher leadership.* Maidenhead, England: Open University Press.

Harrow, A. (1972). *A taxonomy of the psychomotor domain: A guide for developing behavioral objectives.* New York: David McKay.

Hartley, D. (2007). Organizational epistemology, education and social theory. *British Journal of Sociology of Education,* 28(2), pp. 195–208.

Harvey, L. (2004). *Analytic quality glossary.* Available on: http://www. qualityresearchinternational.com/glossary/ (Accessed on 6 September 2008)

Hawes, H. W. (1975). *Lifelong education, schools and curricula in developing countries.* Hamburg: UNESCO Institute for Education.

Hawes, H. (1979). The curriculum of teacher education. In G. Springller (ed.). *Education and anthropology.* Stanford: Stanford University Press.

Hayes, A. (2007). OBE curriculum is not sustainable in PNG. *Papua New Guinea Post Courier,* 25 May, np.

Heller, M. J. and Firestone, W. A. (1995). Who's in charge here? Sources of leadership for change in eight schools. *Elementary School Journal,* 96(1), pp. 65–86.

Herr, K. and Anderson, G. L. (2005). *The action research dissertation: A guide for students and faculty.* London: Sage.

Hoffbauer, D.K. (1992). Why North Carolina? The early history of a teacher renewal effort. In A.G. Rud Jr. and W.R. Oldendorf (eds). *A place for teacher renewal: Challenging the intellect, creating educational reform* (pp. 45–62). New York: Teachers College Press.

Hoffman, R. H., Hoffman, W. H. A. and Gray, J. M. (2008). Comparing key dimensions of schooling: Towards a typology of European school systems. *Comparative Education,* 44(1), pp. 93–110.

Holger, D. (1997). National forces, globalization and educational restructuring: Some European response patterns. *Compare,* 27(1), pp. 19–41.

Hopkins, D. (1993). *A teacher's guide to classroom research.* Buckingham: Open University Press.

Hopkins, D. and Jackson, D. (2003). Building the capacity for leading and learning. In A. Harris, C. Day, M. Hadfield, D. Hopkins, A. Hargreaves and C. Chapman (eds). *Effective leadership for school improvement* (pp. 84–104). New York: RoutledgeFalmer.

Hopkins, D., Hadfield, M., Hargreaves, A. and Chapman, C. (eds). (2003). *Effective leadership for school improvement* (pp. 72–83). London: RoutledgeFalmer.

Hubert, E. and Phillips, D. (2006). Standardization in EU education and training policy: Findings from a European research network. *Comparative Education,* 42(1), pp. 77–91.

International Baccalaureate Organization (1991). *International Baccalaureate Organization CAS Activities Handbook for IB Schools.* Geneva. International Baccalaureate Organization.

—— (1996). *Creativity Action Service.* Geneva. International Baccalaureate Organization.

Jackson, D. and Tasker, R. (2003). *Professional learning communities.* Nottingham: National College for School Leadership. Available on: www.ncsl.org.uk/nlc

Jackson, D. and Temperley, J. (2007). From professional learning to networked learning community. In L. Stoll and K. Seashore Louis (eds). *Professional learning communities: Divergence, depth and dilemma* (pp. 45–62). Maidenhead, Berkshire: Open University Press.

James, M. (2007). Unlocking transformative practice within and beyond the classroom: Messages for practice and policy. In M. James, R. McCormick, P. Black, P. Carmichael, M.J. Drummond, A. Fox, J. MacBeath, B. Marshall, D. Pedder, R. Procter, S. Swaffield J. Swann and D. William (eds). *Improving learning how to learn. Classroom, schools and networks* (pp. 215–226). London: Routledge.

James, M., Black, P., McCormick, R. and Pedder, D. (2007). Promoting learning how to learn through assessment for learning. In M. James, R. McCormick, P. Black, P. Carmichael, M. J. Drummond, A. Fox, J. MacBeath, B. Marshall, D. Pedder, R. Procter, S. Swaffield, J. Swann and D. William (eds). *Improving learning how to learn. Classroom, schools and networks* (pp. 3–29). London: Routledge.

James, W. (1958). *Talks to teachers on psychology: And to students on some of life's ideals*. New York: W. W. Norton.

Jenkins, C.D.O. (1994). Alec Dickson, CBE, May 1914 - October 1994, *Contact, The Journal of the IB Teachers*, 6, December.

Jenkins, D. (1976). Man: A course of study. In M. Golby (ed.). *Design issues: Curriculum design and development – Units 14–15* (pp. 59–104). Milton Keynes: Open University Press.

Jessup, F. W. (1969). *Lifelong learning: A symposium of continuing education*. Oxford: Pergamon Press.

Jin, L. and Cortazzi, M. (1998). Dimensions of dialogue, large classes in China. *International Journal of Educational Research*, 29, pp. 739–61.

Johnson, A. P. (2008). *A short guide to action research*. Boston: Pearson.

Jones, F. (1996). Adding caring to the curriculum. *ASCD Education Update*, 38(7), pp. 2–3.

Jones, J. (1974). *Quantitative concepts, vernaculars and education in Papua New Guinea. ERU Report 19*. Waigani: Educational Research Unit, University of Papua New Guinea.

Kamens, D. H., Meyer, J. W. and Benavot, A. (1996). Worldwide patterns in academic secondary education curricula. *Comparative Education Review*, 40(2), pp. 116–38.

Katzenmeyer, M. and Moller, G. (2001). *Awakening the sleeping giant: Helping teachers develop as leaders*. Thousand Oaks, CA: Corwin Press.

Kauchak, D. and Eggen, P. (2008). *Introduction to teaching: Becoming a professional*. Columbus, Ohio: Pearson.

Kember, D. (1996). The intention to both memorise and understand: Another approach to learning. *Higher Education*, 31, pp. 341–54.

Killen, R. (2003). *Effective teaching strategies: Lessons from research and practice*. Tuggerah, New South Wales: Social Science Press.

Knapp, M. S., Copland, M. A. and McLaughlin, M. W. (2003). *Leading for learning sourcebook: Concepts and examples*. Seattle, WA: Center for the Study of Teaching and Policy: University of Washington.

Knapp, M., Copland, M. and Talbert, J. (2003). *Leading for learning: Reflective tools for school and district leaders*. Seattle, WA: Center for the Study of Teaching and Policy: University of Washington.

Krathwohl, D., Bloom, B. and Masia, B. (1964). *Taxonomy of educational objectives. Handbook II: Affective domain*. New York: David McKay.

Kulundu, F. and Hayden, M. (2002). Creativity, action, service (CAS) activities as part of the International Baccalaureate diploma programme: A case study. *Pastoral Care*, 20(1), pp. 30–36.

Kumar, K. (1979). *Bonds without bondage: Explorations in transcultural interactions*. Honolulu: University Press of Hawaii.

Kwen, B. H. and Chee, K.C. (2002). Enhancing the standard of project work in primary science. *Learning and Growing Through Projects*, 10(3), pp. 15–20.

Lam, C. C. (2003). The romance and reality of policy-making and implementation: A case study of the target-oriented curriculum in Hong Kong. *Journal of Education Policy*, 18(6), pp. 641–55.

Lambert, L. (1995). New directions in the preparation of educational leaders. *Thrust for Educational Leadership*, 24(5), pp. 6–10.

Laurillard, D. (1979). The process of student learning. *Higher Education*, 8, pp. 395–409.

—— (1993). *Rethinking university teaching: A framework for the effective use of educational technology*. London: Routledge.

Lee, J. J., Adams, D. and Cornbleth, C. (1988). Transnational transfer of curriculum knowledge: A Korean case study. *Journal of Curriculum Studies*, 20, pp. 233–46.

Leithwood, K. (1994). Leadership for school restructuring. *Educational Administration Quarterly*, 30(4), pp. 498–518.

Leithwood, K. and Atkin, R. (1995). *Making schools smarter: A system for monitoring school and district progress*. Thousands Oaks, CA: Corwin Press Inc.

Leithwood, K., Jantzi, D. and Steinbach, R. (1999). *Changing leadership for changing times*. Buckingham: Open University Press.

Leithwood, H. and Seashore Louis (1998). Organizational learning in schools: An introduction. In K. Leithwood and K. Seashore Louis (eds). *Organizational learning in schools: Context of learning* (1–14), Lisse: Swets and Zeitlinger.

LeSourd, S. J. (1990). Curriculum development and cultural context. *The Educational Forum*, 54, pp. 205–16.

Lewis, K. S. (2007). Trust and improvement in schools. *Journal of Educational Change*, 8, pp. 1–24.

Lien, L. M. and May, A. L. C. (2002). Storyline approach to project work: The Nan Hua primary school. *Learning and Growing Through Projects*, 10(3), pp. 4–8.

Little, A. (1988). *Learning from developing countries*. London: University of London Institute of Education.

Little, J. W. (1990). The persistence of privacy: Autonomy and initiative in teachers' professional relations. *Teachers College Record*, 91(4), pp. 509–36.

Livingstone, D. W. (1999). Lifelong learning and underemployment in the knowledge society: A North American perspective. *Comparative Education*, 35(2), pp. 163–86.

Logan, L. and Sachs, J. (1998). Primary schools: Educational fringe dwellers. *Education Review*, 6, April.

Longworth, N. (1999). Education is dead. Long live learning. *Journal of Lifelong Learning Initiatives*, 15, pp. 15–17.

Louis, K. S. (1994). Beyond managed change: Rethinking how schools improve. *School effectiveness and school improvement*, 5(1), pp. 2–24.

—— (2007). Trust improvement in schools. *Journal of Educational Change*, 8, pp. 1–24.

Lynch, J. (1977). *Lifelong education and the preparation of educational personnel*. Hamburg: UNESCO Institute for Education.

MacBeath, J. (1998). *Effective school leadership: Responding to change*. London: Paul Chapman.

—— (1999). *Schools must speak for themselves. The case for school self-evaluation*. London: Routledge.

—— (2001). *Self-evaluation, background principles and key learning*. Available on: http://www.ncsl.org.uk (Accessed on 1 February, 2008)

—— (2004). *The leadership file*. Glasgow: Anderson and Sons Ltd.

—— (2005a). *Supporting innovative pedagogies: The role of school leadership*. Paper prepared for the ESRC Seminar IV. Enactments of Professionalism: Classrooms and Pedagogies. Kings College London, 5 July.

—— (2005b). *The self-evaluation file*. Glasgow: Anderson and Sons Ltd.

——(2006). A story of change: Growing leadership for learning. *Journal for Educational Change*, 7, pp. 33–46.

MacBeath, J. and Mortimore, P. (2001). (eds). *Improving school effectiveness*. Buckingham: Open University.

MacBeath, J., Frost, F. D. and Swaffield, S. (2005). Researching leadership for learning in seven countries [The Carpe Vitam Project]. *Educational Research and Perspectives*, 32(2), pp. 24–42.

MacBeath, J., Myers, K. and Demetriou, H. (2001). Supporting teachers in consulting pupils about aspects of teaching and learning, and evaluating impact. *Forum*, 43(2), pp. 78–82.

MacBeath, J., Pedder, D. and Swaffield, S. (2007). Unlocking transformative practice within and beyond the classroom: Messages for practice and policy. In M. James, R. McCormick, P. Black, P. Carmichael, M. J. Drummond, A. Fox, J. MacBeath, B. Marshall, D. Pedder, R. Procter, S. Swaffield, J. Swann and D. William (eds). *Improving learning how to learn. Classroom, schools and networks* (pp. 64–88). London: Routledge.

McCarthy, B. (1990). Using the 4MAT System to bring learning styles to schools. *Educational Leadership*, 48(2), pp. 31–37.

McCrone, D. (2003). Culture, nationalism and Scottish education. In T. G. K. Bryce and W. M. Hume (eds). *Scottish education second edition: Post devolution* (pp. 239–49). Edinburgh: Edinburgh University Press.

MacDonald, B. (1991). From innovation to reform – A framework for analyzing change. Introduction. In J. Ruddock (ed.). *Innovation and change*. Milton Keynes: Open University Press.

MacGilchrist, B. (n.d.). *Leading the intelligent school*. UK: National College for School leadership.

MacGilchrist, B., Myers, K. and Reed, J. (1997). *The intelligent school*. London: Paul Chapman Publishing Ltd.

—— (2004). *The intelligent school* (2nd edition). London: Paul Chapman Publishing Ltd.

McGilp, E. J. (2000). Something special. Australian Catholic University establishes centre for lifelong learning. *Journal of Lifelong Learning Initiatives*, 20, np.

McKernan, J. (2008). *Curriculum and imagination: Process, theory, pedagogy and action research*. Oxford: Routledge.

McLaughlin, D. (1990). *Teaching the teachers of teachers: Tertiary teacher education in Papua New Guinea*. Unpublished PhD Thesis, Institute of Education, University of London.

McNamara, N. (2005). *Choose leaders wisely*. Sydney: Catholic Education Office Sydney, Australia.

McNiff, J., Lomax, P. and Whitehead, J. (1996). *You and your action research project*. London: Routledge.

McPherson, R.B. (1992). Administration for human and organizational growth. In A.G. Rud Jr. and W.R. Oldendorf (eds). *A place for teacher renewal: Challenging the intellect, creating educational reform* (pp. 87–111). New York: Teachers College Press.

Madaus, G. and Keelaghan, T. (1992). Curriculum evaluation and assessment. In P. Jackson (eds). *Handbook of research on curriculum* (pp. 119–54). Boston, MA: Kluwer-Nijhoff.

Mamchur, C. (1996). *A teacher's guide to cognitive type theory and learning style*. Alexandria, Virginia: Association for Supervision and Curriculum Development.

Mangubhai, F. (1984). Fiji. In R. M. Thomas and T. N. Postlethwaite (eds). *Schooling in the Pacific Islands: Colonies in transition* (pp. 167–202). London: Pergamon Press.

Marsh, C. 2008). *Becoming a teacher: Knowledge, skills and issues*. Frenchs Forest, New South Wales, Australia: Pearson.

Marsh, C. and Stafford, K.(1988) *Curriculum: Practices and issues*. Sydney: McGraw-Hill.

Marton, F. and Saljo, R. (1976a). On qualitative differences in learning: 1 – outcome and process. *British Journal of Educational Psychology*, 46, pp. 4–11.

—— (1976b). Symposium: Learning processes and strategies on qualitative differences in learning: 11 – outcome as a function of the learner's conception of the task. *British Journal of Educational Psychology*, 46, pp. 115–27.

Marton, F., Hounsel, D. and Entwistle, N. (1984). *The experience of learning*. Edinburgh: Scottish University Press.

Marton, F., Watkins, D. and Tang, C. (1997). Discontinuities and continuities in the experience of learning: An interview study of high school students in Hong Kong. *Learning and Instruction*, 7, pp. 21–48.

Mayer, E. (Chair) (1993). *Putting general education to work: The key competencies report*. Melbourne: Sands and McDougall.

Mayo, P., Donnelly, M. B., Nash, P. P. and Schwartz, R. W. (1993). Student perceptions of tutor effectiveness in problem-based surgery clerkship. *Teaching and Learning in Medicine*, 5(4), pp. 227–33.

Ministry of Education, Singapore (2000). *The desired outcomes of education*. Singapore: Ministry of Education.

Ministry of Education, Singapore (2003). *Project work: Handbook*. Singapore: Ministry of Education.

Mitchell, C. and Sackney, L. (1998). Learning about organisational learning. In K. Leithwood and K. Seashore Louis (eds). *Organisational learning in schools. Context of learning*. Lisse, The Netherlands: Swets and Zeitlinger.

—— (2000). *Profound improvement: Building capacity for a learning community*. Lisse, The Netherlands: Swets and Zeitlinger.

—— (2007). Extending the learning community: A broader perspective embedded in policy. In L. Stoll and K. Seashore Louis (eds). *Professional learning communities. Divergence, depth and dilemmas* (pp. 30–44). Maidenhead, Berkshire: Open University Press.

Mohammed, R. F. and Harlech-Jones, B. (2008). The fault is in ourselves: Looking at 'failures in implementation'. *Compare*, 38(1), pp. 39–51.

Mooney, L.A. and Edwards, B. (2001). Experiential learning in sociology: Service learning and other community-based learning initiatives. *Teaching Sociology*, 29(2), pp. 181–94.

Morris, P. (2002). Promoting curriculum reforms in the context of a political transition: An analysis of Hong Kong's experience. *Journal of Education Policy*, 17(1), pp. 13–28.

Morris, P. and Lo, M. L. (2000). Shaping the curriculum: Contexts and cultures. *School Leadership and Management*, 20(2), pp. 175–88.

Morrison, K. (2002). *School leadership and complexity theory*. London: Routledge Falmer.

Muijs, D. and Harris, A. (2003). Teacher leadership. Improvement through empowerment? *Educational Management and Administration*, 31(4), pp. 437–48.

Mulford, B. (2005). Editorial. *Leading and Managing*, 11(2), pp. ii–vii.

Munn, P. (2008). Scotland. In T.O'Donoghue and C. Whitehead. *Teacher education in the English-speaking world: Past, present and future* (pp. 61–74). Charlotte, NC: Information Age Publishing.

Murphy, D. (1983). Comparative trends in post-primary curriculum reform. *Studies in Education: A Journal of Educational Research*, 1(1), pp. 7–35.

Murphy, J., Elliot, S., Goldring, E. and Porter, A. (2006). *Learning-centered leadership: A conceptual foundation*. Unpublished manuscript prepared for the Wallace Foundation Grant on Leadership Assessment, August.

NeSmith, R. A. (2001). Four practical applications to improving the teaching of science. *Education News: The Independent Journal of Australian Education*, 119, pp. 51–52.

Neuman, M. and Simmons, W. (2000). Leadership for student learning. *Phi Delta Kappan*, pp. 9–13, September.

Noah, H. J. (1986). The use and abuse of comparative education. In P. G. Altbach and G. P. Kelly (eds). *New approaches to comparative education* (pp. 153–65). Chicago: University of Chicago Press.

Nordic Council of Ministers (1995). *The golden riches in the grass*. Copenhagen: Nordic Council of Ministers.

North Carolina Center for the Advancement of Teaching (2008). *From the mountains to the sea: Advancing education as an art and as a profession*. Culowhee, NC: North Carolina Center for the Advancement of Teaching.

Nuthall, G. and Alton-Lee, A. (1994). How pupils learn. *SET: Research and information for teachers*, 3(2), pp. 1–2.

O'Donoghue, T. A. (1991). Physical education in Papua New Guinea: A case study of an inappropriate national curriculum. *Physical Education Review*, 14, pp. 28–33.

—— (2007). *Planning your qualitative research project: An introduction to interpretivist research in education*. London: Routledge.

O'Donoghue, T.A. and Saville, K. (1996). The power of the story form in curriculum development: An exposition on the ideas of Kieran Egan. *Curriculum*, 17(1), pp. 24–35.

Oduro, G. K. T. (2004). *Distributive leadership in schools: What English headteachers say about the 'pull' and 'push' factors*. Paper presented at the British Educational Research Association Annual Conference, University of Manchester 16–18 September.

OECD (1996). *Making lifelong learning a reality for all*. Paris: OECD.

Ornstein, A. (1995). *Strategies for effective teaching*. Dubuque, IA: Brown and Benchmark.

Ornstein, A. and Levine, D. (1989). Social class, race and school achievement: Problems and prospects. *Journal of Teacher Education*, 40(5), pp. 17–23.

Ortenblad, A. (2002). Organizational learning: A radical perspective. *International Journal of Management Reviews*, 4(1), pp. 87–100.

Osterman, K. (2000). Students' need for belonging in the school community. *Review of Educational Research*, 70(3), pp. 323–67.

Owen, E., Stephens, M., Moskowitz, J. and Gil, G. (2004). Toward education improvement: The future of international assessment (pp. 3–23). In J. Moskowitz and M. Stephens (eds). *Comparing learning outcomes: International assessment and education policy*. London: RoutledgeFalmer.

Owen, R. G. (2001). *Organizational behavior in education: Instructional leadership and school reform*. Boston: Allyn and Bacon.

Paris, D. C. and Kimball, B. A. (2000). Liberal education: An overlapping pragmatic consensus. *Journal of Curriculum Studies*, 32(2), pp. 143–58.

Pedder, D. and MacBeath, J. (2008). Organizational learning approaches to school leadership and management: Teachers' values and perceptions of practice. *School Effectiveness and School Improvement*, 19(2), pp. 207–24.

Perkins, D. (2003). *Making thinking visible. New horizons for learning*. Available on: http:// www.newhorizons.org.info@newhorizons.org. (Accessed on 14 June, 2007)

Perrenoud, P. (1998). From formative assessment to a controlled regulation of learning processes: Towards a wider conceptual field. *Assessment in Education. Principles, Policy and Practice*, 5(1), pp. 85–102.

Pinar, W., Reynolds, W. M., Slattery, P. and Taubman, P. M. (1995). *Understanding curriculum*. New York: Peter Lang.

Pintrich, P. R. (1995). *Understanding self-regulated learning*. San Francisco: Jossey-Bass.

Piscatelli, J. (2005). Sustaining service-learning and youth voice through policy, *Growing to greatness*. Saint Paul, MN: National Youth Leadership Council.

Popham, W. J. (1995). *Educational evaluation*. Boston: Allyn and Bacon.

Postman, N. (1992). *Technology: The surrender of culture to technology*. New York: Vintage Books.

Psacharopoulos, G. and Woodhall, M. (1985). *Education for development: An analysis of investment choices*. New York: Oxford University Press.

Raymond, L. (2001). Student involvement in school improvement: From data source to significant voice. *Forum*, 43(2), pp. 58–61.

Razia, F. M. and Harlech-Jones, B. (2008). The fault is in ourselves: Looking at failures in implementation. *Compare*, 38(1), pp. 39–51.

Reinders, H. and Youniss, J. (2006). School-based required community service and civic development in adolescents. *Applied Developmental Science*, 10(1), pp. 2–12.

Riley, K.A. (2003). Redefining the profession – teachers with attitude. *Education Review*, Vol. 16(2), pp. 19–27.

Ritchart, R. and Perkins, D. (2008). Making thinking visible. *Educational Leadership*, 65(1), pp. 57–61.

Robinson, V. M. J. (2008) Forging the links between distributed leadership and educational outcomes. *Journal of Educational Administration*, 46(2), pp. 241–56.

Rochex, J. Y. (2004). Social, methodological and theoretical issues regarding assessment: Lessons from a secondary analysis of PISA 2000 literacy tests, In G. Green and A. Luke (eds). *Review of research in education, 30: Special issue on 'rethinking learning: What counts as learning and what learning counts'* (pp. 163–212). Washington, DC: American Educational Research Association.

Rondinelli, D., Middleton, J. and Verspoor, A. (1990). *Planning education reforms in developing countries: The contingency approach*. London: Duke University.

Rosenshine, B. (1995). Advances in research on instruction. *The Journal of Educational Research*, 88(5), pp. 262–68.

Rost, J. (1985). *Distinguishing leadership and management: A new consensus.* Paper presented at California Principals' Conference. Anaheim, California, November.

Ruddock, J. (2004). Consulting pupils about teaching and learning. In C. Conors, C. Desforges, M. Galton, B. MacGilchrist, A. Pollard, J. Ruddock, C. Watkins and D. William (eds). *Learning texts* (pp. 79–92). Nottingham: National College for School Leadership.

—— (n.d.). *Pupils voice is here to stay.* Available on: http://www.qca.org.uk\ futures\ (Accessed on 6 September, 2008)

Ruddock, J. and Flutter, J. (2000). Pupil participation and pupil perspective: Carving a new order of experience. *Cambridge Journal of Education*, 30(1), pp. 75–89.

Ryan, J. (2002). Leadership in contexts of diversity and accountability. In K. Leithwood and P. Hallinger (eds). *Second international handbook of educational leadership and administration* (pp. 41–73). Dordrecht: Kluwer Academic Publishers.

Ryan, T. (2000). *Making connections. The use and misuse of information communication technologies in young people's learning.* Paper presented at the international conference on education in the age of the information revolution, Tel-Aviv, June.

Schein, E. (2004). *Organizational culture and leadership*. San Francisco: Jossey-Bass.

Schratz, M. (2006). Leading and learning: 'Odd couple' or powerful match? *Leading and Managing*, 12(2), pp. 40–53.

Schuetz, H. G. and Casey, C. (2006). Models and meanings of lifelong learning: Progress and barriers on the road to a learning society. *Compare*, 36(3), pp. 279–87.

Scribner, J. S., Cockrell, K. S., Cockrell, D. H. and Valentine, J. W. (1999). Creating professional communities in schools through organizational learning: An evaluation of a school improvement process. *Educational Administrative Quarterly*, 35(1), pp. 130–60.

Seashore Louis, K. and Leithwood, K. (1998). From organizational learning to professional learning communities. In K. Leithwood and K. Seashore Louis (eds). *Organizational learning in schools. Contexts of learning* (pp. 275–85). Lisse, The Netherlands: Swets and Zeitlinger.

Senge, P. M. (1990). *The fifth discipline: The art and practice of the learning organization*. New York: DoubleDay.

—— (1995). *The fifth discipline: The art and practice of the learning organisation* (2nd Edition). Australia: Random House.

—— (2000). *Schools that learn*. London: Nicholas-Brealey Publishing.

—— (2004). The leader's new work: Building learning organisations. In K. Starkey, S. Tempest and A. McKinlay (eds). *How organisations learn: Managing the search for knowledge* (pp. 462–86). London: Thomson.

Senge, P., Cambron-McCabe, N., Lucas, T., Smith, B., Dutton, J. and Kleiner, A. (2000). *Schools that learn: A fifth discipline field-book for educators, parents, and everyone who cares about education*. London: Nicholas Brealey.

Sergiovanni, T. J. (1984). Leadership as cultural expression. In T. J. Sergiovanni and J. E Corbally (eds). *Leadership and Organizational Culture. New Perspectives on Administrative Theory and Practice* (pp. 105–14). Urbana: University of Illinois Press.

—— (1991). *The principalship: A reflective practice perspective.* Boston: Allyn and Bacon.

—— (1992). Leadership and excellence in schooling. *Educational Leadership*, 41(5), pp. 4–13.

—— (1998). Leadership as pedagogy: Capital development for school effectiveness. *International Journal for Leadership in Education*, 1(1), pp. 37–47.

—— (2001). *Leadership: What's in it for schools?* London: RoutledgeFalmer.

Shea, C.M. (1992). NCCAT's search for a teacher renewal philosophy: An historical account. In A.G. Rud Jr. and W.R. Oldendorf (eds). *A place for teacher renewal: Challenging the intellect, creating educational reform* (pp. 1–24). New York: Teachers College Press.

Shen, J. and Cooley, V. E. (2008). Critical issues in using data for decision making. *International Journal of Leadership in Education*, 11(3), pp. 319–29.

Shulman, L. S. (1997). Professional development learning from experience. In L. S. Shulman (ed.). *The wisdom of practice: Essays on teaching, learning, and learning to teach* (pp. 503–20). San Fransisco: Jossey-Bass.

Silcox, H.C. and Leek, T. E. (1997). International service learning: Its time has come. *Phi Delta Kappan*, 78(8), pp. 615–18.

Silins, H., Zarins, S. and Mulford, B. (2002). What characteristics and processes define a school as a learning organization? Is this a useful concept to apply to schools? *International Education Journal*, 3(1), pp. 24–32.

Simpson, D. and Cieslik, M. (2002). Education Action Zones, empowerment and parents. *Educational Research*, 44(2), pp. 119–28.

Skilbeck, M. (1989). *Curriculum reform: An overview of trends.* Paris: OECD.

—— (1992). National curriculum within the OECD. *Unicorn*, 18(3), pp. 9–13.

Skinner, B. F. (1969). *Contingencies of reinforcement: A theoretical analysis.* New York: Appleton-Century-Crofts.

Skinner, R. and Chapman, C. (1999). *Service learning and community service in K-12 public schools: Statistics in brief.* Washington DC: National Center for Education Statistics.

Slavin, R. (1983). *Cooperative learning.* New York: Longman.

—— (1995). *Cooperative learning: Theory, research and practice.* Boston: Allyn and Unwin.

Smalley, N. (2003). Chalk, talk, technology and the teacher: Teacher decisions in blended learning. *The Welsh Journal of Education*, 12(1), pp. 53–63.

Smith, D. L. and Lovat, T. J. (2003). *Curriculum: Action on reflection.* Tuggerah, New South Wales, Australia: Social Science Press.

Smith, R. A. and Knight, J. (1978). MACOS in Queensland: The politics of educational knowledge. *The Australian Journal of Education*, 22(3), pp. 225–48.

—— (1981). Political censorship in the teaching of social sciences: Queensland scenarios. *The Australian Journal of Education*, 25(1), pp. 3–23.

Smylie, M. A. and Hart, A. W. (1999). School leadership for teacher learning and change: A human and social capital development perspective. In J. Murphy and K. S. Louis (eds). *Handbook of educational administration* (pp. 421–42). San Francisco: Jossey-Bass.

Smyth, J. (2006). Educational leadership that fosters 'student voice'. *International Journal of leadership in Education*, 9(4), pp. 279–84.

Snowman, J. and Biehler, R. (2000). *Psychology applied to teaching*. Boston: Houghton Mifflin Company.

Soliman, A. (2003). Review of 'Designing the learning-centred school: A cross cultural perspective'. *Comparative Education Review*, 47(1), pp. 128–29.

Southworth, G. (2000). *Leading and developing pedagogies*. Keynote address at the Professional Development network Conference for School Leaders. Surfers' Paradise, Queensland. August.

—— (2002). Instructional leadership in schools: Reflections and empirical evidence. *School Leadership and Management*, 22(1), pp. 73–91.

Spady, W. (2001). *Beyond counterfeit reforms: Forging an authentic future for all learners*. Maryland, USA: Scarecrow Press.

Spillane, J. P. (2005). Distributed leadership. *The Educational Forum*, 69(2), pp. 143–50.

—— (2006). *Distributed leadership*. San Francisco: Jossey-Bass.

Spillane, J. P., Halverson, R. and Diamond, J. B. (2001). Investigating schools leadership practice: A distributed perspective. *Educational Researcher*, 30(3), pp. 23–28.

—— (2004). Towards a theory of leadership practice: A distributed perspective. *Journal of Curriculum Studies*, 36(1), pp. 3–34.

Stenhouse, L. (1975). *An introduction to curriculum research and development*. London: Heinemann Educational Books Ltd.

Sternberg, R. J. (1998). Abilities are forms of developing expertise. *Educational Researcher*, 27(3), pp. 11–20.

Stiggins, R.J. (2002). Assessment crisis: The absence of assessment FOR learning. *Phi Delta Kappan*, pp. 1–10, 6 June.

Stoll, L. and Fink, D. (1996). *Changing our schools*. Buckingham: Open University Press.

Stoll, L., Bolam, R. and Collarbone, P. (2002). Leading for change: Building capacity for learning. In K. Leithwood and P. Hallinger (eds). *Second international handbook of educational leadership and administration* (pp. 41–73). Dordrecht: Kluwer Academic Publishers.

Swaffield, S. (2002). *Contextualising the work of the critical friend*. A paper presented within the symposium leadership for Learning: The Cambridge Network. 15th International Congress for School Effectiveness and Improvement (ICSEI). Copenhagen, 3–6 January.

Swaffield, S. and MacBeath, J. (2006). Embedding learning how to learn in school policy: The challenge for leadership. *Research Papers in Education*, 21(2), pp. 201–15.

Swee, N.H. and Lan, H.G. (2002). Project work using problem-based learning approach in Crescent Girls' School. *Learning and Growing Through Projects*, 10(3), pp. 9–14.

Szabo, M. and Lambert, L. (2002). The preparation of new constructivist leaders. In L. Lambert, D. Walker, D. P. Zimmerman, J. E. Cooper, M. Dale Lambert, M. E. Gardner and M. Szabo (eds). *The constructivist leader* (pp. 204–38). New York: Teachers College Press.

Thaman, K. H. (1991). Towards a culture-sensitive model of curriculum development for the Pacific countries. *Directions: Journal of Educational Studies*, 13, pp. 1–13.

Theakston, J., Robinson, K. D. and Bangs, J. (2001). Teachers talking: Teacher involvement in Education Action Zones. *School Leadership and Management*, 21(2), pp. 183–97.

Thomas, R. M. (1984). American Samoa and Western Samoa. In R. M. Thomas and T. N. Postlethwaite (eds). *Schooling in the Pacific Islands: Colonies in transition* (pp. 67–110). London: Pergamon Press.

Throsby, C. D. and Gannicott, K. (1990). *The quality of education in the South Pacific*. Canberra: National Centre for Development Studies.

Thut, I. N. and Adams, D. (1964). *Educational patterns in contemporary society*. Tokyo: McGraw-Hill, Kogakusha.

Timperley, H. S. (2005). Distributed leadership: Developing theory from practice. *Journal of Curriculum Studies*, 37(4), pp. 395–420.

Timperly, H. A. (2008). A distributed perspective on leadership and enhancing valued outcomes for students. *Journal of Curriculum Studies*, 40 (6), pp. 821–33.

Treagust, D. F., Duit, R. and Fraser, B. J. (eds). (1996). *Improving teaching and learning in science and mathematics*. New York: Teachers College Press.

Tripp, D. (2003). Action inquiry. *Action Research Reports* 017. Available on: http://www.fhs.usyd.au/arow/arer/017.htm (Accessed on 1 March 2006)

Tucker, R. C. (1981). *Politics and leadership*. Missouri: University of Missouri Press.

Tuohy, D. and Coghlan, D. (1997). Development in schools: A systems approach based on organizational levels. *Education Management and Administration*, 25(1), pp. 65–77.

Tyack, D. and Cuban, L. (1995). *Tinkering towards utopia: A century of public school reform*. Cambridge, MA: Harvard University Press.

Uline, C. and Tschannen-Moran, M. (2008). The walls speak: The interplay of quality facilities, school climate and student achievement. *Journal of Educational Administration*, 46(1), pp. 55–73.

UNESCO (1996). *Learning: The treasure within*. Hamburg: UNESCO Institute for Learning.

United Nations (2003). *United Nations charter on the rights of the child*. New York: United Nations.

Useem, J. and Useem, R. H. (1980). Generating fresh research perspectives and study designs for transnational exchange among the highly educated. DAAD Research and Exchange. Proceedings of the German-American Conference at the Wissenschaftszentrum, Bonn, pp. 24–58. November.

Van Manen, M. (1977). Linking ways of knowing with ways of being practical. *Curriculum Inquiry*, 62(3), pp. 205–28.

Vlaeminke, M. (1998). Historical and philosophical influences. In J. Moyles and L. Hargreaves (eds). *The primary curriculum: Learning from international perspectives*. London: Routledge.

Voogt, J. C., Lagerweij, N. A. J. and Seashore Louis, K. (1998). School development in organizational learning: Toward an Integrative Theory. In K. Leithwood and K. Seashore Louis (eds). *Organizational learning in schools. Context of learning* (pp. 237–60). Lisse, The Netherlands: Swets and Zeitlenger.

Vulliamy, G. (1981). The Secondary Schools Community Extension Project in Papua New Guinea. *Journal of Curriculum Studies*, 13, pp. 92–103.

Vygotsky, L. S. (1978). *Mind and society*. Cambridge, MA: Harvard University Press.

Walters, S. (1999). New challenges and opportunities for lifelong learning in South Africa. *Comparative Education*, 35(2), pp. 217–24.

Wasley, P. A. (1991). *Teachers who lead: The rhetoric of reform and the realities of practice*. New York: Teachers College Press.

Watkins, D. (2000). Learning and teaching: A cross-cultural perspective. *School Leadership and Management*, 20(2), pp. 161–73.

Watts, M. and Bentley, D. (1991). Constructivism in the curriculum. *The Curriculum Journal*, 2 (2), 171–82.

Weber, M. (1984). Legitimate authority and bureaucracy. In D. S. Pugh (ed.). *Organization Theories* (pp. 4–27). London: Penguin.

Weir, D. (2003). Her Majesty's Inspectorate of Education (HMIE). In T. G. K. Bryce and W. M. Hume (eds). *Scottish education second edition: Post devolution* (pp. 151–58). Edinburgh: Edinburgh University Press.

West, A. and Pennel, H. (2005). Market-oriented reforms and 'high stakes' testing: Incentives and consequences. *Cahiers de la Recherche sur l'Education et les Savoirs*, 1, pp. 181–99.

West-Burnham, J. (1997). Leadership for learning: Re-engineering mind set. *School Leadership and Management*, 17(2), pp. 231–43.

West-Burham, J. and O'Sullivan, F. (1998). *Leadership and professional development in schools. How to promote techniques for effective professional learning*. Harlow: Pearson Education Limited.

Whitehead, J. and Clough, N. (2004). Pupils, the forgotten partners in education action zones. *Journal of Education Policy*, 19(2), pp. 215–27.

Willett, J. (1992). (ed. and translator). *Bertolt Brecht poems and songs from the plays*. London: Methuen.

Willis, P. (1977). *Learning to labour*. Hampshire, England: Gower.

Wirth, A. G. (1994). A reconstituted general education: The integration of the vocational and the liberal. *Journal of Curriculum Studies*, 26(6), pp. 593–600.

World Bank (1980). Education sector policy paper: World Bank, policy, planning and research working paper WPS 143. Washington, DC: World Bank.

—— (1988). *Education in Sub-Saharan Africa: Policies for adjustment, revitalization and expansion*. Washington, DC: World Bank.

York-Barr, J. and Duke, K. (2004). What do we know about teacher leadership? Findings from two decades of scholarship. *Review of Educational Research*, 74(3), pp. 255–316.

Young, G. (2000). The motivation to learn: Connecting the disengaged. *Journal of Lifelong Learning Initiatives*, 18, pp. 5–8.

Zimmerman, B. J. and Risenberg, R. (1997). Self-regulatory dimensions of academic learning and motivation. In G. G. Phye (ed.). *Handbook of academic learning: Construction of knowledge* (pp. 110–25). San Diego, CA: Academic Press.

Index